BATTLEGROUND CHICAGO

BATTLEGROUND CHICAGO

THE POLICE AND THE 1968 DEMOCRATIC NATIONAL CONVENTION

FRANK KUSCH

PRAEGER

Westport, Connecticut
London

Library of Congress Cataloging-in-Publication Data

Kusch, Frank, 1959–
    Battleground Chicago : the police and the 1968 Democratic National Convention /
Frank Kusch.
        p. cm.
    Includes bibliographical references and index.
    ISBN 0-275-98138-X (alk. paper)
    1. Police—Illinois—Chicago. 2. Riots—Illinois—Chicago. 3. Democratic National
Convention (1968 : Chicago, Ill.) I. Title.
    HV8148.C42K87 2004
    977.3'11043—dc22   2004052155

British Library Cataloguing in Publication Data is available.

Library of Congress Catalog Card Number: 2004052155
ISBN: 0–275–98138–X

First published in 2004

Praeger Publishers, 88 Post Road West, Westport, CT 06881
An imprint of Greenwood Publishing Group, Inc.
www.praeger.com

Printed in the United States of America

The paper used in this book complies with the
Permanent Paper Standard issued by the National
Information Standards Organization (Z39.48–1984).

10 9 8 7 6 5 4 3 2 1

For my brother and sisters
Larry, Pat, and Sharon

and in memory of
Dr. Dave De Brou

Contents

Photo essay follows chapter 5.

Preface

Few periods in American history engender hyperbole like the 1960s. Although those years were indeed turbulent, they actually pale when compared with much of the nation's past. Arguably, the revolutionary era, the opening of the West, the scourge of slavery, the crisis of civil war, the tribulations of Reconstruction, two world wars, a crippling economic depression, and a 1950s ensconced in cold war and civil rights all trump the decade in turmoil.

The 1960s, however, remain an endless source of fascination for baby boomers and those born after the culmination of America's long war in Vietnam. In some circles, the years have reached almost mythical proportions. Elucidating this enduring attraction is that, unlike much of the aforementioned past, the 1960s are sexy. The years charm with Black Power, sexual revolution, unconstrained youth, expansive rhetoric, and unabashed self-expression. Perhaps one of the reasons intrigue holds fast is that the era feeds the mind's attraction to spectacle while assuaging its desire for deeper meaning.

Beyond the fête of psychedelic drugs and free love, however, was the war in Vietnam and the war at home. Consequently, although many are attracted to the era, the loss of 58,000 young Americans in a fruitless war remains a sobering fact. An academic acquaintance once admitted that the reason he avoids teaching any course on the 1960s is that he finds the decade "distasteful." It is clear, however, that the subject, to him and others, goes beyond mere unpleasantness but borders on the taboo. Although the scholar in question knew someone who died in Vietnam, he has not been able to visit the Vietnam Veterans Memorial in

Washington, D.C. When traveling to the nation's capital, he actively avoids the granite walls that rest in the shadow of Lincoln's memorial. He believes a visit would constitute a trespass.

The sixties are unfinished business. Whatever dreams or hopes were imagined during John Fitzgerald Kennedy's stirring 1961 inaugural address fragmented in the immediate years following his death on a Dallas street. His successor's attempt to outrun the ghosts of the New Frontier with an even more ambitious Great Society ended in discontent at home and tragedy in Vietnam. Although some periods were indeed more turbulent in American history, the 1960s cast a pall over those who remember all too well the war and the turmoil that defined the era, the dashed hopes, and a youthful idealism that appeared truncated as the curtain closed on the decade.

Battleground Chicago is an effort to explain the breach called the sixties, when optimism and idealism collided with angst and warfare, when the World War II generation clashed with its rebellious offspring. This book revisits the decade's pinnacle year, 1968, and the protest riots that occurred during the Democratic National Convention that August. Unlike previous studies, however, this book focuses primarily on those whom many commentators have blamed for causing much of the turmoil: members of the Chicago Police Department. By turning its lens on the men who wore the uniform that fateful spring and summer, and the city they called home, this study hopes to move beyond stereotypical images of Irish, Italian, and Polish cops, "storm troopers" with cigar butts between their teeth, beating hippies with batons, spraying mace with abandonment. It ventures past the construct of "pigs" that went "berserk" on the streets of Chicago and places their actions into the context of the time and the culture from which they emerged. As such, the book does not limit its scope to that summer alone, but examines events leading to that dramatic showdown in the Windy City. It strives to see these officers as they saw themselves—men with families, mortgages, and lives—from the perspective of that turbulent time. It is an effort not to excuse police behavior but to explain one of the most legendary clashes of the 1960s, one marred by hyperbole and myth concerning the actions of the Chicago police. In doing so, this book endeavors not only to offer a more accurate portrayal of convention week, but of a paradoxical decade. This reconstruction of events was gleaned in part from U.S. government and city of Chicago investigations, interviews with eighty former officers, print and televised media accounts, police reports, and manuscript sources.

This book would not have been possible without the help of numerous individuals and institutions. Much appreciation goes to retired members of the Chicago Police Department who spoke about their past in such vivid detail. Many thanks to AnneMarie Chase and Robert Medina, from the Chicago Historical Society, for going the extra mile; kudos to the patient and professional research and reference staffs from the Chicago Municipal Reference Library, the Chicago Public Library, the Illinois State Archives, the University of Chicago, the Richard J. Daley Library at the University of Illinois at Chicago, the Lyndon Baines Johnson

Library and Museum at Austin, Texas, Western Michigan University, the University of Iowa, the University of Saskatchewan, and Ohio University. Thanks also go to Bill Creighton from *United Press International,* Eric Behrens of the *Peoria Journal Star,* the Chicago Police Department, and veteran photographer Fred W. McDarrah for access to the photos from that summer. Many thanks to Darrell Seib for his technical assistance with the images. Sincere appreciation also goes to the good people at Praeger Publishers, especially to my editor, Heather Ruland Staines, for the support that gets books published.

Last, I am grateful to friends and family, especially, my wife, partner, and best friend, Jo, who endured the absences (in both body and spirit) resulting from the writing of this book with humor, patience, and support.

Frank Kusch
Chicago, Illinois
October 14, 2003

Timeline

1968

January

- Federal grand jury in Boston indicts Dr. Benjamin Spock, Michael Ferber, Marcus Raskin, Mitchell Goodman, and William Sloan Coffin on conspiracy to "counsel, aid and abet young men to violate draft laws."
- U.S. intelligence ship *Pueblo* is captured in waters off North Korea. Commander and crew are taken prisoner by the North Koreans.
- The Student Mobilization Committee holds planning conference in Chicago.
- U.S. embassy in Saigon is overrun by Vietcong guerrillas. Attack is shown on U.S. television. Vietcong begin Tet Offensive.

February

- Tet Offensive becomes turning point of the Vietnam War. North Vietnamese attack thirty-six cities in the south. Offensive lasts until April. Viewed more as a political disaster, it begins to turn the American public against the war.
- Richard Nixon announces his intention to seek the Republican nomination for president.
- Alabama Governor George Wallace seeks presidential nomination as an Independent.
- State troopers shoot and kill three black students and wound twenty-seven more in Orangeburg, South Carolina. In what became known as the "Orangeburg Massacre," demonstrators had been demanding the integration of a local bowling alley.

March

- One hundred and thirty-nine members of the House of Representatives call for a congressional review of U.S. policy in Southeast Asia. Twenty-one members call for repeal of the Gulf of Tonkin Resolution.
- President Johnson earns narrow victory over antiwar candidate Senator Eugene McCarthy in the New Hampshire primary. McCarthy claims 40 percent of the vote.
- Robert F. Kennedy announces his candidacy for the office of president of the United States.
- U.S. Marines kill unarmed civilians in what became known as the My Lai Massacre.
- General Creighton Abrams replaces Westmoreland as MACV commander in Vietnam.
- Robert Kennedy is booed during St. Patrick's Day parade in New York City. The same day, 30,000 U.S. troops are sent to Vietnam.
- President Lyndon Johnson is told by his advisers that the war is not winnable; announces a cessation to bombing in North Vietnam.
- Johnson chooses not to seek reelection.

April

- Martin Luther King Jr. is assassinated in Memphis.
- Blacks riot in more than 100 cities, including Washington, D.C., Chicago, Detroit, and Philadelphia. In Chicago, nine blacks are killed and twenty city blocks are burned.
- Chicago Mayor Richard Daley orders police to "shoot to kill" arsonists. Daley also publicly criticizes his superintendent of police for not doing enough to quell the riots that followed King's assassination.
- President Johnson calls up 24,500 reservists for Vietnam. The president signs the Civil Rights Act of 1968. The act includes a federal antiriot provision, making it a crime to cross state lines with the intent to incite a riot.
- Columbia University is occupied by antiwar activists. New York police retake the campus in what some call a "police riot."
- On the heels of Daley's earlier rebuff, police attack a peaceful antiwar march in Chicago.
- Hubert Humphrey announces his candidacy for the U.S. presidency.

May

- McCarthy defeats Robert Kennedy in the Oregon primary.

June

- Robert F. Kennedy is assassinated in Los Angeles following his victory in the California primary.
- Boston 5 are found guilty of conspiracy.

July

- Mobe's applications for permits to march and rally at the International Amphitheater, site of the Democratic National Convention, and Grant Park are denied. Use of the Grant Park band shell for a rally is the only permit granted.

August

- Yippies and other antiwar activists finalize plans for demonstrations in Chicago.
- Senator George S. McGovern announces his candidacy for the Democratic presidential nomination.
- Chicago Police Department places its entire 12,000-man force on twelve-hour shifts for convention week, increasing its capacity by 50 percent.
- Five thousand national guardsmen arrive in Chicago; 6,000 army troops are put on alert.
- Soviet troops and tanks invade Czechoslovakia to crush the "Prague Spring" movement.
- Chicago police shoot and kill a seventeen-year-old Sioux Indian from South Dakota prior to the convention. Police say he opened fire at them with a gun.
- Festival of Life begins in Chicago's Lincoln Park.
- Yippies select a pig as their presidential nominee. Seven of the Yippies, plus the pig, are arrested.
- Police and protesters clash for seven days of rioting during the Democratic National Convention.
- Democratic delegates vote down the peace plank.
- Hubert Humphrey wins the Democratic nomination; the party is split.
- During convention week, 308 U.S. servicemen are killed in Vietnam.
- More than 500,000 U.S. troops are in Southeast Asia.
- Milwaukee Fourteen destroy 10,000 draft records.

September

- Hubert Humphrey is booed in New York City. Mayor Daley tells reporters, "The policeman isn't there to create disorder; the policeman is there to preserve disorder."
- Harris poll places Richard Nixon in the lead for the U.S. presidency; Nixon calls for peace with honor in Vietnam and law and order at home.

November

- Richard Nixon is elected president of the United States.

December

- The National Commission on the Causes and Prevention of Violence releases its findings. The "Walker Report" as it came to be known, was the result of the Chicago Study Team, headed by Daniel Walker, to investigate the disturbances during convention week. The report concluded that events in Chicago that August constituted a "police riot."

chapter 1

"An American City": The Roots of a Creed

Chicago *was* America. It was grand. It stood for hard work. It stood for ingenuity. It stood for perseverance. It was a melting pot if you wanted it to be, but it never lost its connection to the old country and a better time. Chicago had real neighborhoods with real personalities and characters that distinguished us from everyone else, and everywhere else, when I was a kid. But somewhere along the way during those years, we lost our way. The 1960s soiled our city—soiled by an entire generation who didn't care about traditional values anymore. Even if they *said* they did, they did not care about our country—*my* country. They were a spoiled generation who only cared about themselves. In the '60s, our city suffered. I was a cop. I wanted the suffering to end.[1]

I n the dog days of 1968, a fractured Democratic Party convened in Chicago to choose a new leader. President Lyndon Johnson's tenure in the Oval Office had become a cross he could no longer bear. Prefaced by the assassinations of the Revered Martin Luther King Jr. and Senator Robert Kennedy, social and political upheaval, and attrition in Vietnam, trouble was brewing for the national convention. In the Windy City battle lines were drawn as Yippies, hippies, and other antiwar activists and radicals converged to challenge the ruling Democrats over their policy in Southeast Asia. Anticipating their arrival was veteran mayor and fierce Democratic Party supporter, Richard J. Daley.

In the wake of growing protests, violent clashes, and riots across the nation, a skittish public called for law and order. In Chicago, Mayor Daley was planning his own brand of law and order by preventing antiwar activists from disrupting the convention and spoiling his party's big show. Doing his bidding were 11,900 members of the Chicago Police Department, 5,000 members of the Illinois National Guard, and an additional 5,000 regular army troops requested by the mayor to help ensure order. Daley had begun to doubt in public his officers' ability to quell civil unrest given their "restraint" in dealing with rioters following King's death that April. The pressure was on everyone—the activists to lobby for an end to the war, the party to agree on a war plank its supporters could accept so that it could regain the White House, a city and its boss that insisted on order, and the police caught in the middle.

The events that followed owed their origins in part to the nature of the city. While modern and progressive in business and infrastructure, Chicago beat with the pulse of the World War II generation, one not ready to accept the birth of the child christened the sixties. What was to transpire during convention week was a clash between the counterculture and the practitioners of a Middle American orthodoxy. When the hippies came to Chicago, the police and city governors were planning to do more than teach a "spoiled" generation a lesson, but to protect their city from the forces of revolution. The seeds for the harsh treatment against protestors on the streets of Chicago during the Democratic National Convention lay in the city's history—a heritage that shaped its police officers long before they wore a badge.

A FRONTIER TOWN

"Chicago," wrote Norman Mailer, "is the great American city."[2] But it certainly did not become that way overnight. Little more than a frontier village in 1833, the future Second City consisted of a small collection of frame houses supplanting log cabins on the edge of Lake Michigan. A sparse population of 400—mostly single men looking for work and adventure in the fur trade—boarded in taverns while others lived above their shops and stores. By the mid-to-late 1830s, the population grew tenfold when scores of merchants, speculators, and lawyers moved to the heartland from the East Coast. The growing town became attractive to businessmen who learned that the state and federal governments had earmarked the village on the edge of the western frontier as a city. The federal government was not only dredging a harbor on the Chicago River, but following the Blackhawk War of 1832, the Pottawatomie Indians were forced into Kansas, making way for more settlers.[3]

By March 1837, Chicago's population had grown to 4,170; the following year, Congress appropriated $200,000 for harbor development. By 1845, more than 1,000 ships entered the city's waterway on an annual basis. Commercial goods were not the only resource flowing into this growing community, as this constant arrival of vessels brought the first significant waves of human capital; scores of immigrants flooded into the region in search of jobs and opportunities. Chicago soon became the gateway for the shipment of produce and livestock from the upper Midwest to ports both east to New York and south to New Orleans. Rapid growth brought rapid change, and some of it wasn't pretty. Chicago quickly gained a reputation as a coarse, nasty city, with an unseemly convention for bawdy houses, saloonkeepers, ramshackle dwellings, and knife fights. In its early days, it was far from a jewel and a Second City rival of New York; for some, it was an unsightly outback. "Having seen it, I urgently desire never to see it again," wrote Rudyard Kipling in 1889. "It is inhabited by savages."[4]

Central to Chicago's economic rise was the development of the city's Union Stock Yards in 1848. With the westward expansion of the railways, the city needed a larger and more efficient stockyard to deal with the influx of both live-stock and meatpackers. As the railroads expanded, Chicago not only evolved into a major railroad center but experienced massive commercial growth. Several meatpacking companies set up operations around the stockyards, including Armour, Swift, Morris, and Hammond. By the turn of the century, the city's meatpacking industry employed more than 25,000 people, producing 80 percent of the meat consumed by Americans. With rich and abundant farmlands to the south and west, Chicago's workers made things area farmers could use, from machinery to fertilizer, while processing the tens of thousands of animals for the market that came in from the countryside.[5] While the steel industry erected tall buildings, meatpacking remained a mainstay of the city's economy throughout the twentieth century, making the city's massive slaughterhouses almost as famous as its baseball teams. According to Norman Mailer, the slaughterhouses not only contributed to the city's economy but helped shape the character of Chicagoans.

Chicago was a town where nobody could ever forget how the money was made. It was picked up from floors still slippery with blood, and if one did not protest and take a vow of vengeance, one knew at least that life was hard, life was in the flesh and in the massacre of the flesh—one breathed the last agonies of beasts. So something of the entrails and the secrets of the gut got into the faces of native Chicagoans. A great city, a strong city with faces tough as leather hide and pavement, it was also a city where the faces took on the broad beastiness of ears which were dull enough to ignore the bleatings of the doomed.[6]

The industry also required large numbers of unskilled workers, providing jobs for thousands of immigrants and their families; there was room for those who wanted to work with their hands and opportunities for the multitudes that poured into the region in the late nineteenth and early twentieth centuries, an influx that created many vibrant and rich ethnic enclaves. Even by 1960, rela-tively distinct communities of Irish, Poles, Germans, Italians, Russians, Swedes, Checks, Austrians, and Hungarians still characterized the city.[7]

The hard toil of slaughterhouse work, to some, distinguished the city as a "working town, rather than a pleasure town."[8] Chicago's poet laureate Carl Sandburg dubbed the city "Hog Butcher for the World, Tool Maker, Stacker of Wheat, Player with Railroads and the Nation's Freight Handler; Stormy, husky, brawling, City of Big Shoulders." Veteran city journalist Studs Terkel called

Chicago "a muscular town. I know I run the danger of romanticization. But it's true. Sandburg was right when he spoke of Chicago as the 'city of big shoulders.'"[9]

Organized labor grew in tandem with industry; the city soon became a cauldron for a clash between big business and trade unions. As was often the case throughout Chicago's colorful history, police found themselves in the middle of violent episodes. In early 1886, the movement for an eight-hour day was picking up steam; on May 1, the unions launched a massive strike to force shorter hours, a move joined by groups of radicals and anarchists. On May 3, during a riot at the McCormick Harvester plant, Chicago police opened fire on a crowd of strikers, leaving one person dead and several injured. The next day during a protest meeting at Haymarket Square to denounce the events of the preceding day, a bomb exploded while police were attempting to disperse the crowd. The explosion took the lives of eight Chicago police officers and injured more than sixty others; police once again fired on the crowd in retaliation. Of the eight men brought to trial over the bombing, the court sentenced seven to death and one received fifteen years in prison. Four went to the gallows, another committed suicide, and the court commuted two death sentences to life imprisonment. In June 1893, Governor John P. Altgeld pardoned the remaining three.[10] In 1889, the city erected a nine-foot bronze statue of a Chicago policeman near the riot's site on Randolph Street near Halsted Street, as a tribute to the officers who lost their lives.[11]

By the turn of the century, Chicago was on familiar terms with violence, confrontation, and tragedy. It had suffered a great fire in 1871, which ravaged the city, leaving 17,000 buildings destroyed (one-third of the city), and 100,000 Chicagoans homeless.[12] Chicago had, however, rebuilt even stronger and forged ahead with a verve born of rapid growth, grit, and hard work.[13] From its days as a frontier town, to an industrial and business capital at the turn of the century, the city gave voice to a credo—a singular hard brand of Middle Americanism.

CHICAGO'S CENTURY

Chicago came into full voice in the twentieth century, a sprawling metropolis that served as both a bastion of opportunity and a haven for opportunists. The city's emerging cadre of heroes and antiheroes also made it difficult to tell one from the other. "Chicago," as Studs Terkel observed, "is an ethically adjustable city."[14] In 1921, the federal government's flirtation with prohibition whetted the city's thirst for opportunity of a different brand. By then, Chicago was on a first-name basis with scandal and corruption—from prostitution to racketeering. In 1919, one of the city's baseball teams became embroiled in the most infamous scandal in baseball history. During the 1919 World Series, the league accused eight players from the Chicago White Sox of throwing the series against the Cincinnati Reds. News of the "black sox" scandal made headlines across the nation. "Shoeless" Joe Jackson, Claude "Lefty" Williams, Eddie Cicotte, Arnold

"Chick" Gandil, Fred McMullin, Charles "Swede" Risberg, Buck Weaver, and Oscar "Happy" Felsch were banned from baseball for life.[15] Less than two years later when the nation went dry, there was more than baseball for Chicagoans to lament. The prohibition of all intoxicating liquors served as a sobering preface for the 1920s as it drew to the surface the underbelly of organized crime.

"Prohibition Is a Business"

Known as a place open to anyone with enough money to buy influence, the rowdy, pugnacious, hard-drinking city made Chicago the perfect place to build a criminal empire. Political corruption and a culture of "two-fisted lawlessness" leant itself to an arm's length consensus and a "spoils system" created by machine bosses such as William "Big Bill" Thompson and Mont Tennes. Political corruption in Chicago was a fact of daily business and one that mobster Al Capone not only capitalized on but turned into a hideous art. When Capone arrived in the Windy City from New York, Prohibition and the city's political machine combined to create one of the most notorious criminal organizations in the nation's history. Capone developed a reputation as a benevolent crime king, providing the people of Chicago with what they craved—beer and liquor—while exerting significant political influence.

The struggles to control booze, the rackets, and prostitution led to bloody turf wars and one of the more infamous gangland killings. Capone's main opposition was Charles "Bugs" Moran, whose headquarters were located in a garage on Clark Street. Capone ordered "Machine gun" Jack McGurn, Albert Anselmi, and John Scalisi to wipe out Moran's operation. Dressing as Chicago police officers, the hit men staged a fake raid on the garage. Believing Capone's men were actual officers, Moran's troops offered no resistance when asked to spread-eagle against the garage wall. The "officers" then riddled their bodies with machine-gun fire. The "St. Valentines Day Massacre" made Capone even more notorious and feared.[16]

In March 1929, with charges of complicity and widespread corruption within the Chicago Police Department, city businessmen prevailed upon President Herbert Hoover to not only repeal Prohibition but put an end to Capone's influence in the city. In August 1929, the Treasury Department assigned native Chicagoan Elliot Ness to the Chicago Police Department to bring Capone down. Ness headed a special investigative unit that the media dubbed "the Untouchables." Although Ness's group dogged the mafia kingpin probing for Prohibition violations and faced both bribes and death threats, the group had little to do with Capone's eventual demise. The less sensational story involved Internal Revenue Service intelligence agents with sharp pencils. Although Ness had developed a cadre of Prohibition law violations against Capone and his associates, the charges with teeth came from officials within the Justice Department that documented numerous income tax violations. Found guilty of tax evasion in June 1931, the city's most infamous mobster was sent to Alcatraz.[17]

Whereas Capone may have been Chicago's dark side in extreme caricature, the city's politics were never far removed from the appearance of corruption. "Chicago, ever since prohibition," wrote Terkel, "has had this remarkable history of no line between what is legal and illegal."[18] Indeed, since the beginning of the city's history, a well-developed system of accommodation shaped its political and social culture. For politicians to be successful, catering to the diverse working-class ethnic communities was a necessity in this "city of nations." Citizens thought of themselves not only as Chicagoans but as members of distinct neighborhoods. Hyde Park, Logan Square, Chatham, Abbey Park, and Canaryville were ethnic enclaves with histories that dated back to the beginning of the city. And diversity was not eschewed but embraced. While radio stations offered listeners Polish and Spanish programming, people lived the American Dream in "self contained sub communities."[19]

While the Irish were historically the city's strongest political force—one that built allegiances and subtle compromises between communities for power and influence—it was Bohemian immigrant Anton Cermak who turned ethnic coalition building into an art. By 1930, the city had grown to more than 3 million people, many of them immigrants who continued to stream into the city. The gregarious Cermak built strong ties to the city's varied ethnic groups and assumed the presidency of the Cook County Board of Commissioners. In 1928, when Democratic Party chairman George Brennan died (the heir to the old-time Irish Democratic organization), Cermak was able to capitalize on his ethnic political ties and take over the party machinery from the Irish. In 1931, he ran against Republican mayor William Thompson, who was linked loosely to Al Capone. In what was to characterize the city's successful machine bosses for the next thirty years, Cermak captured the mayor's office with a "house for all peoples" campaign, while reaching out for the Irish vote. Preaching hard work and discipline, Cermak built the Chicago machine.[20]

One who understood, perhaps as well as anyone, the subtle and intricate pattern of accommodations required to excel in the ethnic patchwork that was Chicago was Richard J. Daley—a man who was to become "the very face of Chicago."[21]

"Hizzoner, Da Mayor"

The son of a sheet-metal worker, Richard Daley emerged from humble beginnings. Raised in a devoted Catholic family in the gritty neighborhood of Bridgeport, Daley cut his teeth in the Irish, working-class eleventh ward near the famous stockyards. Daley excelled at school and later studied law at DePaul, graduating with a law degree in 1934. Ambitious by nature, he began his rise to political prominence as a secretary on Chicago's city council, moving up rapidly through the ranks of the Democratic Party machine. Using charisma and a shrewd eye for accumulating personal power, Daley built a citywide coalition, becoming the party boss in 1954. The following year, with his leadership of the Cook County Central Committee, which oversaw the city's fifty wards, Daley's power became unsurpassed as he ran both Chicago's administrative and political apparatuses. As Milton Rakove observed, "He used his power as mayor to strengthen his role as party chairman, and he used his power as party chairman to strengthen his role as mayor." By 1968, The Cook County Democratic organization controlled the mayoralty, thirty-eight of fifty city council members, the housing authority, the school board, the park board, two-thirds of the county board, including much of the state apparatus, and the governor. As mayor, Daley had the support of the unions through patronage, but he delivered both ways and garnered strong support from the business community as a "creative autocrat," acquiring millions in federal dollars for massive improvements to infrastructure, building expressways, improving street maintenance, establishing new building construction, and making advancements to lighting in the central business district.[22]

Daley also managed to remain unblemished in a city known for political corruption. The biggest challenge for the city boss, however, came in January 1960 when news broke that twenty-three-year-old Richard Morrison, taken into custody by police, revealed that twelve members of the Summerdale police district on Chicago's north side had aided him in his criminal pursuits. Morrison delivered a stunning seventy-seven-page confession outlining a two-year period where police officers helped him rob local businesses. During the operations, cops used squad cars to fence stolen goods; investigators found four truckloads of stolen merchandise in officers' homes. Daley moved fast to contain the damage. Police superintendent Timothy O'Connor took charge of the case known as the "Summerdale Scandal" or the "Burglars in Blue," questioning more than 130 officers.[23]

The investigation put Daley's handling of the department under scrutiny. As the investigation uncovered more fencing rings in the North Damen Avenue Station, Daley faced criticism that he had let the department slide during his first five years at the helm, along with allegations that O'Connor was the superintendent in name only, and the mayor really held the power over the department. Daley, however, sidestepped blame by firing O'Connor and replacing him with University of California professor and head of the criminology department Orlando W. Wilson. In the end, eight Chicago police officers went to jail, and hundreds more were tested by polygraph. Those who refused were suspended.[24] Daley, the consummate politician, managed to turn a scandal into a political victory and gained important friends in the city's business community.[25] His personal power won over the city's establishment, which supported his ambitious construction program, including O'Hare International Airport, an elaborate expressway, and a major redevelopment surrounding the University of Chicago.[26] "Whatever Mayor Richard J. Daley likes is O.K. with a lot of Chicagoans—or has to be O.K.," wrote J. Anthony Lukas, "for Mr. Daley runs the most efficient political machine in America."[27]

It was also a machine that exerted significant influence in the national Democratic Party. Daley's influence and notoriety came to the fore in November of 1960 as John F. Kennedy faced Richard Nixon in the federal election. Republicans claimed that Daley's political machine "stole" the election from Richard Nixon by padding the ballots in precincts it controlled in Chicago and other parts of Cook County to carry the important state of Illinois. In his memoirs, Nixon accused Daley of subterfuge. "The Daley Machine" wrote Nixon, "was holding back the Chicago results until the downstate Republican counties had reported and it was known how many votes the Democrats would need to carry the state."[28] Critics pointed to Kennedy's narrow Illinois victory, as he only won by .19 percent; however, that margin was almost identical to the results nationwide. Of the 68,828,960 votes cast, Kennedy won by a mere 114,673, or 49.72 percent of the popular vote compared to 49.55 percent for Nixon, a difference of .17 percent nationally and indeed, slightly lower than the percentage in Illinois. Had Kennedy actually lost the state, its twenty-seven electoral votes would still not have given the election to Nixon; Kennedy won in the Electoral College, 303 to 219.[29]

Often overlooked is the charge that Republicans stole as many downstate votes as Daley's machine allegedly procured in Cook County. While Kennedy took the Daley-controlled county, statewide election results revealed that Nixon won big in downstate Illinois; Kennedy claimed Illinois by a slim 8,858 votes. Among the most vocal of the challengers was Cook County state's attorney, Benjamin Adamowski. The Daley political rival for the mayoralty led a recount of 863 precincts. Whereas a recount completed on December 9 found that the original tally had marginally undercounted Nixon's votes, 40 percent of the precincts found an overcount for the Republican candidate. Although it is impossible to disprove fraud, election boards found no cause to overturn the election, nor did state or federal judges. In 1961, an Illinois special prosecutor and a study by a group of three University of Chicago academics failed to uncover evidence of irregularities substantial enough to alter the results. In the end, the Republican-controlled state electoral board certified the Illinois election. As the *Chicago Tribune* concluded, "Once an election has been stolen in Cook County, it stays stolen."[30]

Indeed, Daley had gained the reputation for running Chicago "like a Chinese warlord,"—a man who could not only end police corruption, but could get the city to do what he wanted.[31] According to David Halberstam, it was his way or no way:

As his power increased, so did his ability to accommodate people, and his ability to tell them to get on the team or be frozen out. Though Daley was strongly opposed by State Street in his first race, he has since practically destroyed the Republican Party as a force within the city. He has given the business leaders what they want, a new downtown area, an expressway, a decent police force, confidence in the city's economic future. . . . In return he has had his projects carried out with their support, and has gotten their political backing and campaign funds.[32]

Daley was not without his critics. "He's an old-time hack," Terkel told the *New York Times* prior to the convention:

A neighborhood bully. You have to see him to believe him. He doesn't even have the personal qualities of the old Chicago politicians. . . . Daley is great when it comes to things . . . he's great when it comes to building, when it comes to ripping down 800 trees to widen a highway on the South Side, when it comes to urban renewal or what the Negroes call Negro removal. He's great when it comes to zoning a parking lot. He's great when it comes to industry. But when it comes to humans, he's not too hot.[33]

O. W. Wilson's retirement as police superintendent seven years later had also become a source of concern; under Wilson's leadership, the police department had undergone significant and much needed reforms, ones that appeared jeopardized with his exit. As *Chicago Daily News* columnist Mike Royko observed,

In seven years [Wilson] had made visible changes in the Police Department, making it probably the most technically modern unit in the world and eliminating most of the blatant corruption and graft. A strict disciplinarian, he had curbed the natural instinct of Chicago policemen to knock around the poor, the black, and the politically impotent. When he retired, several civil rights leaders expressed regret. They had reason to. Out on the street, the police sensed what Daley wanted and began pushing blacks harder.[34]

Former cop and president of the Chicago Patrolman's Association, Joe Pecoraro, however, plays down the significance of Wilson's tenure. "All Wilson did was change the color of the cars," says, Pecoraro, who suggests that Wilson cleaned up the streets with imaginative bookkeeping. "You want to know how he kept down crime? You take a twenty-story building, downtown, say there are forty different companies in that building, so a burglar breaks in and he robs maybe twenty different companies in the building; you don't list them all under twenty different companies, you list them all under one address. That's one crime."[35]

While Wilson operated at arm's length from the mayor's office, such was not the case for new top cop James B. Conlisk. As Royko pointed out, with Wilson gone, "Daley could now pick up the phone and issue an order that would be obeyed by the police chief." Conlisk "would say 'yes sir' when Daley told him what to do."[36] The city's black population had reason to worry about worsening relations with the city administration and the police. Daley was seen as insensitive and unsympathetic to the concerns of blacks, especially with housing—as black families were sometimes displaced to make room for development. In the 1960s, there was no black or reform power base or "countermachine" strong enough to challenge Daley's political engine. In a city known as one of the most segregated of the northern cities during the 1950s and 1960s, Daley's stance was mostly political as he gave the black community only as much as his white ethnic supporters would allow. As Mike Royko observed, "The only genuine difference between a southern white and a Chicago white, was in their accent."[37]

Daley played to this strong base of support, remaining faithful to his roots, a believer in "keeping the neighborhood the way it's been." The close-knit Irish-American clan, from which the pugnacious city boss emerged, was a formidable political force and one that he constantly nurtured. The Irish not only constituted the longest tradition of involvement in Chicago politics, but remained the most powerful ethnic contingent in Cook County. Daley utilized his "tribal ties" understanding that success came from his ability to maintain a balance between these communities and the greater urban society. Known as the "ultimate ethnic booster," Daley was in step with the city's working-class ideology, championing blue-collar values and the ethnic communities' desire to ensure personalized forms of kinship. As Theodore White observed, Daley was "intuitively linked with the unspoken culture of white workingmen."[38] This broad base of support made him all but unbeatable. Daley's Democratic machine relied on these communities for votes and for financing campaigns; jobs and self-interest created the fuel that made the machine run. As Lewis Chester suggests, "The system ultimately depends on two things: a precise awareness of place among its members and a general feeling among most voters that it works."[39]

Keenly attuned to the city's mood, Daley was wary of the emerging antiwar movement and the youth culture, aware that his base feared that the forces unleashed in the country could threaten traditional values. The sentiment dovetailed with a growing unease among ethnic groups in rapidly changing Chicago that a way of life would be lost in the shuffle of change in a turbulent time. As Melvin Kahn pointed out,

One of the major problems affecting residents of a large metropolis like Chicago is their loss of a sense of community, particularly those who had severed their ties with their respective ethnic groups. Big cities are impersonal, the people living in them can easily feel that no one knows or cares about them.[40]

Daley saw himself as a defender of traditional values and the best man to guide the city and its citizens through an increasingly divisive decade. His uncanny ability to embody working-class resentment toward antiwar protestors and the new youth culture made him not only an unbeatable force, but a crutch upon which many Chicagoans relied.[41] In the end, Daley shared those fears; he was deeply offended by the social movements of the late 1950s and the 1960s, and he was concerned that massive dissent could threaten his authority.

Seen, however, as a politician with national influence in the Democratic Party, Daley also lobbied extensively to host the Democratic National Convention set for the summer of 1968. Playing host to his beloved Democrats was not only a source of pride for the veteran mayor, but he steadfastly believed that his city and his police department could best control the massive protests everyone expected for the national convention.[42] Aware that the choice of Chicago hinged on his influence in the party and his ability to keep a lid on dissent, Daley relied on his police—boys from the neighborhood who lived and breathed the city they called home. Mayor Daley appealed to the men who wore a uniform for the Chicago Police Department as they shared his worldview, his politics, and his determination to protect their home communities.

Although the events to come in 1968 would have them labeled as "storm troopers in blue,"[43] Chicago's police officers during the 1950s and 1960s were also family men, raised in the city's close-knit, working-class neighborhoods, the same as Richard Daley. Many of their fathers and grandfathers had walked a beat since the turn of the century or served in the military—native Chicagoans who had come to the ranks in search of a regular job and an opportunity to don a uniform. These men shared not only a desire to preserve the city of their youth but to protect "traditional Chicago values."

"Defending the City from Outsiders"

Like most police officers, Greg Parzanski grew up in Chicago,[44] and like most of his partners, he wanted to be a cop since he was old enough to walk. "I got a gun from my grandfather for my eighth birthday. I remember that so clearly, and I think that the reason I did was because I wanted one that looked like a real gun. He had modified it so it couldn't be loaded or fired. I wanted one made from metal, that was heavy and felt good and substantial in my hand." Parzanski remembers walking around the house, the yard, and his street with the gun slung on his hip like a marshal out of a Wyatt Erp comic book. He liked to pretend he was policing the town against outlaws; it was a desire that only grew as he became a teenager and saw his neighborhood change. "It had changed even in the years between the time I was ten and the end of high school. I could walk to school, which was four blocks away when I was seven or eight, but when I was fifteen or so, already things were changing. My dad would walk with me and my sisters until he could see the school and would watch until we went through the iron gates. There were already some gangs forming, not like you see today, no guns or anything, but local punks hitting smaller ones up for lunch money, for booze and drugs were beginning to become a problem. There were also more black families moving into the neighborhoods around us, and there were a lot of families like mine that were becoming worried." Like others during those years, his family was pleased when he decided to join the force. "My grandfather who was on the force for twenty-six years was very happy, proud. He thought that being a cop was a man's profession, that I would make a good living, buy a house in the neighborhood and be a good catch for a wife. I wanted to clean up some messes, and I thought that it would suit my temperament. It was also a job with a pension and a brotherhood. It was the job for me."[45]

It was "the job" for numerous young men after the end of the Second World War. The city was growing, and with the inevitable growing pains there were calls for a larger more modern police force. In the 1940s and 1950s, candidates did not need a university education to join the department.[46] Young men who grew up in the city, from Irish, Polish, and Italian backgrounds, "fit right in."[47]

Knowing that there would be quick acceptance for men of particular backgrounds, it was attractive for recruits such as Tom O'Malley. He recalled a sense of brotherhood that went beneath the badge. "We had a sense of community on the force. We were from similar backgrounds, we liked the same food, movies, jokes, and had the same tolerance for bullshit. We knew what we liked and what we didn't like. Most of the guys were Catholic; god-fearing, who drank a little now and then and played some poker, but it never got out of hand. We wanted to keep our neighborhoods safe, and *you bet* we tried to run the riffraff out, or keep them in their own part of town. It was a great city in those days and we wanted to keep it that way. It was an American city. And really, the hell with anyone who complained about our methods. I think they were fine."[48]

Familiarity and commonality were catalysts for a close-knit department; most of their fellow officers were family men who grew up within blocks of each other, played baseball together; their wives were friends, their children played together. "We liked what we had," says cop Warren MacAulay. "We would have done anything to protect that; we were no different than anyone else." Also common among them was a strong desire to protect their neighborhoods from the perception that the world was changing rapidly for the worse. "The only thing that mattered to any of us was our families, and it was like that when I joined the force before my wife and I had kids. And after my daughter was born, being a cop took on a whole new meaning," says cop Jerry Ewaschuck. "There was something to really fight for." Cop Don Holtz agrees. "Having a family, being family men, which was what we all were except for a couple of young guys, meant that what was going on in society and displayed on the streets was big time."[49]

Such attitudes were common—views that helped shape these men as individuals and as police officers. Says cop Dennis Kaminski, "I was a guy who wanted to fix things—it's always the way I was—I still fix cars, houses, and *people* when needed. I was like that when I was a teen, and wanted to find a job that allowed me to be me. The force was great. It gave me opportunities. It gave me a decent wage, and a chance to help protect our neighborhoods." Cop Jack Ochosky says that many of the guys he worked alongside held similar views. He suggests that while there were some "bad apples" in the department, the majority of officers were family men who had the best interests of the city at heart. "There were jerks; there are jerks in every profession; look at what's happened to the priesthood. No one is going to tell me that all priests molest children. What I'm saying is that the vast majority of the guys who wore our uniform were decent, upstanding people who really cared about the health and safety of our city, our neighborhoods, our families, and our homes."[50] Indeed, many officers saw themselves as personal protectors of their city. As Joe Pecoraro points out, "The first word that comes out of anyone's mouth when they're in trouble is 'help police.' That's the first word that comes out of their mouth; they are looking for someone to help them, so we feel like we are their big brothers to someone who is picking on them."[51]

The growing unrest in the late 1950s and early 1960s had many longing for earlier days. Former cop Ernie Watson remembers when a nickel got him a soda down at a mom-and-pop store across the street and down the block from his parents' home. He recalls coming of age in Chicago and walking the streets of his neighborhood without the need for a chaperone. "When I was growing up in this city, things were so much better; I know that's hard for people to understand. But I swear, that's the way it was. But it began to change in the late '50s, and by the time old Lyndon came in, the streets were not safe for no one. I was safer being out by myself when I was eight than when I was sixteen, and by the time I turned twenty-two and joined up, things were unrecognizable, because in those short years the culture changed. When I had kids they didn't go anywhere without us knowing exactly where they were. Sad but true."[52]

Fears rose within the ranks as the 1960s began, fears that they were losing the battle on the streets against "subversive elements" and a culture change that threatened a way of life. Part of their disconcertment came not simply from what they saw on the beat, but the reaction from within their families and neighborhoods. People expressed their concerns over what came into their homes via television and turned to police officers they knew to offer unsolicited advice. Says cop Steven Latz, "And I know that in the early '60s, some of us began to worry about the type of world we were raising our kids in. The city began to change; we began to feel helpless to do anything about it, and shit did we hear it in the neighborhood. We'd get asked, 'What's going on out there and how come you guys aren't doing more to make the streets safe?' Everyone had an opinion." The pressure intensified as protests against the Vietnam War appeared on their televisions and increased on city streets. Recalls cop Tom Freeborn, "We'd hear, 'Hey, you bums, can't you do anything about these freaks?' And this came from our families and friends on our block or from the in-laws. Christ, when the demonstrations began over 'Nam, we were hearing about that from everyone with a hole in his head."[53]

Such criticism was taken to heart, as officers shared the public's fears and at times their sense of helplessness. Cop George Horsley recalls, "The problem was that we agreed with them; we wanted to stop it from spreading and getting worse. But we didn't have a license to shoot people without a reason. We had to watch what we did, and we didn't have the resources to handle all the problems, and the courts, well, they were like a revolving door; we'd bust people and then three months later, the same slimy punks—longhairs often—were back on the streets giving the citizenry nightmares. I had only been on the force for three years when the city began to go down hill—hell, the whole country began to slide."[54]

These former officers maintain that the nation's "slide" became personal. Says cop Grant Brown, "We weren't just putting in our time and collecting a paycheck, there was a way of life to protect; there were our families, our extended families, and then the biggie—the families of our fellow officers. We knew them, where they lived, where their kids went to school. *Everything* on the street gets personal because you know and care about people, and the need to protect them from subversion is powerful and it was right."[55]

These were not the extreme thoughts held by a few Chicago police officers but symptomatic of communities that saw a direct correlation between cultural change and an increase in violent crime. Officers say that this reality afforded them a higher level of respect in those years—an esteem that people from the outside, they claim, simply could not understand. The respect came in part from the reality that as they walked the beat and protected the city, they were "boys from the neighborhood." Former officer Randall Bakker recalls, "You should have seen the reaction we'd get walking down the street. People trusted us, believed us, and looked up to us. Our own people did not hate us. They understood who we were because they were like us." Ex-cop, Brian Ramsey agrees, adding that much of the negative reports and attitudes about police came from "outsiders" who didn't know Chicago or its citizens. "Well, a man gets tired of the know-it-alls who get on their high horse and say, 'Well, you shouldn't do that, and you should do it like we do here.' And that's the thing that just grates a person. We always said, 'Chicago problems—Chicago solutions.' "[56]

The reality for officers was that the nation's problems were becoming Chicago problems, creating a need to thwart social and political chaos from entering their neighborhoods. Some felt that they had become the last line of defense between order and anarchy. Says officer Steve Nowakowski,

People have to remember that when I came on the force in 1951—hell, for the first few years—I thought being a cop was the easiest thing in the world. I wondered why everyone wasn't joining the force. By 1957 or '58, you could feel things beginning to change—not dramatically at first, but, you know, the tension was building, especially in the colored communities. And, you know, I don't blame some of those people; life hadn't handed them many favors. You should have seen some of those poor sons of bitches. And no one wanted to hire them; but we were caught in the middle—what were we going to do: ignore the problem? They [the administration] would have had our hides, and so would every other God-fearing American. You just can't bury your head in the sand or get all touchy-feely when you're a cop. That's for the talking heads and the sops to cry over. And Christ, was there a lot of them. I think that we were realists and we did the job that most everyone wanted us to do even though they didn't always want to admit it out loud.[57]

Making officers increasingly nervous was the forces they saw unleashed during John Kennedy's brief presidency. Even though those in uniform thought well of Kennedy personally, they held that some of his policies contributed to a growing cultural entitlement—a development they felt on the street. As former cop Kelly Fredrickson points out, "It started to get bad when Kennedy came into office and people began to feel entitled to start trouble with joining with the Negroes in the South and civil rights." Officer Henry Nostbakken concurs, "Things began to slide when Kennedy took over; old Ike [President Dwight Eisenhower] was having his trouble in the South but all hell began to break loose when Kennedy took office, and there were some reasons to wonder what the coming years would bring." Officers cared little for the president's polices on segregation and being "soft" on communism. They believed that his presidency had led to "decadence" and a "feminization" of the culture. As officer Orrest Hupka pointes out, "The only thing good about Kennedy was that he was Catholic."[58]

Kennedy's demise, however, brought little comfort to the boys in blue in Chicago, as the prevailing belief was that the president's assassination helped usher in a national, social, and political meltdown. Contributing to their apprehension was their country's deepening involvement in Vietnam. As the war intensified, so did the problems they faced on the streets. Says cop Paul Juravinski, "By the following spring [1964] there was big time trouble brewing—things on the streets began to have an edge to them, and it looked like they were readying for battle on the campuses. And that began to spill out on to the streets and onto our laps." Juravinski's feeling was widely shared. Officer Al Ogilvie recalls, "As the trouble increased over the war that Johnson was getting us into over there in Vietnam, our workload began to rise." Officers knew that their city would not tolerate chaos on their streets—especially from the growing movement against the war, a movement that would be seen as an affront to the citizens of Chicago. "Revulsion against this rabble came from the sweat of the people in this town, in the sweat of their toil," says former officer Milt Brower. "They were hard-working people who would not put up with the things that were beginning to happen, and they expected nothing less from us—they expected us to deal with it."[59]

Police officers shared the city's antipathy to the beginnings of campus protests and to the emerging youth culture, especially when young people began to view them with increasing malice. As cop Tim Markosky remembers, "It wasn't just that kids began to look different; the hair changed, the clothes changed, but the attitude changed—and *that* was the worst. They just hated us, began to call us names in public. I had been a cop for ten years, and no one had ever said anything to us like that, even when I was making an arrest. You walked by a group of these beatniks, the early hippies, and they'd cuss and swear at you like sailors. We wondered what the hell was going on." Former officer Joe Pecoraro agrees. "There was no regard for policemen anymore, not like when I came on the force in 1952. When I came on, the attitude toward the police was very respectful. But that changed; the people changed; the Vietnam War changed everything."[60]

These officers found themselves under siege and worried about not only their city but the nation. They struggled to comprehend the changes they saw on television and before their eyes. In a city built on the backs of immigrants, Chicago did not breed the type of person or police officer that wanted to appear unpatriotic or un-American. The hippie movement was the antithesis of the city's creed of hard work and loyalty to tradition; hippies and antiwar activists were likened to godless transients without respect for traditional values. Says Marlin Rowden, "I don't know what happened to that generation that was coming of age, but they came out of their parent's homes, lazy, disrespectful, without roots, gunning for the government . . . and gunning for us."[61]

The prevailing belief among the city's officers at the time was, "So went Chicago, so went the nation." Faced with race riots and antiwar demonstrations, the men carrying nightsticks on the beat readied for battle. "I knew—I think that we all began to sense that if there was going to be a war, much of it would be fought on our turf, that Chicago would be a battleground," says cop Steve Nowakowski. "So we couldn't lose—or lose face. Our city needed us, our nation needed us; we knew we would have to wage a war of defense in every neighborhood and fight street by street—hippie by hippie."[62]

chapter 2

"Freaks, Cowards, and Bastards": The War at Home

The foundations of authority have been blasted to bits in America because the whole society has been indicted, tried, and convicted of injustice. To the youth, the elders are the Ugly Americans; to the elders, the youth have gone mad.[1]

There were few days in the last half of that decade [the 1960s] when there was not some sort of demonstration activity that we, the police, had to clean up. It was nothing but them pushing the envelope on every front, from having sex in the open park, overdoses, and out-in-the-open-drug use. We're spit on, suffered threats to our persons, the city, the infrastructure, and our very way of life. They were attacking our nation on every front. There was no doubt about it in any of our minds. It was war.[2]

As Lyndon Johnson completed his slain predecessor's term and campaigned for one he could call his own, the "polecat" from the Texas town that bears his name appeared to favor letting the Vietnamese fight their own battles. The veteran politician in essence became the first president for peace, promising during the 1964 presidential campaign not to send young Americans to fight in Southeast Asia, a pledge he made repeatedly across the nation on the election trail while squeezing hands and kissing babies. "We are not about to send American boys nine or ten thousand miles away from home to do what Asian boys ought to be doing for themselves," Johnson told a campaign crowd in Akron, Ohio. His peacenik phase, however, was mostly political and short lived.[3] In August 1964, U.S. ships *Maddox* and *Turner Joy* reported coming under torpedo fire from the North Vietnamese in the Gulf of Tonkin. Seizing the opportunity, Johnson not only launched an air raid against the north but initiated a resolution before Congress that would have long-term consequences for the nation in Southeast Asia.

On August 7, Congress passed the controversial Gulf of Tonkin Resolution with the intention to "take all necessary measures to repel any armed attack against forces of the United States and to prevent further aggression." The legislation became "the functional equivalent" of a war declaration. The official view of the event, while passing almost unanimously in Congress, led to troubling questions. While the administration cast the attacks as unprovoked, at the time of the alleged aggression, the *Maddox* was engaged in covert operations designed to bomb coastal installations in North Vietnam. Three weeks following his inauguration, the president ordered the air force to begin bombing North Vietnam. By the end of the following month, the first American combat troops went ashore in Vietnam. Less than a month later in April 1965, the war at home began—an upheaval that was to consume the remainder of the decade.[4]

Amid a bevy of teach-ins, smoldering draft cards, and protest rallies, Johnson attempted to placate the growing unrest during a speech to students at Johns Hopkins University. "Vietnam," Johnson said, "is far away from this quiet campus. . . . Some four hundred young men born into an America bursting with opportunity and promise have ended their lives on Vietnamese soil. . . . We fight because we must fight if we are to live in a world were every country can shape its own destiny and only in such a world will our own freedom be finally secured." Johnson informed the students that this reality "will never be built by guns and bullets." At the same time, the president reminded the audience that they did not live in that idealistic world and would have to take the long, hard road to war in order to reach peace, freedom, and independence for South Vietnam. "We will not be defeated. We will not withdraw. We know that air attacks alone will not accomplish all of these purposes. We must be prepared for a long continued process." Not only did Johnson's address enliven the burgeoning antiwar movement, but for the remainder of his presidency, there were few places where the commander and chief was able to find a "quiet campus."[5]

Organized activity against the war had begun in earnest in December 1964, when the then virtually unknown Students for a Democratic Society (SDS) called for a march on Washington in April to protest the nation's deepening involvement in Southeast Asia. On April 17, the largest antiwar protest to date took place in the nation's capital as 25,000 protesters dressed in skirts, jackets, shirts, and ties converged to voice their opposition to their country's growing involvement in Vietnam. It was only the beginning of a larger movement. The remainder of 1965 saw demonstrations across the nation, including 15,000 protesters in Berkeley, 20,000 in Manhattan, and another 25,000 for a second march on Washington in November of that year. Although the numbers pale to the

massive demonstrations that took place from 1967 to 1971, the antiwar movement was already in full swing.[6] In April 1965, sensing an unfolding tragedy,
Oregon Senator Wayne Morse predicted that the Vietnam War would drive
Lyndon Johnson "out of office the most discredited president in the history of
the nation."[7] The prediction, while a lone congressional voice in 1965, proved to
be tragically fortuitous as a war of attrition dragged on in the jungles of Vietnam
and on American streets.

The amassed forces did not arise solely due to the administration's policy in
Southeast Asia. Many of the early demonstrators were part of the Old Left and
veterans of the civil rights movement, which saw a natural correlation. While
antiwar groups typically had young faces, protesters came from a cross-section of
the U.S. population, especially a growing number from the working class and
other students most at risk to the draft that began to dominate U.S. campuses by
the mid-to-late 1960s. Protest took on an increased fervor, with committed
activists ready to go to any lengths to disrupt the war effort on U.S. soil. In some
states, protestors laid down on tracks to block troop trains; others took extraordi-
nary means to demonstrate their opposition to their nation's war policy by dous-
ing themselves with gasoline and lighting their bodies on fire.[8] While opinion
polls showed strong support for the continuance of the war prior to February
1968, antiwar activists became emboldened by any hint that they were achieving
results in the struggle for public opinion.

In October 1967, several distinguished citizens turned over a briefcase full of
draft cards to the Justice Department. The forfeiture of more than 1,000 draft
cards resulted in the arrest and prosecution of Dr. Benjamin Spock, Marcus
Raskin, Mitchell Goodman, Michael Ferber, and Reverend William Sloan
Coffin. In a widely disseminated document, the group openly counseled young
men to spurn the draft. Calling the war "unconstitutional and illegal," the document stated that Americans have "a legal right and a moral duty to exert every
effort to end this war, to avoid collusion with it, and to encourage others to do
the same. . . . We call upon all men of good will to join us in this confrontation
with immoral authority. Especially we call upon the universities to fulfill their
mission of enlightenment and religious organizations to honor their heritage of
brotherhood. Now is the time to resist." Antiwar activists on university campuses
across the nation launched "We Won't Go" movements, pledging not to serve in
uniform in Vietnam, while burning their draft cards and encouraging others to
do the same. On October 21, 1967, federal marshals and military police confronted more than 100,000 demonstrators as they rallied in Washington, D.C.,
and marched on the Pentagon.[9]

Some of the worst clashes in the country were those between demonstrators
and city police departments. For the remainder of the year and into 1968, as antiwar activity spread and intensified, protesters were pitted against police with
growing frequency and violence. An all-volunteer army of police had inadvertently become foot soldiers in the war at home.

HOME-FRONT TROOPS

Clashes between citizens and police have been part of the nation's public discourse since colonial times. With the rise of the civil rights movement in the late 1950s and the beginning of the antiwar movement by the mid-1960s, citizen-police conflict took on an intensity not seen for almost a century. As the war at home heated up, the nation's police forces became the frontline forces dealing with all forms of dissent. Police also faced the pressures of city governments that relied on them as the primary means of quelling the excesses of antiwar demonstrations. During the 1960s, these disturbances often pitted police, typically from white, working-class backgrounds, against largely white, middle- and upper-middle class college kids. Although police had little in common with antiwar activists, an even greater gap existed between police departments and the growing cadre of black Americans fighting a system they claimed oppressed them. Carrying over from the civil rights movements of the 1950s, protests in the 1960s intensified as black Americans pushed to eliminate the remaining vestiges of segregation while demanding inclusion into greater American society. They called for an end to what they saw as systemic discrimination and, in some cases, outright racism in housing and employment opportunities. Alongside more mainstream movements headed by the Reverend Martin Luther King were enigmatic figures such as Malcolm X, and the Nation of Islam, and the charge that blacks were a colonized people. Black Americans likened their cause to worldwide Third World revolutionary movements.

Beginning in 1965, race riots occurred in several cities and continued with only the occasional reprieve for much of the next five years. Detroit, Washington, D.C., Newark, Los Angeles, Philadelphia, and Chicago were among the hardest hit cites. That August in Watts, rioting took thirty-four lives, caused 1,072 injuries, destroyed 977 buildings, and produced 4,000 arrests. Thirty thousand blacks participated in looting.[10] For black Americans, however, Vietnam had rapidly become as contentious an issue as poverty. As the number of black men serving in Vietnam was disproportionate to their percentage in the U.S. population, the war became a flash point of dissent and protest throughout the decade. In a growing number of American cities, police faced the brunt of the dissention.

By 1967, hardcore activities were not alone in showing opposition to the war, as even the moderate King broke his silence on the nation's foreign policy. On April 4, 1967, at Manhattan's Riverside Church, the famed civil rights leader delivered one of the most impassioned addresses against the war.

We are taking the young black men who had been crippled by our society and sending them 8,000 miles away to guarantee liberties in Southeast Asia, which they had not found in Southwest Georgia and East Harlem. So we have been repeatedly faced with the cruel irony of watching Negro and white boys on TV screens as they kill and die together for a nation that has been unable to seat them together in the same schools. So we watch them in brutal solidarity burning the huts of the poor village, but we realize that they would never live on the same block in Detroit.[11]

King's words did not move all members of the black community. A growing number of activists no longer felt that King's old guard spoke for them; his mantra of nonviolence, they argued, was unproductive and unrealistic. Over the Labor Day weekend in 1967, the National Conference for New Politics met in Chicago to choose a candidate to challenge Johnson. In the wake of increased rioting in the ghettos, however, young blacks were disinclined to follow the words of white liberals and moderate black leaders. As King gave the conference's keynote address, young blacks uttered threats and insults. Outside the Chicago Coliseum, groups of young blacks with bongo drums chanted, "Kill whitey!" King, along with convention cochairman Julian Bond and the reverend Andrew Young of the Southern Christian Leadership Conference (SCLC), left the convention.[12] That summer in Detroit, rioting and looting left forty-three dead. Police made 7,000 arrests as rioters destroyed 1,300 buildings and looted 2,700 businesses. The mayor thought his city looked like a war zone. Bewildered, Jerome Cavanagh simply uttered, "It looks like Berlin in 1945."[13]

Deadly and destructive riots and corresponding confrontations with police raised tensions across the country and seemingly pushed the system closer to chaos. The impact of the disturbances was not lost on some black activists who believed that they had to fight the system and the police, which in their view were propping the system up while suppressing them. Their stated objective was not only to prevent young blacks from serving in the military abroad but battling police and other civilian forces at home in a "racist America."

Black Power

Moving well beyond King's call for nonviolent disobedience, younger activists called for confrontation when dealing with the government and its police forces. Black activists made it clear that they were going to confront police at every opportunity, proclaiming that they had no respect for "white" laws relating to the draft for the Vietnam War or any other issue connected to civil rights or civil disobedience. Among the most radical of this organized opposition came from the Black Panthers. Formed in Oakland, California, in 1966, the Panthers became a magnet for police scrutiny for what they said, wrote, represented, and appeared. The organization, headed by Stokely Carmichael, Huey Newton, and Bobby Seale, called for blacks to not only refuse to serve their country in the military, but to wage war against the state at home by "any means necessary" to achieve equal treatment. "Black people should and must fight back," wrote Carmichael and Charles Hamilton in 1967, suggesting that it was time for black Americans to break away from King's call for nonviolence. "White people," they maintained, "must be made to understand that they must stop messing with black people, or the blacks *will* fight back!"[14]

As with other commentators, Carmichael stressed the troubles that blacks faced in the North, especially those who had immigrated from the South since the turn of the century, crowded into the urban ghettos of Philadelphia, Detroit, and

Chicago. Like several other northern cities, racial tension festered in Chicago as the ghetto expanded, dating back to the turn of the century and erupting in violence in 1919 when violent racial disturbances led to a five-day riot and claimed thirty-eight lives. Police were blamed for doing little to curb much of the white-on-black violence.[15] Black leaders, such as Carmichael, claimed that little had changed in Chicago in the intervening fifty years, where a severe lack of decent housing and poverty fed growing ghettos, where charges of unfair treatment by police was the norm.[16] Carmichael, writing in *Black Power* in 1967, was clear about what was needed:

It is difficult, if not impossible, for white America, or for those blacks who want to be like white America, to understand this basically revolutionary mentality. But in the final analysis, white America would save itself a lot of trouble if it did try to understand and to come to terms with this new black-oriented mentality. Because one thing stands clear: whatever the consequences, there is a growing—a rapidly growing—body of black people determined to "T.C.B."—take care of business. They will not be stopped in their drive to achieve dignity, to achieve their share of power, indeed, to become their own men and women—in this time and in this land—by whatever means necessary.[17]

Police forces were not alone in their concern for what they saw unfolding on American streets. The Pentagon worried also about a convergence of black and antiwar movements. Some officials believed that this development not only threatened the national peace but the public's support of the war. National Guard commander George L. Jackson revealed the detrimental effect it had on military capabilities:

This coalition [of civil rights and antiwar organizations] has spearheaded the shift of public opinion away from support of the Vietnamese conflict. . . . Just as the civil rights movement has served as a restraint upon the ability of American forces in Vietnam to complete their mission, so it has altered and restricted the use of military resources. The most apparent effect that the civil rights movement has had upon military force employment has been the necessity of using troops to quell civil disturbances.[18]

This reality was not lost on black activists. Panther Eldridge Cleaver knew that black militancy could severely hamper the war effort in Vietnam by forcing the expenditure of resources to confront protest at home. Cleaver stated that President Johnson not only faced trouble in Vietnam but a "Negro revolution at home." Evoking the late Malcolm X, he maintained that black Americans were justified in protecting themselves. "We shall have our manhood," Cleaver wrote. "We shall have it or the earth will be leveled by our attempts to gain it."[19] Cleaver blamed police forces for keeping blacks in their place. Increasingly, he likened the role of the police to the U.S. military. "The police," Cleaver wrote, "do on the domestic level what the armed forces do on the international level: protect the way of life of those in power. . . . The policeman and the soldier will violate your person, smoke you out with various gases. Each will shoot you, beat your head and body with sticks and clubs, with rifle butts, run you through with bayonets, shoot holes in your flesh, kill you. They have unlimited fire-power. . . . The policemen and the soldier will have the last word."[20]

"WE WERE BLAMED FOR EVERTHING"

For thousands of men wearing a police uniform during the mid-to-late 1960s, Cleaver's words confirmed some of their worst fears. The idea of antiwar groups joining, however loosely, with elements of the black power movement led to alarm in the ranks. Recalls officer Kurt O'Grady: "It was a real unsettling time; lots of us knew damn well what they [those in the radical black movement] thought of us. They weren't marching with the longhairs, but they shared a vision of destroying this country and they knew they had to get through us first. The stuff they wrote and said at those rallies that we covered sent a chill down the guys' spines."[21] Black activist H. Rap Brown, for example, had simple and chilling advice concerning white people. "Don't love him to death. Shoot him to death."[22]

The language and the attitude also fed many of the officers' base attitudes about blacks, impressions heightened as they viewed them as an extra violent appendage to the antiwar movement. "Hippie" challenges to "traditional values" had coupled with the worst images of black-on-white violence and racial stereotyping. Recalls cop Len Colsky, "The black movement had made it clear that all authority was the enemy. And they were giving even the real peace-loving hippies ideas—and that was scary. It was a loose joining together, a sort of convergence, however tenuous, and that was the real problem in those days. We had to get that rabbit back in the hat. It became an us against them thing." Panther Eldridge Cleaver agreed. "Everywhere the whites are fighting to prolong their status, to retard the erosion of their position. In America, when everything else fails, they call out the police."[23]

"Pigs"

As clashes between war demonstrators and police intensified, so did the rhetoric. The language of the more militant black activists infiltrated the words of the mainstream antiwar movement. Police officers became aware that the type and level of insults, along with spitting, taunts, and bottles and bricks, had increased dramatically. As a result, many officers began to blame young white radicals sympathetic toward the plight of blacks for the increase in antipolice hostility. There were reasons for those in the counterculture to see a natural bridge between their causes and those faced by black Americans; they began to see the police as a common enemy. Indeed, leaders, including Cleaver, challenged young white protestors: "The genie of black revolutionary violence is here, and it says that the oppressor has no rights which the oppressed are bound to respect. The genie also has a question for white Americans: which side to you choose? Do you side with the oppressor or with the oppressed? The time for decision is upon you."[24]

A growing number of officers were also becoming aware that the language used to describe them in underground publications and in speeches by black activists was bleeding into the terminology of the still predominantly white anti-war movement. In fact, many in the movement, even those who had not yet faced anything comparable to the history of blacks with police, began to see themselves as similarly victimized, labeling police "pigs," and speaking of oppression by a dominant culture. College newspapers and campus protest speeches increasingly reflected this mantra.[25]

The convergence and increased identification of the mainstream antiwar movement with black activists made many Chicago police officers nervous. Cop Paul Juravinski spoke to the issue:

We knew that a lot of the shit coming at us from those in the antiwar movement was because of black activists and them making such a public spectacle of their plight. So it wasn't just the war that these kids were against; they took on the cause of racial injustice and intolerance. And since they blamed us for that, for keeping them in their place, there was this strange convergence, where since we were to blame for blacks—and they linked the causes of oppression, between racial segregation and the Vietnam War as one cause brought about by the oppressors—that way, we were to blame for the Vietnam War, too. How about that? It's more true than anyone has the guts to say.[26]

Other cops agree that as movements converged, the police had become universal domestic symbols of the oppressors. Ray Mihalicz recalls:

We were the guys they faced on the streets and thus became equated with all social problems they took up the torch for, and foreign policy—you know, the war in Vietnam. If a protest rally went wrong, they faced us. When blacks rioted in their neighborhoods, they saw us controlling it. It became that we were the cause.[27]

Police officers bristled when they first heard white college kids begin to adopt "the language of the ghetto." Officer Sheldon Bartowski recalls, "Can you imagine some young, rich white brat calling us 'honky pigs' and 'the man'? The first time I heard it, I couldn't believe it." Cop Tom Freeborn concurs. " 'Pigs' was what the blacks called us when there was trouble. 'Pigs' was what the white kids called us when there wasn't yet trouble. They began to dress, act, and look like their 'black brothers', and, man, we were blamed for everything, it seemed. Things began to change so quickly then, and it was worlds apart from what I remember when I joined up. We had a level of respect that in just a few short years had evaporated."[28] For several police officers, the change from the time they joined the force to the mid-sixties was staggering.

Former Chicago police officer Ronald Adler, for one, joined the force in 1957. He said that he might have never made that decision had he known what was in store for him within a few short years. The city, as he recalled, had its share of big city problems, and he was tough and could take whatever the job required. But he hadn't prepared for the civil disturbances that came with the Vietnam War.

I knew, hell, five years before I joined the force, when I was in the tenth grade, that there was going to be trouble with African Americans; that was just a reality. But you know the war turned out to be a hell of a lot more divisive than I thought; I thought it would be like Korea; no one wanted to fight, but they did anyway. I was twenty-eight and Uncle Sam wouldn't be knocking on my door in 1964, but I would have gone even though I would have hated it. It wasn't like WWII where there was something to get fired up about with the Japs and the Krauts; who the hell were the Vietnamese? Anyway, when your country asks you to serve, you serve, and you don't ask questions. But these snot college kids said "hell no," and got the double AAs [African Americans] to get all riled up so we had both barrels of the shotgun pointed at us. They [blacks] were already calling us "motherfucking pigs," but then the college kids began to copy them calling us that and worse, pretending that they were being oppressed like the blacks because some of them were subjected to the draft. And since we were "oppressing" blacks, then we were suppressing them when we arrested them for antiwar demonstrations that got out of hand. So they blamed us for the war, too.[29]

Several former officers say that as the youth culture emerged, people became more strident with their opinions, deciding those who wore a uniform were not only indictable for many of society's ills but were akin to the worst characters in history. Ronald Lardo says that from 1957 to 1967 he no longer recognized his city, his nation, or his job description. "I hadn't signed up for the crap we put up with. Yes, we were supposed to control crowds and keep the peace, but they were not paying us enough to be spit on and have bags of excrement hurled at us. To be called fascists and Nazis and killers. We fought the fascists and the Nazis in the war and these punks who refused to serve had the nerve to call us by those names."[30]

As the war dragged on in Southeast Asia, so did the condemnation from the movement, as antiwar radicals and demonstrators blamed police for prolonging the war machine by restricting public gatherings against the war. Criticized for a foreign policy out of their control, those in the rank-and-file felt that they were caught between their commanders' demands to preserve law and order and those who blamed them for acting as the instruments of the government. The confrontations began to get personal. Former officer Hank Peterson recalls, "We were called in to quell a disturbance on Friday or Saturday night in Grant Park. Nothing much to it; a couple of longhairs had set up a band, pissing off some of the local hotels and restaurant managers; there were complaints, so we went in there to stop things before too big a crowd got going there, and then shit would hit the old fan. They were screaming at us before we got thirty feet from them— telling us that they were fucking our daughters, making fun of our haircuts, and calling us 'Nazis.' My family fought against those Kraut sons of bitches, and that just pissed me off like nothing else. I thought, the nerve of these little flee bag shits, and we shut 'em down."[31]

Former officers are quick to point out that there was no option to "shutting them down" as their watch commanders would not have it any other way. Carl Moore states, "As things progressed, each year and each month, say from late

'65 to '68 or so, we were told not to take any prisoners, that we were in a war, and that the taxpayers were not going to pay us to watch their city go down the shitter. It was the way Mayor Daley wanted it, and it was hard not to agree with him. And *I* agreed; so did a lot of the guys. You didn't have to tell us twice to do our job, and that is what we were doing." Officers claim that few understand what they faced on the streets during the 1960s. As a result, commentators condemned them from the safety of their homes and their broadcast booths, while police "took the hits" and stood in their defense. Eddie Kelso recalls:

The way we saw it—well, I'll only speak for myself here—is that the whole country was going to hell faster than you could wipe your nose. We had shit to clean up every night— and no one writes about that—human garbage with a mouth. And the press, they just wrote everything that these bastards said—and the biggest words that they used against us was "police brutality." My *ass* it was. We were not the ones breaking windows and throwing bottles and tying up traffic and making it so that an honest man could not make a living because they were disrupting things all over the damn place. And what were we to do about all the other crimes that were taking place? We were thinly spread, over-worked, stressed out—and when things weren't fixed right, or at least the way people thought they should have been, we took hell in our own neighborhoods; boy do I know it. We got friggin hell.[32]

"They Pissed on the Flag"

As protest rallies and marches increased in frequency and intensity, officers felt a growing pressure from their own communities and families to act. Officer Norm Nelson recalls, "It was like, when we went to my mother's house and the TV was on, it was like, 'Christ, turn the goddamn thing off before there was going to be a fight.' Who wanted to see a damn fight—the news would come on and punks and blacks were wrecking our city and spitting on the flag, and they say, 'Hey, Normy, why don't you guys wise up and stomp these bums. If you guys were real cops like Uncle Michael, this would not be happening.'" Other cops, such as Don Holtz, recall that they continuously faced doubt when television, newspaper, and radio reports detailed the troubles in U.S. cities. "People always knew better—we were getting free police advice in our own homes. Let me tell you, it wasn't fun. It got on your nerves and played with you at night when you were trying to sleep. There may have been a point when it all got to be too much and you decided to do something about it, and in a way it wasn't that we disagreed with what had to be done, it was that no one knew how much *had* to be done. You could crack guys' heads all night, every night, and the next week there would be a new crop of assholes waving placards, shitting in the park, and wearing our flag like it was a diaper or a snot rag—it was disgraceful."[33]

These were not the isolated feelings of a few cops. As public protests and displays of disobedience increased, so did the level of frustration. As one former officer says, "the harder we swung, the more they came." There were days when many in uniform did not want to see another person with long hair, another set of beads, another cross around a hippie's neck, or another peace sign. Former officer Henry Nostbakken recalls, "Even things that I liked, that I respected, were being denigrated like never before. Nothing was sacred. We had these peaceniks calling people who served their country in arms 'baby killers.' " Cop Sam McMaster agrees. "My brother and nephew served in Vietnam, and they were not baby killers, they were soldiers—*true* Americans who did what their country asked of them. And then there are all these kids—some of them who grew up right in our neighborhood, not outside agitators from San Francisco—who said these things, and because we wore a uniform, we were called the same thing. They wore the flag on the back of a dirty jean jacket, as if it was a badge of honor, and shit upon those who died to defend that flag. It made you sick some days, and it just got worse year after year, month after month."[34]

Increasingly, these officers believed that police departments were targets of those in the movement and their "black agitators." They maintain that speeches given by some at public rallies not only encouraged counterculture violence against those in uniform but against the entire "law-abiding" country. Indeed, Stokely Carmichael, among others, made it clear exactly what white America and the police faced. In his speech "Black Power," delivered at Berkeley in November of 1966, Carmichael took the rhetoric a step further. "This country is uncivilized. It needs to be civilized. . . . And so we must urge you to fight now to be the leaders of today, not tomorrow. . . . This country is a nation of thieves. It stands on the brink of becoming a nation of murderers. We must stop it. We must stop it." Such brazen attitudes were not lost on police in Chicago, who began to view organized black activists with increased scrutiny. While secret investigative units, including the infamous Red Squad, had followed, bugged, and wiretapped various dissident groups in Chicago since the 1920s, the city police department began to examine not only speeches, but fliers and newspaper and magazine articles. Mainstream, college, and underground publications, and even books, became required reading by some officers who felt that it was in their interests to scrutinize known "subversives." This included the Black Panthers, and those who may have shared some of their stated objectives, such as the increasingly militant words emanating from the core of the antiwar movement. As such, these "enemies" of law and order were associated *increasing* as the same.

Although the department's subversive unit usually monitored what was written in the underground press, much of the material was disseminated to members of the rank-and-file as confrontations with demonstrators increased. Officer Will Gerald was one of many who made it a point to read what was written by black militants and antiwar activists: "I just saw it as good police work. I wasn't targeting Negroes; I read all the crapola that came down the pike or out the pipe. But a lot of the real rabid stuff was from people like those Panthers, but not just them, mind you. There were all kinds of local wannabees and kooks with a cause who were hell bent on destroying our city just to spite us." Cop Herbert Bile knew that the police had real enemies on the street. "They were all against our society; blacks and the antiwar crowd, they were all the same. Some of them may have had a legitimate beef, but most of what I saw and read was pure baloney dressed up like steak. It was like they thought that we had a war going against them, but it was them that had declared war on us, and we were not about to say the hell with our neighborhoods; we had a duty to stop it, and the best way was to get inside their heads."[35] Although officers admit that not every cop in their district read the material, a dedicated core wanted to know more "about the enemy." While some of it was filtered down from the subversive unit, several of those in uniform made it a practice to not only share information on their own but form ideas from what they read.

Even officers who didn't read material from the underground and radical press usually knew of some who did. Says former officer Archie Pasis, "I didn't read the shit, but there were guys, you bet, that did. Sometimes it was brought into the station and left for the men to read, you know, to know what we were up against. The subversive, intelligence unit guys liked to let us know what to look for and what we were up against." As with other officers, Pasis suspects that the material was used to "fire up the troops," while allowing them to justify what they had to do on the streets. He stresses, however, that the material was taken seriously. "They make it look like we were trying to keep blacks in their place and uphold-ing segregation. It was nothing like that. They were all part of the antigovernment war and more so, antilaw and order. Blacks used their plight to attack the country and the war and we saw them the same as any of those longhairs that were ruining the country. What were we to do? Go have coffee while they burned the city to the ground? People were being counseled to break the law and ignore our com-mands." Ira Freyling speaks to the difficulty cops faced. "It became increasingly impossible to get anyone to do anything. You had the black agitators and the SDSers [members of Students for a Democratic Society] joining hands and getting all those little unwashed punks all fired up for a cause, and then we took the brunt of it 'cause we had to control it. It had become a fine mess."[36]

Some officers, such as Terry Novicki, took the material they read personally. "It was one of those things where you didn't want to know anymore what was to come, but a couple of us could not resist reading it, and even out loud to whomever wanted to listen. And Christ, some of it was so personal and so *out there* that you wondered if you were gonna get shot stepping out of your house in the morning." The wariness increased with rallies, protests, and concerts fre-quented by ever larger numbers of youths, especially those from the antiwar movement. Says Cal Noonan, "Each year it got simply worse and worse. The rhetoric was more violent, directed increasingly not just against the administra-tion and what was happening with the troops in Vietnam or the draft, but against us. They thought that if they were speaking while disrupting the public peace and we shut 'em down, then we were shutting their speech down. That isn't right. They can say whatever the hell they wanted but not block the damn street at the same time. They just thought that they could do whatever they wanted and we should have just gone away, but that was not our job. No sir."[37]

By the beginning of 1968, televised images made the situation in the nation appear as if it were sliding toward anarchy. In the hearts and minds of some who wore the badge on the streets of Chicago, their fears seemed to be coming to fruition. The frequent battles with the antiwar movement were combined with their own worries about those fighting in Vietnam and a growing sense of dread about the war. Like the rest of the population, many officers had relatives and friends serving in Southeast Asia. For police, discussion of the war in their own homes had become increasingly uncomfortable. "It was not a topic that went down well around the dinner table," says former officer Victor Olafson. "Even those who were gung ho for the war were beginning to have their doubts, and after [newscaster Walter] Cronkite bit down on a lemon and gave his big kiss off to the war on national TV, there was more trouble. There was because all those antiwar, anti-*everything* pukes knew there was blood in the water. There was a lot of blood spilled already, and there was a lot more to come. These kids took advantage of our nation when it was weak and turned on the afterburners. That was 1968 to come."[38]

As trouble and confrontations with the movement increased, so did the level of anger and even hatred with anything or anyone connected with the antiwar movement. Among these officers, there appears to have been a volatile mixture of fear and contempt. "It was hard to know what to expect from them," says Fred Jeffery. "I think that there were some good kids out there, but they were mixed up with the lunatic fringe. They could get whipped up into a frenzy, and that was scary because these agitators had all these flower children, and some of them did mean well and were for peace, but those opportunists had too many of these kids believing that we were Nazis and brown shirts. That made dealing with the '60s people very unpredictable." Other police officers were even more direct in their feelings about the movement. "I knew this *peace* movement," states Steven Latz, a ten-year veteran of the force at the time. "They were a rotten generation, and they made each day we went to work harder and our communities less safe. They joined with the black militants and that was nothing but trouble, let me tell you. From then on it was all-out war."[39]

Adding to the animosity police felt toward to the movement was their belief that demonstrators were giving their enemies aid and comfort in Vietnam while flirting with communist agents in America. Police saw the movement against the war as a national embarrassment. "It was a disgrace how they pissed on the flag," recalls cop Eddie Kelso. "It seemed like everything that was right about the country—saluting the flag, protecting our nation, they were against; it was wrong." Other officers felt that the behavior of the antiwar movement was not only reprehensible and an affront to the nation's image but was to blame for the unfolding disaster. Some Chicago police officers believed the biggest obstacle to victory in Southeast Asia was not the Vietcong but American demonstrators. Says former cop Ronald Lardo, "As those protests increased, so too did the second guessing at home among the government and the military, and then those peace talks and calling for an end to the bombing—those punks had went and scared the commander and chief, and old Lyndon was a hard guy to spook."[40]

Despite the cost and loss in Vietnam and the growing rage at home, opinion polls on the eve of 1968 revealed that the majority of Americans still supported their country's war effort. Though there were some cracks in the armor of resolve, there was one man who steadfastly refused to entertain the idea that the United States was embroiled in a war it could not win. In late 1967, the commander of U.S. forces in Vietnam, General William Westmoreland, provided an optimistic assessment of the war effort. As Westmoreland looked into the new year, he saw America winning the war. "The friendly picture," he advised, "gives rise for increased success in 1968."[41] For police manning the frontlines at home, however, a new year did not appear to present much of a reprieve internationally or domestically. Indeed, as 1968 loomed, they held that the antiwar movement and the counterculture were a dangerous and subversive element that threatened to plunge the nation into anarchy. "As another year of shit ended," recalls Milt Brower, "I remember thinking, what now—what's next? Is there going to be a meltdown, a civil war? We knew already that we were in trouble over there in 'Nam. There was a lot of trepidation as 1968 began." Officer George Horsley felt a similar dread. "I don't know why, just a feeling of dread—that things were building to a head at home while so many of our guys were putting their lives on the line in Vietnam. And then look what happened."[42] For cops including Orrest Hupka, the dominant feelings were anger and fear. As 1967 came to a close, both the war aboard and the one at home had become personal.

We seemed to be in it over our heads on the streets at home, and then there was the damn war—and it hurt my family. I had two friends killed here in the city, and then a cousin, and two friends—longtime friends—dead in Vietnam. I supported the war, most of the guys I knew did. But it was tough, and then these antiwar people were calling returning veterans baby killers. How did they know what was happening? They weren't in those jungles. I heard what it was like. At the beginning of that year, 1968, I still supported the war. But that war made the one we were fighting on the streets here all the worse. Every crackpot with a gripe came out of the woodwork that year. The wheels had come off. . . . It was nothing but freaks, cowards, and bastards.[43]

chapter 3

"What's America Coming To?": January–June 1968

There was growing trepidation in the district. The year began badly, and we didn't know what to expect next. There was a sense that events were going to slip out of control, that there was going to be a meltdown and chaos was going to emerge. There was no sense anymore of law and order, at least none that I could see. No sense that as a nation and as a people, we all believed in the same thing, or wanted the same thing for our country. And the so-called *future* of this country was going to be taken over and run by a bunch of long-haired animals that were in college and were inciting everyone else to do dangerous things, and it was up to us to make sure that they didn't plunge our nation into anarchy. Each month there were new reasons for fear. We did not know what was going to happen next. There was no doubt in our minds that there was cause for alarm.[1]

History took on a vicious pace as the nation moved into 1968, dashing the hopes many Americans held for a better year from the one that passed. By summer, the nation was not only reeling from military defeats in Southeast Asia, but riots, assassinations, and spreading chaos at home. With the succession of calamities, a wary nation waited for the next shoe to fall. So jarring were events that former Students for a Democratic Society (SDS) member Todd Gitlin referred to the year as a "series of exclamation points."[2]

The first of a string of events occurred on January 31, when any lingering hope for a timely American victory in Vietnam crumbled. The launch of a massive attack by the Vietcong on the Tet holiday signaled the beginning of the end of Americans' appetite for their president's lament of "more cost and more loss in Vietnam," as more than 60,000 Vietcong troops invaded dozens of cities and towns throughout the south. While U.S. and Vietnamese forces recaptured most of the urban areas within days of the initial attacks, the war effort had never looked more hopeless, as even the American embassy in Saigon proved vulnerable to enemy forces. The attack came on the heels of General Westmoreland's assurance that U.S. forces were winning the war. Although Johnson relieved him of his command in favor of General Creighton Abrams, he was not able to forestall a growing military disaster abroad or political chaos and division at home.[3]

Demonstrations ensued in more than 100 American cities and on the majority of college campuses. Contributing greatly to the burgeoning opposition to the war was an unexpected on-air editorial from veteran CBS News anchor Walter Cronkite upon his return from Vietnam:

It seems now more certain than ever that the bloody experience of Vietnam is to end in a stalemate. This summer's almost certain standoff will either end in real give-and-take negotiations or terrible escalation; and for every means we have to escalate, the enemy can match us, and that applies to invasion of the North, the use of nuclear weapons, or the mere commitment of one hundred or two hundred or three hundred thousand more troops to the battle. And with the escalation, the world comes close to the brink of cosmic disaster.[4]

The first person who understood the importance of these words was the president. Johnson knew that Cronkite's address would ripple through the American heartland. "If I've lost Walter, then it's over," Johnson said. "I've lost Mr. Average Citizen." Six weeks following Cronkite's unprecedented commentary on a futile war, other canons of the media establishment, including the *Wall Street Journal* and *Newsweek*, joined in the call for immediate de-escalation, further isolating the president.[5] Johnson found no sanctuary from the growing foreign policy disaster at home, as his administration faced growing protests, civil disobedience, an upswing in race riots, militant Black Panthers, and daily demonstrations outside the White House. There were even placards that read: "Lee Harvey Oswald, where are you now that we need you." On February 8, 1968, the war at home turned tragic, as state troopers fired on unarmed students on the all-black campus of South Carolina State College in Orangeburg. In what became known as the "Orangeburg Massacre," twenty-seven unarmed students were wounded and three were killed in a hail of gunfire.[6]

In an attempt to grapple with the growing unrest, Johnson's staff went about preparing the National Advisory Commission on Civil Disorders. But as much as the president tried in vain to quell the rising tide, there was no reprieve from the deepening social and military quagmire or the growing divisions within his party; even Johnson's hold on the presidency soon came under direct challenge. The first challenger to emerge was Eugene McCarthy.

"THE PARTISAN DIVISIONS"

It was only a matter of time before the political and social turmoil played into the hands of Johnson's detractors within the Democratic Party. Buoyed by a small army of youthful volunteers dubbed the "children's crusade," Minnesota Senator Eugene McCarthy surprised even some of his most avid supporters by capturing

40 percent of the vote in the New Hampshire primary. The young "clean for Gene" volunteers that shaved, cut their hair, and donned more conventional clothing had grown so rapidly that McCarthy's campaign workers began to turn some away. His supporters, who favored the senator's call for a speedy negotiated settlement to the war, believed that McCarthy represented the strongest voice in the Democratic Party to challenge the incumbent president. McCarthy's support, however, owed more to the opposition against an unpopular sitting president and a growing foreign policy disaster than to McCarthy's political appeal.[7]

Soon after McCarthy's "win," in New Hampshire, Robert Kennedy decided that the political waters were right to join the race. While Kennedy claimed that his decision was based on a desire to stop "disastrous" and "divisive polices," his candidacy for the Democratic ticket only created more division within his party and on the streets. The day after his announcement, New Yorkers booed Kennedy during his appearance at the city's St. Patrick's Day parade with shouts of "opportunist" and "coward" lacing the parade route. The same day, 30,000 additional troops were sent to Vietnam. While Senator Fulbright's Foreign Relations Committee hearings concerning the war continued on Capitol Hill, the president's own inner circle provided him with a sobering dose of reality. In late March, in a meeting of Johnson's friends and advisers (later dubbed the "Wise Men"), the president heard the grim news on the war. The group, which included McGeorge Bundy, Henry Cabot Lodge, General Maxwell Taylor, Dean Acheson, George Ball, General Omar Bradley, and Abe Fortas, informed Johnson that it was not possible to win the war for another five to ten years at the minimum, and more so, the public no longer supported the war.[8] The president felt under siege from all sides, and he was plagued by personal demons. Central to his fears was Kennedy's decision to seek the presidency. "I felt that I was being chased on all sides by a giant stampede," Johnson admitted years later. "I was being forced over the edge by rioting blacks, demonstrating students, marching welfare mothers, squawking professors, and hysterical reporters. And then the final straw. The thing I feared from the first day of my Presidency was actually coming true. Robert Kennedy had openly announced his intention to reclaim the throne in the memory of his brother."[9]

On March 31, the man who held lifetime presidential ambitions, told a nationwide audience that he would not seek another term in the Oval Office. Johnson prefaced his startling announcement by admitting to a growing split in the country and his desire to stem a dangerous tide. "I have concluded that I should not permit the presidency to become involved in the partisan divisions that are developing in this political year. . . . Accordingly, I shall not seek, and I will not accept, the nomination of my party for another term as your president."[10] Johnson's decision was the hardest of his life. He would later say, "The only difference between the Kennedy assassination and mine is that I am alive and it has been more torturous."[11] In Chicago, Mayor Daley was "shocked" by the president's decision. "It was a historic moment in the Presidency for an American Chief of State to put the unity of his country and passionate desire for peace ahead of personal feelings and politics."[12] Unity and peace, however, were far from what followed Johnson's monumental decision; his stunning retirement ushered in six of the most violent months of the war at home. The president left the nation with the spoils of a degenerating war and teetering on the edge of anarchy. "American politics became unhinged," wrote Theodore White, as power drifted into the streets across the nation. In Chicago, the police were about to face one of their biggest tests, one that would have direct consequences later that summer.

April

In 1968, Americans had reason to agree with T. S. Eliot's lament, "April is the cruellest month." Five days into the month a rifle shot silenced the heart, soul, and voice of the civil rights movement in Memphis, Tennessee. As the news spread of Martin Luther King Jr.'s assassination, leaders issued pleas for calm. Among the voices for restraint was Robert Kennedy. The former attorney general, who knew as much as anyone about personal tragedy, attempted to stem the rioting and violence that he knew would surely follow the news that King's assassin was a white man, James Earl Ray.[13] "For those of you who are black and are tempted to be filled with hatred and distrust at the injustice of such an act, against all white people, I can only say that I feel in my own heart the same kind of feeling," said Kennedy. "I had a member of my family killed, but he was killed by a white man. But we have to make an effort in the United States, we have to make an effort to understand, to go beyond these rather difficult times."[14] Few, however, heeded Kennedy's impassioned pleas.

The rioting in the days immediately following King's death nearly eclipsed all of 1967. Before the end of the month, the nation suffered 202 racial disturbances in 172 cities, forty-three deaths, 3,500 injuries, and a staggering 27,000 arrests.[15] A machine gun nest was set up on the steps of the U.S. Capitol while army troops patrolled several cites. Chicago joined Washington, D.C., Detroit, and Philadelphia as the worst hit. In Chicago, where some of the more severe rioting ensued, nine blacks lost their lives and twenty city blocks were lost to the fires. There were scores of break-ins, rampant incidents of arson, and looting was widespread. Mobs broke the windows of city buses, drivers were hurt in breaking glass, and others were beaten. Schools and businesses closed. The day of King's assassination, Mayor Daley pleaded for an end to the violence. While his firefighters and police faced sporadic sniper fire, sometimes pinning them down, members of the National Guard took to the streets.[16] The next day, as army troops arrived to help restore order, Daley set a 7 P.M. to 6 A.M. curfew for everyone under twenty-one; incidents of looting and arson raged on.[17]

The following day, with 5,000 army troops on patrol, the mayor surveyed the damage to his city from a helicopter.[18] Not helping Daley's mood nor endearing the antiwar movement to the city of Chicago, activist Rennie Davis decided to lead a demonstration during the middle of some of the worst rioting in the city's history. Officers, already under stress and lacking resources, responded with teargas.[19] The fire department fared little better, as firefighters not only faced sniper fire, but on Friday of that turbulent week, they experienced the worst day since the Great Fire of 1871. The department reported that a new fire broke out every fifteen seconds.[20] By April 7, police had made 2,000 arrests, including 400 juveniles; one-third of the arrests were for looting. Officers charged twenty with arson. The police department placed their officers on twelve-hour shifts, up from the regular eight.[21] The violence finally abated, and by April 11, Daley lifted the curfew for those under twenty-one; the following day, federal troops left the city. The days of rioting took the lives of nine people.[22]

While clashes did occur between police and rioters, by most accounts, Chicago's police acted with restraint, despite the ferocity of the riots and the department's less than exemplary reputation in dealing with the city's black population. While police made dozens of arrests, there were few claims of undue force during the weeklong rioting. As Daley lifted the curfew, he commended city police for doing an "outstanding job in trying times."[23] But there were grumblings that Daley had failed to take the measures necessary to control the arson and widespread looting. One of the calls came from black State Senator Charles Chew (D) from Chicago. "I would like to see the law enforced at all costs, and I don't care whose toes are stepped on."[24] Letters in the *Tribune* readers' forum included instructions on how the city should handle riots in the future. "Let's change the rules," wrote one outraged Chicagoan. "No decent person wants looting. All over the world, the order 'shoot to kill all looters' has always been the only effective deterrent to this dastardly crime. Make it clear that all looters are to be shot on site." An editorial from the same day appeared to agree with the need for a tougher stance, along with the implied criticism of the mayor and the police. "Until the army restored order," said the *Tribune* commentary, "we had anarchy in Chicago."[25]

Two days later, on April 15, Daley laid down the gauntlet, issuing some of his toughest language during his long tenure in the mayor's office. The feisty city boss made headlines when he ordered his officers to "shoot to kill" arsonists and "shoot to maim or cripple" looters.[26] Taking his superintendent of police, James B. Conlisk Jr., to task, he publicly rebuked him before members of the media. Daley said that he was "very much disappointed to learn that every policeman pounding a beat was to use his own discretion. He should have had instructions to shoot arsonists and shoot looters." And what was seen as a public dressing down of his superintendent of police, Daley stated "In my opinion, there should have been orders to shoot arsonists to kill, and to shoot looters in order that they be detained." When reporters asked if Conlisk would be asked to step down, the mayor did not exactly give his top cop a ringing endorsement. "I wouldn't want to discuss that at this time," Daley said. "I want to await the report of my committee." The mayor added, though, that he was "disappointed" in his superintendent, as there was "no reason for this lawlessness and immorality. An arsonist is a murderer and should be shot right on the spot." Daley was critical of both his officers and their commanders for failing to take what he saw in hindsight as the necessary action. When reporters inquired as to why a shoot-to-kill policy was not in place, Daley responded, "I assumed the orders were given. I would assume any superintendent would issue orders to shoot any arsonists on-site. I'll surely take action to improve the police department."[27] Conlisk reacted quickly to Daley's demand, sending the following signed message over the department's Teletype to all unit commanders:

Arson, attempted arson, burglary, and attempted burglary and forcible felonies. Such force as is necessary including deadly force [gunfire] shall be used to prevent the commission of these offenses and to prevent the escape of perpetrators. Commanding officers will insure that the above and general order 67-14 [governing the use of force by police] are continually reviewed at all roll calls beginning immediately and continuing thru April 22.[28]

According to reports in the *Tribune*, some officers were miffed over the order as it clashed with order 67-14, which limits the use of firearms in crowds, a factor in much of the looting and incidents of arson during the April riots. The *Tribune* article indicated, however, that most officers praised the order. Indeed, Joseph J. LeFevour, president of the Fraternal Order of Police, sent Daley a telegram of thanks. "I can assure you that you will have the fullest cooperation of the Chicago policemen in carrying out your orders," LeFevour wrote, adding, "you have our deepest respect and admiration for the unequivocal stand you have taken with respect to the anarchy that is threatening to destroy our society."[29] Daley also received important backing from former superintendent O. W. Wilson. "I have great respect and a very high regard for Mayor Daley's judgment," said Wilson, who held the top cop position prior to Conlisk. "And if in his judgment this is the action that should be taken I certainly would back it."[30]

The people of Chicago also wholeheartedly agreed with Daley's "strong stand."[31] In the first three days following his shoot to kill orders, city officials received more than 10,000 letters backing Daley by a count of fifteen to one.[32] "He's talking my language," said city alderman Vito Marzullo. "If the order had been issued April 5 there would have been less trouble, and it would have been ended quickly." Even though Daley modified his directive a few days later, people remembered his original orders much more than his subsequent "clarification."[33] Indeed, his original news conference sent shockwaves through the police department, as officers knew they were going to be under pressure to act.

While Daley criticized his officers for their lack of gunplay, a *Sun-Times* editorial a day later criticized police for their "indiscriminate" use of their weapons. The editorial suggested that the police instead should have been more aggressive in using their chemical mace.[34] The vast majority of police believed that increased use of their guns would only lead to more trouble and conflict with order 67-14 implemented by former superintendent O. W. Wilson, a order thought sensible by many officers. The lesson that was driven home, however, was that they were expected to be much more aggressive from the outset of any future disturbances. While U.S. attorney general Ramsey Clark and New York mayor John Lindsay condemned Daley's orders, city officials in other locales endorsed similar measures. Miami's chief of police Walter B. Headley, for example, recommended his officers shoot arsonists and looters on sight to curb further riots. Headley stated, "It is a matter of common law that looters and arsonists may be shot on sight. That is the quickest way to contain it."[35]

Government and civic leaders had more than race riots to contain, however, as they faced a rise in both the frequency and intensity of campus protests. While there were numerous violent clashes between police and students across the nation, one of the more poignant of these took place in New York City on the campus of Columbia University, where mayor Lindsay was about to face his own civic crisis. Lindsay had criticized Daley's directives for dealing with disturbances, adding that New York would handle turmoil with a more even hand. The mayor stated, "We're not going to turn disorder into chaos."[36]

The Siege of Columbia

As protests spread to more than 200 universities across the country, a foreshadowing of Chicago's violent summer took place at Columbia University. On April 23, the local chapter of SDS together with a cadre of antiwar radicals occupied the president's office and buildings housing classrooms and kidnapped the acting dean of Columbia College, Henry Coleman. The actions were related to the university's decision to expand, a move affecting a large area of neighboring black housing. For a week, protestors ransacked administrative and faculty offices and occupied buildings causing the cancellation of classes. When it became clear that order was not forthcoming, university officials called in the New York City police to end the stranglehold. Police action, however, only radicalized the remainder of the student body. A massive student strike forced the university to close for the remainder of the term. Contributing to the siege was the protestors' charge that the university's administration was unduly rigid when dealing with dissent. University officials, however, feared that the increasing chaos on campus would spread into nearby Harlem, thereby creating a larger and perhaps deadly disturbance.[37]

Those in the movement criticized officials for creating a "police riot," arguing that police seriously overreacted to events. More than 1,000 officers, the largest police action to date at an American university, charged the occupied buildings, first clearing students from doorways before entering with nightsticks, which, according to various accounts, they used freely. Police countered that they only made arrests when students ignored a warning to leave. During the melee, cops clubbed, knocked to the ground, occasionally kicked, and threw students into paddy wagons. And much like later conflicts between the police and the media in Chicago, Robert Thomas, a reporter for the *New York Times,* was beaten by uniformed and plainclothes officers after being identified as a journalist. Thomas required twelve stitches to close a gash to his head. Reports indicated that some officers wore trench coats with concealed batons. The officers in question either refused to show identification or were not carrying ID, and waited outside until their uniformed counterparts pushed people out of the buildings. Once outside, plainclothes officers moved in with their nightsticks. The battered included faculty members, such as history professor James Shenton, who was beaten, kicked, and had an elbow broken.[38]

Compounding the incidents of violence was that after police ended the occupation of the campus buildings—the stated reason for the action—officers swept the college grounds where students and other onlookers were watching the unfolding drama. The police charged the crowds, clubbing everyone in sight, arresting more than 700, and prompting 120 charges of police brutality with the New York City Police Civilian Complaint Review Board.[39]

The result was not all bad news to some in the movement. In fact, a major confrontation with authorities was what some activists wanted to see replicated. "Columbia opened a new tactical stage in the resistance movement which began last fall: from the overnight occupation of buildings to permanent occupation," wrote Tom Hayden in *Ramparts,* following the actions in Columbia. "From mill-ins to the creation of revolutionary committees; from symbolic civil disobedience to barricaded resistance. Not only are these tactics already being duplicated on other campuses, but they are sure to be surpassed by even more militant attacks." Hayden suggested that in the future, protestors would need to threaten the destruction of buildings as "a last deterrent to police attacks." Further, he suggested, "Columbia's problem is the American problem in miniature. . . . A crisis is foreseeable that would be too massive for police to handle . . . what is certain is that we are moving toward power— the power to stop the machine if it cannot be made to serve human needs."[40]

Hayden pledged to "bring the war home" with an expansion of the acts seen in Columbia, while fellow activist Jerry Rubin stated "We're now in the business of wholesale disruption and widespread resistance and dislocation of the American society."[41] Such pronouncements were not lost on members of the police, certainly not those in the Chicago Police Department. The force was becoming increasingly alarmed with movement rhetoric directed at their city following the events in New York. Former Chicago police officer Sam McMaster remembers well the tensions that were building in the ranks as his fellow officers worried about similar riots at Chicago's university campuses. "That Columbia thing got a lot of press; it was like, shit, I hope that doesn't happen here; but we knew that it would. We had it up to here with the shit after King's killing, and the mood was just going to hell."[42]

Although few officers recall reading or hearing about Hayden's words, they knew there were threats to launch similar action in Chicago that summer for the convention. "We knew they were coming," says cop Norm Nelson. "It was the buzz on the street. Guys were reading these pronouncements, how they were going to make it so we had little choice but to listen to them because they were going to begin to destroy what they occupied. Well, it didn't sound anything like peaceful assembly and peaceniks wanting to end the war. They wanted to have a war on our streets."[43] Officer Sam Ivanchenko agrees. "It's not fair; those guys in New York were doing their jobs. They gave those kids fair warning and then they did what they had to do. You got a few jerk reporters who stick a microphone in front of kids' mouths and take a picture and make it look like they are a bunch of Nazis. And damn it, I knew the freaks were on their way here. We all did."[44] Indeed, there is some indication that New York and Chicago police were communicating formally or informally about the actions of the Yippies following the Columbia incident. The particular concern surrounded what the Yippies may have been planning for the August convention. Following the arrest of Jerry Rubin in June, New York police questioned the Yippie leader about the group's plans for Chicago.[45]

Police knew that they did not have to wait until summer for trouble, as the level of antiwar activity in the Windy City had grown steadily. Still in the shadow of the riots following King's assassination, police faced pressure from

Mayor Daley and their own commanders to take a tougher stance against any disturbances. With internal demands and a sizable antiwar protest rally set to take place in Chicago within days, the stage was set for what was to become a dress rehearsal for convention week.

"We Were under Pressure"

The message that Chicago was going to be an unfriendly place for the antiwar movement came home loud and clear on the afternoon of April 27. What began as a peaceful march of 5,000 demonstrators against the war turned into a violent tussle with police. Following the two-mile trek from Grant Park, protestors planned to gather on the grounds of the Civic Center Plaza. When marchers arrived at the site, they discovered it roped off. Police refused to allow anyone into the plaza area, claiming that workers were caulking—an assertion rejected by a reporter from *United Press International* who said that no workers were in sight when the protestors arrived. As marchers began to circle the Civic Center, some cut into the ropes. When demonstrators breached the barriers, officers under the command of Superintendent Conlisk hustled them off the plaza grounds and onto nearby Washington and Clark streets. Two hundred and fifty marchers refused to move and staged a sit-in. Police again moved in, forcing them across the street, breaking them into smaller groups, and using mace when they faced resistance. The situation worsened when police ordered marchers to drop their placards; instead, some threw the heavy signs at nearby officers. A female marcher struck Commander James Riordan in the head with a sign, sending the veteran officer to the hospital. Fourteen others required medical treatment, including a *Tribune* city news bureau reporter.

Approximately 1,000 officers moved in swinging nightsticks and spraying mace. Several of the fifty demonstrators arrested by police showed their displeasure by spitting on arresting officers. Riordan later complained to the media "many policemen were kicked, pummeled and spat on."[46] Some witnesses, however, claimed that it was not only marchers who were clubbed but spectators and local area shoppers. Among the victims was *Sun-Times* photographer Jack Lenahan, who was struck by police batons after trying to photograph a woman knocked down by an onrush of police. The assistant city editor with the city news bureau was also hit in the head during the scuffle with police.[47] The *Tribune* reported that approximately fifty counter-demonstrators watched the melee and "exchanged curses" with marchers. Some of the locals encouraged police to "Sock it to 'em." It took police forty-five minutes to quell the disturbances.[48]

While there was much condemnation of police actions, the department and Daley's office all but ignored the incident. Individual officers believed that they had, in fact, done nothing for which to apologize. Former cop Ernie Bellows recalls, "There were thousands of these kids on the street. The place, as I remember, was roped off. We had other barricades up, and we weren't stopping the march, but at the end of it, they insisted on breaking through the barricade. They didn't have to go those last few feet around the Civic Center; they could have stopped there, but there's always a few agitators who push it, and there was noth-ing we could do." Cop Bob Nurnberger agrees, adding that police felt they had to stop protestors from doing what they wanted. "If we let them through the barricade, then there is nothing stopping them from doing whatever the hell they wanted. And, of course, when we tried to stop them, they fought back."[49]

Police also play down claims of attacks against innocent bystanders and members of the media. "When things are moving that quickly, and when there's people hit-ting you and running every which way, it's hard to tell who are the protestors and who are the bystanders," says former cop "Sash" Sadowski. "Bystanders should get the hell out of the way, but they just stand there and let the crowd run over them. The press, well, those SOBs, they like to move right into the thick of things, right into the area we are trying to clear, and get themselves hurt. Well, they are adults, aren't they? Then they get roughed up and cry police brutality."[50]

Officers such as Harold "Hank" Pacnik blamed demonstrators for starting the violence and for doing more damage than the police. "They took swings at our guys—spit and started swinging their goddamn signs; a commander was hit on the head and needed medical attention. A bottle just missed my ear. They could have listened to our commanders, but they wanted to cause trouble, that's why they crashed the barrier and broke the law. I think that this was blown way out of proportion by some who wanted to make it look like we were brutalizing people out there and what it was, was textbook crowd control."[51]

The commission that looked into the event disagreed. It concluded that the police "badly mishandled their task. Brutalizing demonstrators without provoca-tion." While finding that police failed to act in a professional manner, the report placed the ultimate blame with city officials. "The April 27 stage had been pre-pared by the Mayor's designated officials weeks before. Administrative actions concerning the April 27 Parade were designed by City officials to communicate that 'these people have no right to demonstrate or express their views.' Many acts of brutal police treatment on April 27 were directly observed (if not commanded) by the Superintendent of Police or his deputies."[52]

Indeed, some officers feel that the commission that looked into the peace march was right. Says former cop Ira Freyling, "The trouble—the widespread crapolla that took place after King got killed—bled into the Civic Center thing. Sure. We were on notice—and I don't think that's a secret." Cal Noonan, already a fifteen-year vet-eran of the department, agrees. "Look, this was no big thing happening on the streets that April. The superintendent [James Conlisk] had got his hide tanned in public by Daley, and the thumb was on us to make sure that it didn't happen again. And everyone knew that the big show [the Democratic National Convention] was on that summer. We were under pressure to shut down the movement in Chicago."[53]

Officer Brian Ramsey concurs, adding that he and his fellow officers, while not specifically ordered to assault marchers, understood that it was the desired outcome. "Stuff was defiantly happening. We were getting reamed for not doing our jobs all month, especially after the King assassination in the black areas; the word through the food chain was that there was not going to be any more 'Mr. Nice Guy' when dealing with protestors of any kind. I think that someone wanted to put the fear of

God in any and all demonstrators, especially with the convention that summer. I think that we did not do our jobs that day." Reg Novak agrees. "It was crummy police work. It was because of fire from above—the mayor's office. Our commanders got leaned on and they leaned on us, and there it is."[54] The pressure to arrest did not sit well with all cops. One officer said later, "Each one of us was told that we had to make an arrest. I couldn't believe it. There was nobody bad there."[55]

While police felt that the media was often against them when dealing with blacks and the peace movement, they had little cause for animosity following the Civic Center incident. Chicago newspapers did not provide in-depth coverage of the peace march riot.[56] Officers also knew that they received some internal congratulations following the event. Says cop Gord Stensill, "We had done what the powers that be wanted, and it was clear that that was the way we were to deal with demonstrations and demonstrators. Don't let them move. We were told that we had done right."[57] The incident's impact not only helped to foster a climate where police could rough up demonstrators with virtual impunity, but it served as an eerie foreshadowing of events to come during the Democratic convention in August.

"On to Chicago"

In announcing his intention to seek the Oval Office, Hubert Horatio Humphrey appeared to have little understanding of the deep divisions gripping the nation, or even what year it was. "Here we are, the way politics ought to be in America," said Humphrey, "the politics of happiness, the politics of purpose and the politics of joy."[58] Detractors would use the vice president's words to dog the remainder of his campaign. Furthermore, Humphrey had made it clear that he supported the administration's policy in Southeast Asia, one that was already being soundly discredited by the president's own advisers. Although he harbored private doubt about Vietnam, his public support of Johnson and his war policy made him a favorite of party bosses and a target of other liberals.[59] The vice president was not only heading for a head-on clash with antiwar activists but with challengers within his own party.

However, while Eugene McCarthy and Robert Kennedy hammered it out against each other on the campaign trail, Humphrey waited on the sidelines, knowing the party bosses would use their control of delegates to nominate him despite the primaries. It was also in part a strategic move, as the vice president attempted to stop a bandwagon coronation for Robert Kennedy by allowing Eugene McCarthy to capture as many delegates as he could.[60] Democratic Party leaders believed that Humphrey had the best chance against Republican Richard Nixon in the fall. A *United Press International* poll in April also found that the party leadership believed that Humphrey could, in fact, beat any Republican contender.[61]

The only challenger with a legitimate chance of upsetting Humphrey's coronation was Robert Kennedy. The junior senator from New York garnered enthusiasm for which other candidates could only hope. McCarthy drew little of the passion that surrounded the Massachusetts native. "Gene wasn't much," said activist Abbie Hoffman about McCarthy. "One could secretly cheer for him the way you cheer for the Mets. It's easy, knowing he can never win. But Bobby, there was the real threat."[62]

Indeed, Kennedy's entry into the race and his frenzied campaign supporters made him a divisive candidate in a highly divisive year. Early in his campaign in Los Angeles, Kennedy told a crowd that "the failure of national purpose . . . is not simply the result of bad polices and lack of skill. It flows from the fact that for almost the first time the national leadership is calling upon the darker impulses of the American spirit—not, perhaps, deliberately, but through its action and the example it sets."[63]

That all changed with Johnson's decision not to seek reelection and the assassination of Martin Luther King Jr. mere days later. Following King's death, Kennedy tried to soften the campaign rhetoric by appealing for reconciliation. Kennedy may have had the best chance of any to reconcile the disparate groups, as he drew support from both white working-class and black voters, and he pandered to both as he set his sights on being a legitimate "other" voice for the middle class. Kennedy remained, however, in a heated contest with Eugene McCarthy for the antiwar vote, and there was little chance of pragmatism and cooperation heading to Chicago. The remaining four primaries pitted Kennedy against McCarthy in Indiana, Nebraska, Oregon, and California. Kennedy took Indiana and Nebraska; McCarthy won in Oregon.

On the night of June 4, 1968, Kennedy won a narrow victory over McCarthy in the all-important Golden State. There was a planned meeting between the two campaigns for the following morning in an attempt to heal some of the wounds before the convention took place. Some within the Kennedy camp held out hope that they could avoid the growing dissension within the party as they headed to Chicago with various radical groups already talking about a showdown at the Democratic National Convention. Shortly after midnight, hopes for reconciliation crumbled.[64] As Robert Kennedy completed his victory address before his faithful supporters at the Ambassador Hotel in Los Angeles, California, the youthful candidate, who had seen so much family tragedy, was minutes away from adding to the legacy. "I think we can end the divisions within the United States," Kennedy said in acceptance. "What I think is quite clear is that we can work together. . . . We are a great country, an unselfish country, and a compassionate country. . . . So my thanks to all of you, and it's on to Chicago, and let's win there."[65]

With football star and bodyguard Roosevelt Greer leading the way, the Democratic hopeful made his way off stage and through the hotel's kitchen to make a quick exit. Waiting for him was Sirhan Sirhan, a fanatic Palestinian national. After the assassin's bullets found their mark, a mortally wounded Kennedy, splayed on the floor, tried to speak. With his head cradled by seventeen-year-old busboy, Juan Romero, blood streaming through the bewildered kitchen worker's hands, Kennedy, lucid for the last moment in his life, still managed to ask, "Is everyone safe? Okay?" Romero replied quickly "Yes, yes. Everything is going to be okay."[66] It was thirteen minutes past midnight, June 5, 1968, and events in the nation were far from okay. "No, no, no, no, no," groaned a distraught male voice.

Amid the screams and confusion, a grief-stricken witness asked in incomprehension and despair, "What's America coming to?"

chapter 4

"On to Chicago": Countdown to August

We cried as a family. But not just for the death of one man, but for what the nation had become. Bobby Kennedy's assassination was the cherry on a poison cake. It said to us that there was no more law, order, or even sanity. Our nation teetered on the brink. His death said that anything could happen. What was going to happen next? God, we were scared.[1]

Boys in Little League uniforms, caps in hand, veterans, women in aprons, the young and the old stood alongside the tracks of the 226-mile funeral train that took the body of Robert Francis Kennedy from New York to his final resting place in Arlington, Virginia. Some waved the flag; others bowed their heads and held hands over hearts. Kennedy's death not only cast a pall over much of the nation but also had an immediate effect on the fortunes of those vying for the Democratic ticket. The senator's premature passing not only virtually assured Hubert Humphrey's nomination but dismayed challenger Eugene McCarthy. The Minnesota senator "looked weary beyond belief," wrote Norman Mailer, who observed him following the assassination. "His skin a used-up yellow, his tall body serving no more than to keep his head up above the crowd at the cocktail party. . . . McCarthy looked like the victim in the snow when the St. Bernard comes up with the rum."[2] The mood among many Democrats was beyond somber; it was grim. Even with the charismatic Kennedy gone and the party machinery behind him, Humphrey lacked broad popularity in his own party, and new polls indicated that McCarthy would fare better against Republican Richard Nixon in November. Enthusiastic crowds and polls, however, were not about to convince the party bosses that Humphrey wasn't their man. "Facts are pitiless," wrote James Reston in the *New York Times*. "After all the crying, the problems will remain and the delegates will probably turn to Humphrey and Nixon. Only an outcry from the people now will stop them."[3] But for activists like Carl Ogelsby, there was little hope for intervention from the people. "Given the assassination of King and Kennedy, there was no more basis for a big-party coalition on the left. In came Hubert Humphrey, with his incredible debt to Lyndon Johnson and everything that was corrupt and sick about the Democratic Party, and then we had Nixon. We were supposed to have Bobby Kennedy!"[4]

The Democrats were heading to Chicago with little hope for anything resembling unity. Instead, as summer began there was a growing rift in the party; Kennedy's passing only added to the shadow descending on the pending convention. The remaining antiwar candidate worried about Chicago. Two weeks prior to the convention, McCarthy urged his supporters to stay away. "This would be a tragedy—a personal tragedy for any hurt or arrested and a tragedy for those of us who wish to give the political process a fair and peaceful test."[5] McCarthy issued his warning after speaking to Mayor Daley by phone several times. A *Sun-Times* editorial agreed that protestors should stay away and do nothing to strengthen the hand of Richard Nixon.[6] Activists, however, planned to deliver one last "outcry" in protest before the November elections.

MOBILIZATION

The assassination of Robert Kennedy did two things for the antiwar movement: it helped fracture it, while sending the fragments on to an even more violent showdown in Chicago. Movement leaders believed that Kennedy's assassination meant a crippling blow for the cause, as they had pinned their last best hopes for an end to the war in Vietnam on his political coattails. The night before his funeral, former SDS leader Tom Hayden, who had serious disagreements with Kennedy, sat in the back of St. Patrick's Cathedral in New York City and wept.[7] Among those standing as an honor guard close to the senator's coffin was Richard Daley, head down, weeping.[8] Despair crossed political boundaries. "Another Messiah crucified!" stated Oglesby. "How long would people sit still for this?"[9] The veteran activist believed that Kennedy's death meant that there was no longer anyone to bridge the gap between the movement and the party. "[T]he RFK assassination had changed the whole strategic equation, had changed the lay of American politics deeply, perhaps irreversibly, and, from the movement's standpoint, vastly for the worse."[10] Abbie Hoffman felt similar anger. "A week after Kennedy's assassination I became convinced that I was going to Chicago."[11] With even normally level-headed activists such as Tom Hayden beginning to talk openly about violence, Oglesby was aware that RFK's death had shaped "a new attitude. . . . This new attitude welcomed the prospect of violence in Chicago . . . violence was no longer avoidable. . . . If the movement went to Chicago, it would be to fight in the streets."[12] In those gloomy early days of summer, it seemed that little mattered anymore for those in the movement. "With King and Kennedy dead, a promise of redemption not only passed out of American politics, it passed out of ourselves," wrote Todd Gitlin. The assassinations of King and Kennedy, Gitlin recalled, constituted the "murder of hope."[13]

The day following RFK's funeral, however, the planning for the political fight continued on various fronts. In East Lansing, Michigan, on the campus of Michigan State University, SDS delegates met for their annual convention. In a meeting room decorated with the images of Lenin and Trotsky, members (donning red armbands and holding copies of Chairman Mao's Little Red Book), young radicals, and political idealists prepared for battle. They were simply one of many such groups across the country that planned to voice an opinion on the pending leadership of the Democratic Party and make a stand in Chicago. The challenge for movement leaders was to unite the disparate groups under one banner for the August convention. Many had already come loosely together under the umbrella of the National Mobilization Committee, or Mobe. As early as November 1967, Mobe began to plan for Chicago.

In December of that year, Mobe met in New York City for a planning session. David Dellinger and ex-SDSers Hayden and Davis wanted concerted protests on the streets of Chicago during convention week. They envisioned hundreds of thousands of people battling against the policies of the sitting president. Dellinger knew that what took place in the Windy City that summer would need to move beyond "business as usual" and "raise official fears of uncontrollable social disorder."[14] During the gathering that also included Sidney Peck, Robert Greenblatt, and Carl Oglesby, little of any substance was planned as there was more concern with what may await them if they arrived en masse in Chicago. Like McCarthy, Oglesby worried about the convention's site, believing that the group should declare Chicago a "death city" and stay away. However, in February 1968, Davis and Hayden opened an office on South Dearborn Street in Chicago to prepare for the convention.[15] The pair published a position paper entitled "Movement Campaign 1968—an Election Year Offensive," which appealed for "sustained, organized protests" during convention week. Although it stated that protests should be legal and nonviolent, they were personally planning and hoping for more. It had become clear that the answer depended on the audience. Indeed, when Dellinger traveled to Chicago on a recruiting mission, he was asked if Hayden and Davis wanted a "bloodbath." Dellinger argued with them over their "waffling" on nonviolence.[16]

One of the biggest hindrances to the movement's plans for Chicago was Johnson's decision not to seek reelection. For all of its plans, Mobe struggled for a period over what exactly to protest during convention week. "We didn't have Lyndon Johnson to kick around anymore," said activist Sam Brown. "I was devastated by it. . . . Rationally, it was a tremendous victory. Emotionally, it was like, 'Oh, my god . . . tomorrow morning we have to get up and see what all of this means, and this afternoon it was so simple.' . . . We had this guy that we could point a finger at, and now it's more diffuse, it's impossible to get a handle on it, you can't see it anymore. It was a crazy emotional reaction. It was like the loss of a valued enemy. I was crushed."[17] Johnson's impending retirement also seriously hampered the movement's efforts to recruit new members for Chicago. "As long as Johnson was going to be the nominee you never had to convince anyone to go out and demonstrate," opined founding member of SDS Paul Booth. "Johnson did all our persuading for us. People just read the newspapers and got mad. Organizing in those days amounted to picking the days and renting the buses."[18]

Some activists thought that Johnson's decision would not only hurt recruitment, but would result in a calmer convention with fewer demonstrations. Dick Gregory said the president's leaving "should have a tremendous effect" on protests in Chicago, adding that the streets will probably be "a little quieter." Chicago activist Chester Robinson agreed. "I don't see a big demonstration now," said Robinson, who headed the West Side Organization. "We have to decide if we are going to do anything at all. I think plans for disruption are off." One of the reasons, Robinson stated at the time, is that they did not want to hurt the chances of Kennedy and McCarthy.[19] Those thoughts changed with the death of Robert Kennedy.

Other than to have a massive presence, Mobe struggled to come up with a coherent plan for Chicago. The only definitive plans came near the end of July when organizers decided that activities would include picketing outside the Conrad Hilton Hotel, where many of the delegates were staying, and marching to the amphitheater, the site of the convention. From the beginning, however, efforts for Chicago were plagued with poor planning, indecision, and disagreement over how strong a stand to take. As activist David Dellinger remembered, the planning for Chicago was anything but coherent. "Our plan began to flounder in the last frantic month before the convention, as we were forced to wrestle with the multiple problems created by external attack and internal uncertainty." The effort, said Dellinger, "suffered from inadequate preparation and attention and energy was drained into uphill efforts to get permits, housing, facilities for movement centers—and recruits." Adding additional strain to convention planning was the reality of competing agendas. While serious-minded Davis and Hayden believed they were in a "prerevolutionary period," others arrived bent on tossing the movement into greater chaos. The instigators were none other than the new Youth International Party, or the Yippies.

Yippie!

However much Mobe leaders hoped to control and coordinate protests during the convention, they could not have completely foreseen or prevented the actions of the Yippies. The group, formed in 1967 and led by Jerry Rubin and Abbie Hoffman, stood in sharp contrast to the likes of Tom Hayden and David Dellinger. While the former SDS members viewed political action as a method for social change, Hoffman wanted to have a revolution for "fun." Hoffman, also known as George Meteskey and "Free," teamed up with Rubin in 1967 during the march on the Pentagon. A veteran of Berkeley and the Student Nonviolent Coordinating Committee (SNCC), Hoffman took his "theater of the absurd" to New York's Lower East Side where he joined Rubin in a thriving hippie community. The pair devoted themselves to a revolution by drugs and sex, creating

absurd situations, uttering outrageous statements, and provoking public demonstrations and stunts—all designed to attract media attention. In many ways, Hoffman and Rubin were bookends of nihilism. "Just as Che needed Fidel and
Costello needed Abbot, Jerry Rubin and I were destined to join forces," said
Hoffman. "We both had a willingness to go beyond reason."[20] As Todd Gitlin
observed, "Abbie and Jerry Rubin, like Abbot and Costello, might as well have
been sent over from Central Casting."[21]

The Yippies made it clear early on that they were going to provoke anarchy in
Chicago. Their major stated goal was to hold a "Festival of Life," while the Democrats were holding their "Convention of Death." Their well-publicized threats
included placing LSD into the city's water supply, nominating a pig as their candidate for president, floating 10,000 nude bodies down Lake Michigan, dressing as
hotel bellboys to try to seduce the wives of delegates, and picking up delegates in
fake cabs and dropping them off in Wisconsin. They also threatened to slash tires
along the freeway while releasing greased pigs throughout the city. The press eagerly
consumed the rhetoric and created a myth larger than the group itself; all of this,
naturally, played into the hands of Rubin and Hoffman. Yippie antics, of course,
were exactly the opposite of what Hayden and Dellinger planned as they struggled
to secure march permits while working with the city and the Democratic Party.[22]

An indication of the disunity and the chaos to come dated back to March when
Mobe invited Yippie representatives, black organizations, and several other dissident groups to Lake Villa, Illinois, in an attempt to bring the entities under a united
banner for the Chicago convention. Already facing disorganization and dissention,
the interjection of Yippie temperament only exacerbated the strife. Mobe was
essentially falling apart. The various groups could not decide between acts of civil
disobedience and open violence. Mobe's idea was to facilitate all avenues of protest
by bringing the various factions together for a massive "funeral march" on the
amphitheater. However, while Hayden and the pacifist Dellinger debated the merits of violent versus nonviolent methods and other political strategies, the Yippies
were having none of it. From the beginning, Hoffman and Rubin made it clear the
meeting would be a farce. They sat in the corner and ridiculed the process. "For
two days the MOB debated whether or not they should go to Chicago in August,"
Hoffman mused. "We laughed at them. . . . While they argued back and forth
we got stoned, made love to all the pretty girls . . . refused to pay for our meals,
and in general carried on like bad, crazy niggers. After two days of bullshit they
postponed a decision until sometime in July."[23] The Yippies had walked out,
declaring that they would head to Chicago alone, while black groups decided that
protesting at the convention was not in their interests. Regardless of the impact on
the movement and Mobe, the key for Hoffman was putting Yippies on the map. It
was something he had been trying to accomplish since early spring.

Hoffman also saw the violent clash between the Yippies and New York police
in March as an indication of what officers could expect in Chicago in August. The
Yippies had called for a spring equinox celebration at midnight on March 22 at
New York's Grand Central Station. Six thousand people arrived. Many of those

who showed up, however, had more on their minds than to mark the cycle of the seasons. As cherry bombs went off, some climbed atop of the information booth and chanted: "Long Hot Summer, Long Hot Summer." Without warning, fifty New York police officers waded into the crowd and attacked with nightsticks. People were kicked as they fell, while the crowd yelled, "*Sieg Heil.*" Police rammed *Village Voice* reporter Don McNeill's head into a set of glass doors, hard enough to break the glass, after he was identified as a journalist; another young Yippie, ostensibly trying to protect Abbie Hoffman from a group of police, was thrown through a plate-glass door. Police then knocked Hoffman unconscious. Whereas some commentators referred to the episode as a police riot, others were more prophetic. "It seemed," wrote McNeill, "to be a prophecy of Chicago." Despite his beating, Hoffman was pleased with the image the clash created. These images, he said, "were powerful enough magic to separate the hippies from the Yippies." Hoffman was also aware that it would send a message of what Chicago could expect during the convention. "It is debatable whether or not the Grand Central Massacre helped or hurt our chances in Chicago. I maintain that it helped tremendously. It put Yippie! on the map. . . . The Grand Central Station Massacre knocked out the hippie image of Chicago and let the whole world know there would be blood on the streets of Chicago."[24]

Yippie antics were not only spreading to Chicago by the underground and university presses but increasingly through the mainstream media. When Hoffman laid out the Yippie's plans for Chicago in an article for the July 7, 1968, edition of *the Realist,* excerpts of the piece appeared a week before the convention in the *Chicago Sun-Times.* "Police, meanwhile, are reading YIP literature and that of the New Left movement in general—and they don't like what they read," stated the *Sun-Times* article titled "Police Keep Watch on Top Yippies." Hoffman boldly pronounced, "We will burn Chicago to the ground. We will fuck on the beaches; we demand the politics of ecstasy; acid for all; abandon the Creeping Meatball; Yippie! Chicago—August 25–30." As *Sun-Times* reporter James Casey pointed out, "Police here are accepting such writings at face value. That is why they are not viewing lightly the prospective invasion of the hippies, which they feel may be merely camouflage for organized violence."[25] Hoffman understood well the image they were creating, proclaiming how they had "learned to manipulate the media."[26] On other occasions he admitted, "I constantly hustle the media. . . . I realize that the media has tremendous power."[27] Hoffman's goal was to create "advertisements" for a Chicago rebellion.[28]

Although Hoffman had effectively distanced himself from the hippies and organized groups such as SDS with his "flower in a clenched fist" attitude, his antics had also made it more difficult for a city administration and its police department to make distinctions between legitimate protesters and anarchists.[29] "Clarity, alas, is not one of our goals," Hoffman admitted. "Confusion is mightier than the sword."[30] The message to the police and the public was that the movement was a dangerous mix of "communist-racist-acid-headed freaks, holding flowers in one hand and bombs in the other."[31] This quite conscious effort blurred the line between fact and fiction and fed the fear, hatred, and genuine paranoia of those within the Chicago Police Department.

"A Longhair Was a Longhair"

By early 1967, police officers admitted that they had difficulty separating radicals from counterculture enthusiasts. Cop Ray Mihalicz remembers that each day his job became increasingly difficult. "I remember the years before—the radicals used to wear black all over or turtlenecks when it was hot enough to fry an egg on the hood of your car and sunglasses on cloudy days. By the time the war heated up, mid-decade, I suppose, the bad ones and the normal kids—if you can call them normal—all looked the same. It was like they wore this uniform that said, 'I don't belong in this society, look out for me.' They might as well put a bull's eye on their back."[32]

Other officers suggest it was as simple as "a longhair was a longhair." Says Ernie Bellows, "I'm not sure how people think that we should have been able to tell these people apart; they didn't look any different, they didn't speak any different, dress any different, their signs said the same thing; they were trouble—we read about them, and they spoke of causing trouble in our city for the convention. Poisoning things, having sex on the streets, and hurting delegates. It was all bad, and we could hear it coming down the pike, and smell it, too."[33] Other officers agree. "There was no distinguishing hippies, Yippies, Diggies, SDSers, and all of those radical groups," recalls former cop Mel Latanzio. "They went under different names, but we kept our eyes on all of them. I think they were pretending that they were different at times, but that was just a ploy, because when they got on the street, they all behaved the same way. Your regular patrolman was not going to be able to tell these people apart, and they didn't seem to care what we thought, anyway; even if they weren't trouble, they wanted to look the part."[34]

Considering the Yippie efforts to blur the line between flower children and political activists, such police attitudes are not surprising. Indeed, Hoffman had no illusions about himself. In a letter to Stokely Carmichael, he made light of his peace and love credentials. "We are working on a huge Youth Festival in Chicago at the time of the Democratic Convention. I hope to get to participate. I'm currently on trial for supposedly hitting a cop with a bottle in a demonstration. I can't imagine what they are talking about, me being a flower child and all that."[35]

Many in the movement knew that they were getting under the skin of those in authority. "Yippies are voluntary Niggers," observed *Realist* editor Paul Krassner. "We live outside the system, and those inside it despise and fear us."[36] Krassner was more right than perhaps he even knew. Hoffman had gotten his way, making police believe that hippies were unpredictable and dangerous, and therefore would more likely bring about a crisis mentality on Chicago streets as the convention neared. Police officer Grant Brown was one of many cops who didn't know what to expect. "The problem for all of us was that we didn't know what or where the hit was going to come from. We worried about the delegates, we worried about the infrastructure, the power, the water, and worried about them putting acid in the water—we didn't know what was going to happen, and there was fear, all right, as silly as some of that fear may seem now."

At issue was the belief that anyone donning counterculture dress was a threat. There were no more "innocent flower children." Former cop Norm Nelson, for example, viewed the Yippies as what the hippies had become, having now abandoned all pretense of flower power and peace. Nelson had read about them in the local papers. "We knew who they were—they had metamorphosed into the real thing. Yippie was the myth. It was the coming of war; from '67 on it was a battle, and they were showing their true colors in the weeks and months leading up to the convention in our city. . . . Let's put it this way, we were ready for those SOBs."[37]

Though less strident in their opinion, other former cops, such as Len Colsky, tend to agree with the basic sentiment. Colsky recalls that even though police tried to distinguish between peaceful protesters and troublemakers, the process had become increasingly difficult. "We were not branding everyone the same. There were peaceniks that a lot of us knew would not hurt a fly. You moved in on them and arrested them and they went like Raggedy Ann dolls in your arms; and [there were] others who were holding protests. And in America, if you don't do damage to private property, you're okay, and we could tell them apart often." Colsky recalls, though, that situations became more difficult to interpret as the decade wore on. "Things became very confusing. I remember well in 1968 where it was hard to distinguish the hippies from the criminals; they all looked the same. And the ones who were causing trouble and promising to do damage looked and dressed like hippies."[38]

Other cops admit, however, that there may have been a desire to see hippies and the counterculture as the same—radicals looking to do harm. Says former officer Warren MacAulay, "I know people who wore a uniform who really didn't care—they hated the entire generation and they used any excuse they could find to go after them and teach them a lesson. These Yipps with their tough talk were making that very easy for some of the members."[39]

Indeed, Yippie actions during the March Grand Central Station incident in New York City had made its way to members of the Chicago Police Department. Evidence of specific communications between departments came following the arrest of Jerry Rubin by New York police in June. Rubin filed a charge of police brutality against officers at the Ninth Precinct following the incident where police allegedly kicked him during his arrest. Abbie Hoffman also accused three of the arresting officers of making "verbal and physical attacks" against him "for political reasons." During a press conference, Rubin complained, "all their questions centered on my politics." He made it clear that the officers asked specific questions on Yippie plans for a major demonstration in Chicago that August.[40]

Some Chicago police officers recall colleagues having conversations with other jurisdictions beginning in 1967 after the march on the Pentagon. What increased communications was the radical Yippies. Officer Marlin Rowden recalls that some in his district had friends in other cities with whom they had regular correspondence. "I don't think that is too difficult to believe, especially when things began to get out of control. Guys would talk shop, sometimes with some of their brothers they had in the academy, cousins, friends, hunting buddies. It was all kind of informal, but it picked up after what happened at the Pentagon and with some of the members in Oakland. We wanted to know what was going on with some of these extremist groups. So, there was some talk back-and-forth, but all of that increased prior to the Democrat's convention. We wanted to find out what was happening with some of these fringe groups, such as the Yippies. If we could scare them from coming in the first place, so be it."[41]

There are indications that discussions were much more formal. "I think that it was tactical," recalls Kelly Frederickson. "We exchanged intelligence and information all the time. Especially between district commanders. What was important filtered down to us, the rest, and the volume of traffic, I don't know, but remember, this is just part of good police procedures. It's not a conspiracy."[42] Indeed such practices were part of the routine work of police intelligence divisions, such as Chicago's infamous subversive unit dubbed the Red Squad that worked to infiltrate radical groups to discern firsthand the plans of "radical elements."[43]

In the weeks and months leading to the August convention, paranoia and hatred were fueled by pronouncements emanating from the fringes of the movement. Fringe material became fodder for police with an ear to the ground or an eye on the local paper. "The press loved these crazies," writes historian Allen Matusow. "Frightened officials took their wildest fantasies literally; and the myth of the Yippie grew."[44] The most telling reaction was how Mayor Richard Daley seized on the threats to restrict permits for marches and ordered curfews for city parks. These threats, which included the absurd Yippie boast to place LSD into the city's water supply, had predictable results. Daley placed police officers at the city's filtration plants twenty-four hours a day. Police were ordered to guard every pumping station and filtration plant starting the Saturday before the convention.[45]

Chicago quickly became an inhospitable place for would-be demonstrators, as Daley refused all permits for marches and parades. Rennie Davis enlisted the help of the Justice Department, arguing with good reason that permits would lower the threats of violence between protesters and police. Although justice official Roger Wilkins met with Daley and city officials, he got nowhere. With one week before the start of the convention, Mobe organizers went to federal court to gain permits for the convention, but they were denied there as well.[46] Organizers also learned that police would enforce a strict 11 P.M. curfew.

There was no doubt that Hoffman and Rubin had succeeded by not only worsening an already tense situation but by helping to create a showdown between protesters and city officials over marches and gatherings. Bowing to fatalism, Hoffman admitted that from the start he knew Chicago was going to result in a fight. "My feeling that Chicago was in a total state of anarchy as far as the police mentality worked," Hoffman admitted later while on trial for conspiracy. "I said that we were going to have to fight for every single thing, we were going to have to fight for the electricity, we were going to have to fight to have the stage come in, we were going to have to fight for every rock musician to play, that the whole week was going to be like that. I said that we should proceed with the festival as planned, we should try to do everything that we had come to Chicago to do, even though the police and the city officials were standing in our way."[47]

All of this made planning for Chicago next to impossible. Hayden and Davis even failed in their last-ditch efforts to allow protesters to sleep in the parks. They knew that allowing protestors to camp overnight would keep the kids off the streets and avoid a housing shortage for visitors. Daley, however, did not intend to make concessions to demonstrators. Since April, he made it clear with his public statements that police would deal harshly with dissenters.[48] The cantankerous mayor instead denied all permits and transformed the city into an armed camp.

"Fort Daley"

A week before the convention, the city of Chicago mobilized for combat. The special Chicago Police Department Task Force prepared for battle with 300 members patrolling in cars, armed with service revolvers, helmets, batons, mace, tear gas, gas masks, and one shotgun per car. Five hundred of these masks were delivered to the CPD one week prior to the convention. "No one is going to take over the streets,"[49] blasted Daley. His cops were to be stationed on every street corner and the middle of every block in the downtown area. At the Conrad Hilton Hotel, which served as campaign headquarters and hosted Vice President Hubert Humphrey and Senator Eugene McCarthy, federal agents were to patrol the rooftops and the corridors, as well as the kitchen and service areas. Agents were to guard the candidates' suites around the clock, checking everyone entering and exiting elevators. Police afforded similar protection to the Sheraton Blackstone across the street, where Senator George McGovern was to stay. The police warned the media not to take pictures through open windows in the area for fear of being mistaken for snipers.

It was no different at the amphitheater. The police sealed all the entrances on Halsted Street, while the owners of nearby buildings were ordered to close their windows during the convention. The department placed 1,500 uniformed officers outside the amphitheater, including snipers atop with binoculars and walkie-talkies. Telephones would connect officers to their counterparts inside, who were installed on catwalks overlooking the convention floor with binoculars.[50] Security also included a cyclone fence topped with barbed wire (at the request of the Democratic National Committee) and sealed manhole covers. The streets surrounding the amphitheater were barred except for VIP vehicles.[51] The readiness of Chicago's fire department was also stepped up as Daley ordered the city's 4,865 firefighters to work extra shifts beginning on the Sunday before the convention. The men would only have twenty-four hours off between shifts instead of the usual forty-eight, increasing the on-duty force by 600. One hundred and seventy-five men from the Fire Prevention Bureau were to be on duty inside the amphitheater, with twelve others at the hotels that were housing delegates.[52]

For the president's safety, the Secret Service planned to take Johnson to the amphitheater by helicopter. The surrounding airspace was turned into a no-fly zone for an altitude of 2,500 feet, except official convention business and police helicopters equipped with high-intensity lights to scan the tops of buildings near the amphitheater. This wall of security was not confined to the outside, as inside, delegates were to be joined by several hundred security personnel, some mingling among the delegates, while others watched from catwalks; female security personnel were stationed in the ladies' washrooms. The security measures extended to protect the delegates traveling to and from the convention site. Delegates would travel in buses escorted by police motorcycles, followed by unmarked squad cars, with a police helicopter scanning the route from overhead.[53] Even though the city spent $500,000 to beautify the area around the convention site, it could not hide the reality that the city encased the amphitheater in barbed wire. Making the site even less hospitable was its unfortunate location right next to the city's stockyards. Two blocks away stood a pile of manure, seventy-feet wide and ten-feet high. The smell in the area was often overpowering.[54]

Also overpowering was the amount of firepower assembled for the weeklong convention. The usual police contingent of 6,000 officers on the streets grew to 11,900 on twelve-hour shifts, up from the usual eight. The city requested the mobilization of 5,649 Illinois National Guardsmen, with an additional 5,000 on alert, bolstered by up to 1,000 Federal Bureau of Investigation (FBI) officers and military intelligence officers. Waiting for signs of trouble in the suburbs would be 6,000 army troops, including members of the elite 101st Airborne Division. The men were to be equipped with bazookas and flamethrowers. While the military protected the suburbs, an unspoken fear was that black militants would try to disrupt the convention by firing on delegates from the decrepit high-rise public housing projects that overlooked portions of the Dan Ryan Expressway. Police helicopters patrolled the stretch looking for any sign of trouble.[55]

Although the mayor's office did not speak openly about this fear, there were concerns of rioting in the black neighborhoods, with the possibility of it spreading to the center of the city. This was especially true since significant police resources were to be pulled away from those areas of the city to protect the convention sites and the downtown parks. In the days leading to the convention, there were threats to attack police if they moved into black areas in force.[56] Most black groups, however, did not intend to become involved in convention-week demonstrations. Calvin Lockeridge, who led the Black Consortium, an amalgamation of thirty-nine national and local black groups, made it clear that the convention was not for them. "We feel basically that this is a white folks' thing."[57]

Most of the security precautions were not secret but highly publicized efforts to intimidate would-be travelers to Chicago. The precautions sent shockwaves through the movement. David Dellinger recalls the trepidation. "The two questions I was always asked were: (1) is there any chance that the police won't create a bloodbath? (2) Are you sure that Tom and Rennie don't want one?"[58] Indeed, Daley's saber-rattling dampened much of the earlier expectations for a huge influx of protesters into Chicago. Even two weeks prior to the convention, J. Anthony Lukas wrote in the *New York Times* that a "conservative" estimate of protesters was 50,000 while the prediction of more than a million was "seemingly inflated." Dellinger and the other Mobe leaders, however, had already abandoned their desire to bring large numbers of protesters to the convention. Racked by dissension and lack of direction, Daley's tactics of stalling on permits and "shoot to kill" orders made the prospect of going to Chicago unattractive for other than the most ardent in the movement.

About 500 SDS members—a fraction of their number—planned to travel to Chicago, along with members of the Chicago Police Council, the Communist Party, the Fifth Avenue Peace Parade Committee, and the Cleveland Area Peace Action Council. One group that planned to stay away was the Chicago Area Draft Resisters. Founder Richard Boardman said the decision to stay away reflected the organization's attitude toward major protests.[59] SDS had feared a bloodbath on the streets of Chicago and was reluctant to travel to the Windy City. For a while, this fear had strained relations between the organization and its former head, Tom Hayden, who believed that the convention was an important stand. SDS wanted highly organized, small groups of demonstrators, or "squad action."[60] The *Chicago Seed,* however, advised people to avoid the city. When it became apparent that the Yippies were not going to secure a permit for the Festival of Life in Lincoln Park, the *Seed* issued a statement urging people to stay away. "Don't come to Chicago if you expect a five-day festival of life, music, and love. The word is out. Chicago may host a festival of blood."[61]

Awareness also grew of a rift within the Yippie leadership, including Jerry Rubin and Paul Krassner, who were thought to want to provoke violence with police, and the Chicago-based Yippies, who wanted to keep the festival peaceful and "life affirming."[62] However, as the convention neared, it looked as though there was little prospect for peace, with rumors within the movement that Rubin and Hoffman hoped police would turn the convention into a riot.[63] Indeed, Rennie Davis admitted that the aim was "to force the police state to become more and more visible, yet somehow survive it."[64] Todd Gitlin knew that a hardcore element of the movement was ready for a fight. "Part of the New Left wanted a riot, then, but the streetfighters could not by themselves have brought it about," wrote Gitlin. "For that, they needed the police. The sleeping dogs sat bolt upright, howled, bared their teeth, bit."[65]

News of how Daley's police had treated peace marchers in April also had a negative impact on those willing to travel to Chicago. The belief was that if Daley felt that marchers had no right to express their views during a seemingly harmless peace march comprised of local Chicagoans in April, how would they react to thousands of out-of-town demonstrators during a national party convention with the eyes of the nation watching?[66] In the days leading up to the convention, Daley tried to strike a more conciliatory tone, suggesting that protests would be permissible as long as they were done "peacefully and legally and rationally." Two days later, the mayor made a point of welcoming all to Chicago.

It is only fitting that during this dynamic democratic process, there is present in our city a cross-section of representation of the voices of America—liberal, moderate, conservative and radical, young and old, hawk and dove, hippy and square . . . and this is the way it should be because this is America.[67]

Few bought Daley's egalitarian prose such as when in July, speaking before the American Legion, Daley promised, "as long as I am Mayor of this city, there will be law and order in the streets."[68] Daley knew he had the support of the citizens of Chicago. As Allen Matusow has deftly pointed out, "Daley knew that if push came to shove, the great mass of white Chicagoans who bathed, prayed, and pledged allegiance to the flag would have backed him all the way."[69] The mayor's tough stance also had the support of the press. A week before the delegates' arrival, the *Sun-Times* praised Daley's "forthright" manner in establishing tough "ground rules." The editorial said Daley was correct to eliminate any "irresponsible activities" on the part of demonstrators during convention week.[70]

The veteran mayor also knew that the people of Chicago expected nothing less. On convention eve, citizens in the mayor's neighborhood warned Yippies to stay away. Even minors were issuing warnings. "They better not come down here," a thirteen-year-old boy told a reporter for the *New York Times*. "We'll get scissors and cut all their hair off." A ten-year-old added, "We'll take their hippie chains and strangle them." A neighborhood woman predicted ominously, "There will be slaughter. Just slaughter. On both sides, I guess. They better not come where they're not wanted." Another man who lived across the street from the mayor's house believed that the city would let police handle demonstrators. "I'm Polish and I don't have much use for these people who sympathize with the Communists. [But] most people will just sit on their porch and watch."[71]

The veteran mayor was acutely aware that massive disturbances would damage his city's reputation; losing control of protestors during the convention, he believed, would tarnish his Democratic Party and hurt its chances in the November election. Daley feared relenting and turning the streets over to the movement. Moreover, says Milton Viorst, little eclipsed Daley's "loathing for young, white radicals."[72] To mitigate any possible damage, Daley also set out to restrict the media's ability to cover the convention. He not only limited the numbers of press passes to the convention floor, but he restricted the press's ability to cover street disturbances; Daley refused to let the networks run the cables necessary to operate the portable generators for their color cameras on the streets in front of the downtown hotels.[73] Although the mayor hoped to control the action on the streets, there was little he could do to forestall the growing split within the Democratic Party.

"Dump the Hump"

Few believed that the national convention would pass without incident either inside or outside the amphitheater. With Humphrey as the likely candidate, there was little hope that the ruling Democrats would be able to silence the antiwar crowds. A week before the convention, Senator George McGovern, head of the convention's platform committee and a candidate for the party's leadership, said that he didn't think Humphrey could move away from Johnson's policy even if he had wished. McGovern believed that the only way he could dislodge Humphrey from Johnson was by giving him a plank he could embrace. Although McGovern stated that the plank could not contain "any implication that we've been on the right course for the last four years," he did not believe it was necessary to have one that would constitute a denunciation of the administration, thereby making it easier for Humphrey to accept.[74]

The plank proposed by Senator Eugene McCarthy a week before the convention, however, left the front-runner with little room to maneuver. McCarthy's plank declared, "The war in Vietnam has been an enormous cost in human life and in material resources. It has diverted our energies from pressing domestic problems and impaired our prestige in the world." As McCarthy believed that neither side could win the war, his plank called for a negotiated settlement. He insisted that a new Democratic administration must immediately halt the bombing of North Vietnam, as well as all other attacks on its territory. Such a plank he said was "fully consistent with the expressed ideas of the late Senator Robert F. Kennedy."[75]

For his part, Humphrey tried to make the case that prior to the senator's assassination, he and Kennedy held similar views on Vietnam. Richard Goodwin, McCarthy's campaign coordinator for the presidency, who also worked for Kennedy at the time, said that if it were in fact true that Humphrey agreed with Kennedy, then the vice president should accept McCarthy's plank. As the convention neared, it appeared that McCarthy wanted to exploit the issue for his own advantage. Humphrey was in a no-win position on the war, a looming issue threatening to divide the party, and one that the vice president was at pains to avoid. Humphrey's aims were to deliver a war plank that was broad enough to bring together the party's dissident factions, yet ambiguous enough to discreetly separate him from the polices of his soon-to-be-former boss. It was, for many reasons, a difficult proposition. "There is no difference of opinion on whether the objective is to get out of Vietnam," stated a Humphrey adviser. "No one favors a strong hawkish position. The only problem is how to phrase a plank that looks ahead, emphasizes peace and does not gratuitously stab the Johnson administration."[76]

Humphrey, however, was associated not only with the administration's polices of the previous four years, but with the decade's failings, particularly the racial divisions and riots that racked numerous cities. With the charismatic Kennedy gone, McCarthy was seen as the last best hope in the Democratic Party to redress the racial divide. This division was especially acute in Chicago, still one of the most racially segregated of the bigger northern cities. One week prior to the convention, crowds cheered McCarthy during an appearance in a black Chicago neighborhood. Speaking in the city's South Side, McCarthy drew warm applause as he endorsed black power. "No people," McCarthy told a crowd at the Tabernacle Baptist Church, "have more reason and more right to organize politically. . . . I'm not really asking [for] your endorsement, but I hope you will consider my candidacy with a sound, harsh judgment." Aware of Humphrey's vulnerability, McCarthy received the most enthusiastic applause when he stated that the system of party bosses made it difficult to challenge incumbents. Democrats, McCarthy explained, are "afraid to change the system. We tried to change it and whether we changed it or not we gave it one or two shakes and kept it alive." He told the all-black crowd that if the Democrats select Humphrey to run against Nixon, the nation will be faced with choosing "between two echoes."[77]

By convention time, the antiwar movement reviled Humphrey more than anyone in the party. Sans Johnson, protestor wrath turned on the vice president. Protestors dogged his appearances, waiting for him following speaking engagements or in receiving lines. When Humphrey arrived to speak to a Liberal Party forum on August 17 in New York City, a hundred protestors confronted him on the street. When his motorcade appeared, they shrieked, "Killer!" and "Murderer!" while chanting "Dump the Hump."[78] At Stanford, an antiwar mob attacked his car yelling, "War Criminal!" and "Murderer!" Demeaning placards, gestures, and being spit in the face characterized much of his campaign.[79] Despite the animosity, the veteran politician refused to turn his back on policies that he had followed (in public at least) so loyally for the previous four years. Such an act would be akin to admitting that he had been wrong on the war all along. Prior to arriving in Chicago, Humphrey made an appearance on *Meet the Press* and told a national television audience that there was no reason to disavow the president's "basically sound" polices. The vice president naturally found little agreement in the antiwar movement that readied for battle in the Windy City.

"My Hand Twitched on My Nightstick"

Police helicopters hovered over Lincoln Park on convention eve as the tension rose and sides postured for position. From the viewpoint of the police, the arriving antiwar crowds looked and acted like those Daley had been warning about for months. With helicopters circling, groups of long-haired young men practiced karate and judo in Lincoln Park, a mere three miles from the delegates' hotels. Although much of the action was *wash-oi* (a series of protective maneuvers designed to ward off attacks inline with David Dellinger's practice of nonviolence), many of those practicing in the park were expecting and even welcoming violence. David Baker, a Mobe leader from Detroit, said that passivity in Chicago would get them nowhere. "To remain passive in the face of escalating police brutality is foolish and degrading. The advice used to be that you should give police a flower and say, 'Hello brother.' But it didn't stop the brutality, and people continued to get hurt." Finding unique ways to avoid injury was on the mind of some of those in the park that afternoon. A young graduate student there to help train Mobe's marshals for convention week told the *New York Times,* "We're still dedicated to peaceful methods, but I can tell you there are some doubts in the movement these days about the old-time nonviolent stance—you know, rolling yourself up in a little ball on your side and getting clubbed. Some of the guys who've done that have been very badly hurt. Let's just say we're planning more active and mobile forms of self-defense."[80]

While the park activity continued, a phalanx of uniformed officers, some on motorcycles, watched from nearby. Former cop Eddie Kelso clearly remembers the arrival of the first crowds of protestors. "They actually seemed to appear out of nowhere. I don't think we were monitoring the bus station, and most probably came in by car, but there they were in the park, sitting in circles, smoking, and I remember them going through their fight sequences; it didn't look too harmless to me; it looked like they were preparing for a riot and meant to do some harm."[81]

The sight must have appeared at least a bit ominous as about seventy-five young men and women *wash-oi* snake-danced in formation across the baseball field with news cameras filming the display. *Sun-Times* reporter Brian Boyer thought the kids looked like a "football team going through summer practice." As plainclothes officers moved about the perimeter snapping photographs, Boyer's colleague Hugh Hough sensed that the young demonstrators meant business. "It was immediately evident that they planned something more than fun and games during next week's Democratic National Convention."[82] The silent policemen looking on were not amused. Former cop Dennis Pierson recalls, "We were about seventy-five yards away and they were doing those flying kung fu kicks, and we could overhear them as well, saying what they were going to do to us if we tried to arrest them. 'These *pigs* were going to *squeal*,' I heard more than once. When I heard that, my hand twitched on my nightstick."[83]

Adding to the trepidation for police and city officials was the extremely violent Republican National Convention that had just ended in Miami. Snipers had fired on policemen, armored personal carriers were on the streets, and three people lost their lives. "We watched the news reports on TV and it looked bad," says Orrest Hupka. "The guys were expecting even worse here as the Democrats were the ones in power and were the ones the radicals blamed for the war. The Miami stuff put the force on edge."[84] Indeed, deputy superintendent of police James Rochford had traveled to Miami to observe security measures and learn how to prepare for convention week in Chicago.[85] Some officers recall that Rochford returned with more than just an insight of convention security techniques. Says Reg Novak, "I heard that he was scared as hell, and that made people nervous for what was going to happen here, because nothing scared that man; so we knew we were in for hell."[86]

The reports from across the nation were also making police apprehensive. The August 9 edition of the *Sun-Times* reported that in the previous five weeks, eight of their fellow police officers had been killed and forty-seven wounded in disturbances nationally. Commentators blamed much of the violence during the Miami convention on "outsiders" set on making trouble for the Republican convention.[87] Adding to the mood were ominous reports that outside groups were plotting assassinations. Grand jurors probed rumors of an alleged assassination plot against Democratic candidates, subpoenaing sixteen people, including members of the Youth International Party. Letters to the editor in the *Sun-Times* warned of violence from the so-called peace demonstrators suggesting that they were little more than "dupes" for "infiltrated Communists."[88]

There was also reason to be nervous when on the night of Thursday, August 22, Jerome Johnson, a seventeen-year-old Native American from Sioux Falls, South Dakota, dressed in hippie garb, was shot and killed by police near Lincoln Park. A pair of detectives had stopped Johnson and another man, eighteen-year-old Bobby Joe Maxwell of Columbia, Tennessee, for possible curfew violations on North Avenue near LaSalle in Old Town. Johnson drew a .32 caliber revolver from a flight bag and fired a shot, narrowly missing one of the officers. "We were passing North and LaSalle and stopped to question these two because they might be curfew violators. Maxwell showed us a draft card. The other youngster reached in his flight bag, pulled a pistol and fired one shot," reported detective John Manley, who, along with fellow officer Frank Szwedo, returned fire on the fleeing Johnson after he "turned around with his gun raised again." The officers fired three times, striking Johnson; one bullet passed through his heart. Manley was treated in the hospital for powder burns between his chest and left arm from Johnson's bullet. Officers arrested Maxwell on a weapons charge after police found a ten-inch hunting knife strapped to his chest.[89] For police, the shooting was an unsettling incident only four days before the beginning of the national convention. The force was on edge with the influx of new faces, veteran protestors, and rumors of trouble.

Movement leaders made a last-minute attempt to secure march permits as Mobe, the Yippies, and political activist Allard Lowenstein sued the city in U.S. District Court. On Friday before the convention was to begin, federal Judge William J. Lynch (Daley's former law partner) ruled that there would be no permits. The only permit that was allowed at all for convention week was granted to Mobe for a rally at the Grant Park band shell for the afternoon of Wednesday, August 28, and that was only granted on Tuesday the 27th, after the convention was already under way. Antiwar leaders including David Dellinger were defiant in the face of the judge's ruling. "We'll march with or without a permit," Dellinger told members of the media. "When those 1,000 persons come here, they will constitute a permit. They are people who are determined to be at the Amphitheater." The Mobe leader was not interested in holding an alternative rally in Grant Park. Dellinger said that the park was suitable only as a "staging area for the march."[90]

Police knew that violence with demonstrators was inevitable. "We understood there would be violence and showdowns," says Carl Moore. "Even though there wasn't the crowds we expected, a few thousand people congregated where they were not going to be allowed to be after dark, well, hell, it didn't take a brain surgeon to predict violence."[91] Most police officers, indeed, expected trouble, as they knew that protestors would not heed the curfew and would try to march on the convention site. Several officers recalled that their district units were nervous on convention eve. Tim Markosky recalls, "We didn't know what to expect except trouble. You could feel the tenseness among the members, less laughter, or too much laughter; it was not this 'just wait so we can crack some hippie head.' It was nothing like that. Nobody was looking forward to a riot."[92] Officer Frank Froese agrees, but like most officers, he knew that they would be out in force and would do what they had to do for their superiors. "We had our orders.

We knew what we were going to do. There were no permits for marches. No one was allowed to be in the parks after 11 P.M. and they were not going to be allowed to march on the convention site and wreck the thing, so we were ready and we mixed it up with them before the convention even started. That's when we knew it was going to be a long week."[93]

The same day, Brigadier General Richard T. Dunn told a news conference that the 5,500 members of the Illinois National Guard set to move into Chicago had been given orders to "shoot to kill" if disturbances got out of hand with looting and arson, or because of attacks on police or firemen. Dunn, however, said he hoped his troops would have a "boring week."

The first incident with police took place three days before the start of the convention. On Friday the 23, the Yippies, showing their complete contempt for the political system, nominated their own Democratic candidate: a 145-pound black and white pig dubbed "Pigasus." The Yippie candidate for president was "released to the public" at the Civic Center Plaza and was promptly "arrested" by police as he was being "interviewed" by waiting journalists. Editor Abe Peck of the underground Chicago paper the *Seed* told a reporter for the *New York Times* that after the nomination, they were "going to roast him and eat him. For years, the Democrats have been nominating a pig and then letting the pig devour them. We plan to reverse the process."[94]

A Yippie calling himself Wrap Sirhan stated that the group had sent President Johnson a telegram requesting Secret Service protection for their four-legged candidate.[95] Five Yippies were taken to jail, including Jerry Rubin and Phil Ochs, while the pig for president's new official residence became the Chicago Humane Society. The Yippies were released after they each posted a $25 bond. "The only moment of levity between Chicago policemen and the Yippies that week occurred after we were arrested and were in jail and went in to be booked," said Rubin, following the convention. "One of the Chicago policemen came in and shouted out all of our names and then said, 'You guys are all going to jail for the rest of your lives—the pig squealed on you.'" The department had already put Hoffman, Rubin, Krassner, and some of their associates on 24-hour surveillance, sometimes uttering warnings that sounded to Yippie leaders like threats.[96]

The only real incident of violence on Friday occurred in the evening when a Vietnam veteran assaulted two members of the group Joe and the Fish in a downtown hotel.[97] Those watching national television, however, were seeing the political rhetoric reach an acute level. With Soviet tanks crushing protestors in Prague, Czechoslovakia, some members of the media found the comparisons to the mood in Chicago irresistible. On the *CBS Evening News with Walter Cronkite,* commentator Eric Sevareid voiced his frustrations with Daley's media restrictions. "The city of Chicago runs the city of Prague a close second right now as the world's least attractive tourist attraction. The Russian soldiers in Prague may feel slightly more frustrated than the Democratic Party delegates, the reporters, and hangers-on in Chicago, but the Russians, at least, have tanks in which to travel from A to B." The comments prompted Daley's director of special events, Colonel Jack Riley, to ask, "Who's Eric Sevareid?"[98] Executive producer for NBC's convention coverage, George Murray, was even more direct than Sevareid in affixing blame. "Things are getting impossible. There's no question that the police are obstructing our coverage." The comments of Sevareid and Murray did not sit well with police or their families. "Those son-of-a-bitches had no right to compare us to the fucking commies," blasts former cop Jerry Melton. "That's the way it was even before the convention began; they were against us, so there was no reason to treat them like independent observers."[99]

All three major networks had complained loudly for days that Daley and his administration were enforcing restrictions that would make it impossible for them to provide adequate convention coverage. On Friday, the issue came to a head when police ordered the network's mobile units and vans equipped for onsite taping of events away from the convention site and off the streets. CBS News president Richard S. Salant was outraged. "This is one more shocking barrier in the way of an open convention. Open in the sense that the public, the people of America, have every right to see and hear what is newsworthy as close in time to the event as possible." Police spokesperson Frank Sullivan said that security not censorship was their main concern. "Our first responsibility is to the delegates. The TV trucks would impede the orderly transportation of delegates to and from the hotels."[100]

By the next afternoon, Saturday, August 24, the first real indication of the trouble that lay ahead appeared. At Lincoln Park, as the first crowds began to assemble, a young college student asked one of the officers where the Yippies were. "Over there," said the officer. "You can smell them."[101] The gathering was peaceful, with police watching from the periphery. Poet Allen Ginsberg was holding court in the center of the crowd, encouraging the gathering to join him in chanting "Om, om, om." The chant, Ginsberg said, had the twin effect of calming and connecting people, enabling them to transcend present circumstances. While the chants went on, plainclothes police officers roamed the grounds looking for trouble, monitoring Yippie leaders, and trying to look inconspicuous.[102] Patrolman Cal Noonan recalls their appearance: "The plainclothes guys were a hoot. They were just cops in casual clothes and there was no way they were fooling anyone. But we were watching them [demonstrators] as closely as we could, we wanted to be everywhere they were, and *we* were."[103]

With the realization that gatherers did not have a permit to remain in the park after 11 P.M., tension began to build as afternoon turned to evening. Ginsberg and his group continued chanting until about 10:40 P.M. before rising to lead people out of the park in the hopes of avoiding a confrontation with police. Approximately 1,000 people had already left the area by that time. Ginsberg led all but a couple of hundred out of the park. Encouraged by Yippie leaders and others not to make a stand before the convention even began, the majority of the crowd dissipated prior to the 11 P.M. curfew leaving only about 200 hardcore gatherers. Police soon moved in. With motorcycles in the lead, they cleared the park, and in the process they arrested eleven people for failing to disperse.

Although there was little trouble in the park that night, a more surprising development occurred on the streets outside. The bulk of the crowd that had already moved several blocks away from the park, without provocation, suddenly began to run toward Wells Street—the main street in Old Town—yelling "Peace now! Peace now! Peace now!" Some of the Saturday night throngs, mostly young Chicagoans with both long and short hair—soon joined them. Drivers in their cars honked their horns and displayed the peace sign out their windows. Even with the large crowd in the middle of the street, the assemblage did not rock cars or break windows. Indeed observers described the spontaneous demonstration as a peaceful march of citizens in their own city or a "joyful and exuberant release from the tension of the day." The crowd moved unmolested by police for ten blocks down the middle of the street until officers, apparently caught off guard, caught up to the end of the parade to make a small number of arrests. When the bulk of the crowd realized that they had gained the attention of police, some yelled, "Get back on the sidewalk! Don't give the pigs a chance to bust you! This is only the beginning." Marchers quickly blended into the evening and into the regular crowds on the sidewalks. The march evaporated as quickly as it began.[104]

The spontaneous march, however, reverberated throughout police ranks. Officer Ronald Lardo remembers it well. "We caught major shit for that, let me tell you. That Old Town shit, well, we heard about that that night and the next day before our shifts began. We were reamed out. The word was that there was not going to be any people marching down the middle of the street anywhere stopping traffic, peaceful or not. Word was it didn't matter. Disperse everyone, no matter who they were, quick and sure, no screwing around. No Mr. Nice Guy."[105] Other cops such as Milt Brower, said that the Old Town episode sent shock waves through the department. "We had been hearing for weeks how crowd control was everything, and then before the convention even began, while we were napping on that nice Saturday night, a damn march began right there in the main street, stopping traffic, and the press is there taking photos. I think that the reason shit hit the fan was that one of those photos made its way to someone at city hall, or Daley's desk, and someone had a fucking conniption, and it went down the food chain. From then on, we were going to be there before they were and if they stepped onto the street we were going to knock them all the way back on or else. We were not going to wait for the crowds to pour in and overwhelm us."[106]

Given Daley's extreme precautions, the numbers of protestors in Chicago on convention eve were far from overwhelming. Although Yippie organizers had estimated attracting 10,000 to 15,000 followers to their five-day Festival of Life in Lincoln Park, the numbers averaged only between 8,000 and 10,000 and never eclipsed 10,000 in total.[107] Movement leaders had repeatedly warned people to stay away. Todd Gitlin recalled "Just before the convention opened, I wrote a front-page headline for an eleventh-hour *Express Times* advance piece on Chicago: 'If you're going to Chicago, be sure to wear some armor in your hair.' Hayden was unhappy about the public foreboding, mine among them, but the warnings piled up. . . . Most of the movement stayed away."[108] Indeed, a disbelieving Hayden realized how much Daley's saber-rattling had set back their efforts. On the Saturday before the convention, Hayden exclaimed, "My God, there's nobody here."[109] Given the increase in the numbers of police, army troops, and National Guard units, it had become clear that the forces amassed against demonstrators were somewhat disproportional. As columnist Mike Royko dryly observed, "Never before had so many feared so much from so few."[110]

SUNDAY, CONVENTION EVE

While 5,000 people turned out at Chicago's Midway airport to welcome Eugene McCarthy, chanting "Gee-yene!" "Gee-yene!" protestors assumed a more aggressive stance with police from the pervious day.[111] The trouble began at 5:30 in the afternoon in Lincoln Park when police refused to allow the use of a flatbed truck as a stage for the scheduled bands. While police and Yippie leaders, including Hoffman discussed the issue, a crowd formed around them; members of the media pressed in for interviews. A police sergeant, upset with their aggressiveness, ordered them away. The sergeant also complained that someone had handed one of his officers a sandwich filled with human waste. Some in the crowd climbed atop the flatbed, hanging over the side. The police ordered the truck moved to an approved area; as the truck began to pull away, others in the crowd began to taunt police. While one yelled, "Who's fuckin' your wife this afternoon, pig?" another protestor planted himself in front of the truck and encouraged others to block its movement. "Don't let the truck out," he yelled, before officers arrested and dragged him to a nearby paddy wagon. Another took his place, ordering others to "Sit in front of the paddy wagon" and "get their guns." As plainclothes officers arrested the second man, the surging crowd screamed, "Let him alone" and "Kill the Pigs! Fuck the pigs!" Uniformed officers moved in from the park command post and formed a double line moving in against the growing crowd. Suddenly, demonstrators rushed the police lines, prompting a call for backup as officers feared the crowd would trap them. As reinforcements arrived, the officers on the scene clubbed open gaps in the crowd, forcing demonstrators back.[112]

Police were surprised by the increase in demonstrator hostility from the previous night. According to journalists from *Ramparts,* the crowd appeared ready to attack the arresting officers. "As the cops dragged away the two men they had arrested, about 300 of the park people moved to follow them, and for a moment it looked as if the police would be attacked." The remaining officers in the park quickly moved in and formed a line as their colleagues placed their detainees in an unmarked squad car. Backing 300 of the more aggressive protestors was a supporting cast of several thousand more who stared down the small line of police. Those in front resumed their taunts of "Pig, pig, fascist pig," and "pigs eat shit, pigs eat shit." The rest of the crowd, however, backed off and sat down on the grass when reinforcements arrived. Police did not retaliate for the name-calling, and within minutes the line of demonstrators broke apart and the incident was over without violence.[113]

Emboldened by the events in Old Town and the face-off in the park with the officers, however, some protestors became more strident, deciding that the cops had no legitimate authority over them. Pressures soon built between protestors and police near the field house. There, a dozen officers stood with their backs to the wall under the glare of the field house lights. They quickly became targets for rocks and lit cigarettes, while fielding taunts of "Mother fuckers!" "Shitheads!" and "Pigs!" The crowd pressed in, continuing its barrage of obscenities for thirty minutes. Police did not react until two squads of reinforcements arrived. Then, without warning, officers charged the crowd. Removing their nameplates, police swung their batons at everyone in their path, including a dozen Yippies who received blows to the head. Police beat some after they fell to the ground.[114]

At 11 P.M., police issued a warning via bullhorn to clear the park. The announcement instructed the crowd, "This is a final warning. The park is closed; all persons now in the park, including representatives of the news media, are in violation of the law and subject to arrest . . . you are in violation of the law. Move out *now!*"[115] Some demonstrators yelled back, "The park is ours! The park is ours!" Others argued over whether to avoid bloodshed and leave or fight for the park. Most decided to leave, among them a crowd of approximately 600 to 1,000 that followed a long-haired man holding a flag of the Vietnamese National Liberation Front, who was atop the shoulders of another. Chanting, "Follow me! To the streets! To the streets! The streets belong to the people!" they led a crowd out of the dimly lit park onto LaSalle. Moving south, the crowd poured into the middle of the street, arm in arm, chanting "Ho, Ho, Ho Chi Minh."[116]

A small squad followed behind the marchers as they continued with the chant: "Two, four, six, eight, organize to smash the state!" Unlike the Old Town crowd of the previous night, the mass heading out of the park was more political and militant; many wore helmets. Crossing State Street, the crowd headed onto Michigan Avenue on a trajectory toward the delegates' hotels. Marchers were not content to simply march, as some threw garbage cans into the streets, blocked traffic, and pounded, rocked, and stomped on cars. The crowd only dispersed when it met head-on with a wall of police blocking the Michigan Avenue Bridge. As officers advanced across the bridge, some broke ranks and charged at fleeing demonstrators. Caught in the middle of the action was *Sun-Times* photojournalist Duane Hall wearing a helmet and press credentials and carrying two cameras. Hall was clubbed in the left jaw and shoulder, and his camera was broken while he attempted to photograph an officer pursuing a demonstrator.[117]

The worst of the violence did not begin until ninety minutes following the 11 P.M. curfew when the bulk of police presence coalesced on the edge of the park and watched the remaining 1,500 demonstrators who had decided that the park was theirs and others who had regrouped after skirmishes on the streets. A police official instructed those remaining that they had thirty seconds to clear out before officers would use force to remove them.[118] Former officer Hank Pacnik recalls that the department was extremely lenient and reasonable with the time allotted for demonstrators to leave the park. "We gave them time to get out of there. We didn't just go in there swinging like so many people think. Hell, even almost two hours after curfew, we went in there slow in formation; all any of them had to do was fall back and move out and no one would have gotten touched. But they wanted a confrontation."[119] Other officers were not so sure. "We should have left them where they were that first night, and permit or not, it would have all fallen apart, and we could have prevented some of the violence we saw later," recalls Paul Juravinski. "And they did not have a lot of time; when we went in we went in quick; people were tripping over themselves trying to get away. Some of them were just stupid kids; they were scared, and they didn't know where to go. I don't know where some of them went. A lot of them were just scared kids who wanted to be part of something and found themselves in the middle of events beyond their comprehension in the dark in the park."[120]

A phalanx of police then moved in from the east, motorcycles in the lead, foot patrolmen, some carrying shotguns, following behind, driving everyone before them onto Clark Street. Some witnesses heard police yell, "Kill the commies" and "Get the bastards."[121] As police lines faced the throngs of defiant protestors, journalists moved in to capture the action. To police, the press were simply "interfering" with their duties. Officers on the scene complained loudly that media strobe lights blinded them, while bottles and rocks struck them repeatedly. Says Darrell Novakowski, "Those guys think because they had a job to do it was okay to fuck up ours. It wasn't." While fending off the barrage, police heard cries of "Oinks," "Pigs," "Motherfuckers," "Pig fuckers," "Fascists," and "Shitheads." Some journalists were struck when they failed to disperse with the rest of the crowd. At 12:20 A.M., police charged, batons swinging, some yelling, "Get out of the park, you motherfuckers!" People broke and ran, shouting back, "Pigs, fuck pigs, oink, oink, oink, pigs, pigs."[122]

One officer cannot forget what took place next in the park. Al Ogilvie recalls what occurred as he and other officers chased the crowd to a parking area adjacent to Clark Street. Police then broke off their pursuit, having achieved their aims of clearing the park. However, as they turned back to find stragglers, they noticed that the demonstrators had reversed their direction and were charging back. "It's what scared the heck out of us a bit on Saturday—their unpredictability, and more so on Sunday later on," says Ogilvie. "They became very aggressive and came after us."[123] Indeed, as a witness would later tell government investigators, crowds were openly defying police.

The thing about this crowd was that since it thrived on confrontation it behaved in a way much different than any other crowd I've ever seen. During racial riots, the police would break up the crowd and the crowd would stay broken up. It might regroup in another place but rarely would it head back for direct confrontation with its assailants. This was a most unusual crowd . . . the police would break people's heads but the crowd would not run away. [It would] regroup and surge back to the police and yell more epithets, as much as saying: "Do it again."[124]

The clashes of Saturday and Sunday had a bearing on convention week. Police believed that they would have to continue to chase demonstrators after they left the park and splinter them into smaller groups in the hopes of keeping them from re-forming in the park and marching on the delegates' hotels or the amphitheater. "It was bewildering," says cop Steve Nowakowski. "I couldn't believe what was happening. Just as we got them going back, they turned and came back for more."[125]

As the crowd surged back, police charged once again, driving demonstrators into Clark Street. Ugly hand-to-hand combat ensued, with police cracking people on the head and even kicking and striking some repeatedly after they fell. Some victims curled into a fetal position in an attempt to ward off the worst of the blows. As before, police clubbed journalists who were trying to cover the chaotic scene.[126] Demonstrators scrambled to form a wedge against the police coming out of the park. Eugenie Triangle and the Old Town Triangle became jammed with people, forcing cars to a stop. Drivers began to blast their horns, adding to the cacophony of screams, angry shouts, and the sickening sound of batons meeting flesh and bone. Two squads of officers moved north to clear Clark Street, while another police line extended from the Eugenie Triangle past Lincoln Avenue on the eastern side of Clark. Then came the rocks. A reporter described the scene in his notes. "They're [the police and the protestors] in Clark Street and it's a mess and now the nastiness really begins. The crowd is picking up rocks and throwing them at the police."[127]

As many in the crowd screamed, "Fuck the pigs and kill the pigs!" officers moved in to clear the sidewalks and the streets. As the police pushed the crowd out into the glare of the streetlights, a huge mass of bodies came together, momentarily trapping the crowd; police moved in, leading with their batons, connecting with shoulders, rear ends, legs, and arms; many of the protestors fled down side streets where the police let them escape.[128] The cops manning the side streets showed restraint. "I remember, I think it was Sunday, when we let them run right by us, thirty or forty of them, they had their hands guarding their faces, and we let them drift on into the night which was best—they were not up to a fight," recalls Tom Freeborn. "As soon as the park and the major intersections were clear of protestors, the rest were let along to disperse."[129]

Some journalists, however, were not as fortunate. Police clubbed *Newsweek* reporters John Culhane and Monroe Anderson despite credentials pinned to their coats and struck reporter Claude Lewis of the Philadelphia *Evening Bulletin* in the head after he took notes of a particularly vicious beating in which a police officer repeatedly jabbed a young blond woman in the stomach with his baton until she collapsed on the street screaming. One of the officers spotted Lewis and demanded, "Hey, you dirty bastard, give me that goddamn notebook." After the officer relieved him of the book, he struck Lewis with his baton. Two *New York Times* reporters took Lewis to the hospital.[130] By 1 A.M., however, most of the remaining crowd had disappeared down side streets and into the night. The violence was over. The injured sought treatment in local hospitals, others found emergency housing in nearby churches, or in homes the movement secured for demonstrators from outside Chicago.[131]

For police, the evening of violence was a foreshadowing of the nights to come. Aware of the threats received over the previous weeks, the clash had proven to them that the antiwar movement had come to fight. Even Tom Hayden's tone in the days leading up to the convention had become increasingly hostile and fearful. Among his pronouncements was his charge that protestors "are coming to Chicago to vomit on the politics of joy, to expose the secret divisions, upset the nightclub orgies, and face the Democratic Party with its illegitimacy and criminality." Hayden also understood, however, that those heading to Chicago were going to be isolated from much of the mainstream movement and trapped inside an armed camp with Daley's cops. As convention week was about to begin, the former SDS leader said that he was "expecting death, expecting the worst."[132]

Several officers felt the same trepidation. Sam Ivanchenko, like many in the Chicago Police Department, worried about what was to come. He saw the week ahead as violent theater. "We were put together like cocks or dogs fighting; the worst of the antiwar movement and the good ole Chicago PD in the ring for five days, and we were going to see who was the last man standing. And I didn't know what to expect." The buildup to convention week led to sleepless nights for some in uniform. Like several other former police officers, Randall Bakker recalls his apprehension on convention eve. Although he says his police background trained him well, nothing could completely prepare him for the barrage of taunts and threats. "I remember late Sunday, could have been early Monday, and I knew it was, God, twelve hours a day for a week of trouble and spit and being asked how I like to suck my fellow officers' cocks. The convention had not even begun yet, and already it was looking like shit."[133]

Other former cops remember the end of their long shift Sunday evening, dreading the next day, Monday and the first day of the convention. "Let me tell you plain that only a fool looked forward to battling with those freaks," says Darrell Novakowski. "We would all have been just fine with not doing a damn thing, drinking coffee, talking about the [Chicago] Bears, women, and collecting our paycheck. I don't know one man personally who was itching to mix it up." Brian Ramsey agrees. "I heard that some of the guys were talking it up a bit before going out and even so after getting out there, but I personally never heard any of it. And some of that was because we were getting these pep talks on how to handle things and that our asses were on the line. It's not a good situation, and there were some real fears about knives and guns."[134]

Former officer Murray Sheppard was so upset he threw up in his district stationhouse washroom after his Sunday night shift. "There was trouble at home, and I'm not using that as an excuse, but I knew damn well that I was going to be on my feet all week, twelve-hours a day, and I had just been through hell out there for all but about an hour of my shift. My heart was hammering in my chest." Adding to his stress was that he almost withdrew his service revolver on two occasions. "I almost drew my gun twice—and that's saying something. It was something that rarely happened on my eleven years in the department; we were not cowboys—we were human beings. You laughed and smiled, and told jokes, but it was a way of cutting the tension." Others were also keenly aware of the media who were on the sidewalks, watching, taking pictures, trying to interview people as they fled. Police recall that the constant scrutiny made their jobs more difficult and added to the stress. Says Jerry Ewaschuck, "You could feel the cameras on us already—every time you looked over your shoulder, there were journalists there, and they were looking at us, even when we were not engaged, more than they were on the hippies and their placards. They were waiting for us to slip up a bit—just an inch, and then flash their bulbs and go running after the hippies for a comment. It was unfair from the beginning. They portrayed us as storm troopers before the convention even got under way. They were judging us and it was only Sunday."[135]

Abbie Hoffman was already making judgments on the police. At 2 A.M. on Monday morning, armed with the home number of Deputy Mayor David Stahl, Hoffman decided to give the city official a call and relate personally his disgust with police tactics. "I said, 'Hi, Dave. How's it going? Your police got to be the dumbest and the most brutal in the country. The decision to drive people out of the park in order to protect the City was about the dumbest military tactic since the Trojans let the Trojan horse inside the gate and there was nothing to be compared with that stupidity.'"[136]

Some officers knew that park curfews would lead to unnecessary confrontations. They admit that the crowds could not do any harm if left alone in the park. The reality that they were not going to let protestors march out of the park or remain after the 11 P.M. curfew, essentially forcing a large number of people out onto the streets at the same time, had some officers understandably worried about what was to come. "My hands were shaking while I was taking off my uniform," says cop Archie Pasis recalling his shift early Monday morning,

and I started to black out. My hands shook some days anyway; I'd get these premonitions the odd time before going out, of death; getting shot, or stabbed, leaving my kids behind without a father, sort of like those feelings you get stepping on a plane sometimes. They were sure shaking that morning. Then I got out onto the street to get home. They were deserted. I smelled the air, the look of the street; it was still warm, muggy. I saw this—and I will always remember—a cat dashed across the street and into the alley. Before it disappeared down the lane, it stopped and shot me a cold look. I knew that look. It sounds stupid but everything felt wrong early that Monday morning, like something approaching—you know . . . like a gathering storm.[137]

chapter 5

"A Perfect Mess": Convention Week

We were characters taking the stage—complete with costumes and legends; they wore black, we wore white, the cameras rolled, some director called "*action*," and we were maneuvered around that windy set according to our prescribed roles. We did—both sides—what everyone expected us to do.[1]

Oh, Dad, help them![2]

Chicago's battleground for the weeklong Democratic National Convention spanned a seven-mile stretch along the shores of Lake Michigan, from Old Town in the north to the stockyards to the south. While the Yippies holed up in Lincoln Park, members of Mobe set up camp roughly two miles to the south in Grant Park across from the Conrad Hilton, the site of the Democrat's headquarters. Five miles farther south near the stockyards was the amphitheater, the site of the convention. In and around the parks, on the streets of Old Town, through the Loop, to the convention site in the south, stood Daley's cops.

A shadow had descended on the Second City in the form of hippies, Yippies, various antiwar groups, conventioneers, and members of the national media. The commission that later investigated events during convention week described that motley crew as including "communists, anarchists, peace advocates, revolutionaries, New Leftists, bizarre flower folk, draft resistors, radical militants, professional agitators, moderate but disconnected liberals, disaffected straights, housewives opposed to the war, black power militants—all with their own motivations and objections."[3]

The mood in the city was tense and grim seemingly with little room for compromise politically or civically by police, politicians, or protestors. The only factor shared by delegates and demonstrators during the 1968 Democratic National Convention in Chicago was that both arrived deeply divided. Adding to the surly mood was that on the heels of a citywide garbage strike, Chicago's cab drivers decided to go on strike mere days before the beginning of the convention. They were joined by the city's bus drivers, who went on strike at 12:01 Sunday morning. As a hundred magistrates prepared for emergency duty to form "a judicial assembly line to process cases on an around-the-clock basis,"[4] the cops looked on the growing crowds with undisguised distain. "What I knew for sure that Monday with the arrival of the hippies," says cop Archie Pasis, "was that the city started to smell a hell of a lot worse."[5]

MONDAY, AUGUST 26

There was little doubt that convention week was going to be difficult for the leaders of Mobe, plagued not only by inflated egos, competing visions, and infighting, but with plainclothes officers tailing key members around the clock. Tom Hayden found himself shadowed by detectives Ralph Bell and Frank Riggio, allegedly uttering not so veiled threats of physical violence; the prospect of arrest at any point became routine. This was certainly the case for Hayden, arrested twice on the first day of the convention. On Sunday evening, he narrowly escaped capture after his partner, Rennie Davis, managed to slip his followers; Hayden, with some gamesmanship, maneuvered behind his pursuers. When the detectives realized what had happened, they pounced on Hayden and threw him into the back of their sedan, threatening to "beat the shit out of him." The car never made it anywhere as a demonstrator had let the air out of the tires. When police blamed their detainee for the act, Hayden began screaming for help, and help came pouring out of the park, surrounding the immobilized car. Riggio and Bell let Hayden go.[6]

On Monday, Hayden was not so fortunate. Near 2 P.M., police went looking for the activist in Lincoln Park. They were armed with a warrant for his arrest thanks to Bell and Riggio who had launched a complaint against him. Two plainclothes officers, accompanied by two others in uniform, grabbed Hayden near a baseball field in the park and marched him to a squad car through the middle of Mobe's own security marshals without incident.[7] Police officers recall that this was also part of a strategy to take control from the beginning. "It was exactly what we were planning to do," says officer Tom O'Malley. "We were letting them know that *we* were in charge from the get-go, and we could and would grab their so-called leaders when we chose to, and any one of them could be next, and that included the press."[8] As they did on Sunday, the police showed remarkably little patience with members of the media. When an ABC-TV crew attempted to film Hayden's arrest, a cop struck soundman Walter James in the back with his baton and destroyed a $900 camera lens belonging to cameraman

Charles Pharris. ABC launched a formal complaint with the police over what the *Sun-Times* referred to as action "without reason."[9]

By most accounts, police used arrests as a form of intimidation—as one officer put it, to send the message "down the food chain" to other protestors of what they could expect if they were to get out of hand. Police made it a point to scare Hayden during his first arrest in the hopes that words of intimidation would spread through protestor ranks. In a squad car on his trip to headquarters, Hayden claimed an arresting officer threatened him: "You motherfucker, we're going to wipe you out. We're going to kill you. . . . We're going to take you into a dark alley and you're never going to come out."[10]

Within minutes of Hayden's arrest, 500 to 1,000 of his compatriots, led by Rennie Davis, descended on police headquarters. When the crowd, some carrying Vietcong flags, arrived at the station, the building was already surrounded by a wall of police, prompting one marcher to quip, "It's wall-to-wall pig." Protestors then locked arms and chanted, "Pig, pig, oink, oink, soo-ee, soo-ee," before moving in the direction of the Loop and the delegates' hotels near Grant Park.[11] Contrary to the alleged threats by police, however, the arresting officers did not take Hayden into an alley or beat him. The officers simply drove him to the station where they charged him with resisting arrest, obstructing police, and disorderly conduct; they released him later Monday evening after he posted bond.[12]

Throughout the day, police made numerous arrests both in the park and on the streets. The word came down from commanders that arrests were to be frequent and obvious. As cop Archie Pasis remembers, "It was made clear to us that when we made arrests, it was going to be in a place where it got a lot of attention, and people could see that we were not going to screw around."[13] More specifically, the department stated that it was actively keeping a round-the-clock watch on particular individuals, among them, an editor of an underground paper, a black militant from the city, and two members of Mobe.[14]

Trouble, however, began late Monday afternoon when protestors laid claim to the statue of Illinois Civil War major general Jonathan Logan, which sits on a small hill across Michigan Avenue from the Conrad Hilton Hotel in Grant Park. Demonstrators draped the statue in the red and black flag of the National Liberation Front, while hanging on to it like a captured trophy.[15] Those on the statue began to yell "Pigs!" "Fuckers!" and "Kill the pigs!" at the police who stood at the bottom of the rise.[16] When the utterances reached the ears of waiting police, they quickly rushed up the hill, a move that prompted most of the demonstrators to clamber off the statue. One young man with a McCarthy button pinned to his shirt, however, went higher as the police surrounded the statute, batons tapping in their hands.

According to journalists from *Ramparts,* march leaders pleaded with one of Daley's representatives (who followed police throughout the week to ensure they acted within the law) to allow the young man to come down and submit to arrest. The representative agreed and instructed police to comply. According to witnesses, the police ignored Daley's commissionaire, climbed the statue, hauled the protestor down, and tossed him into a patrol car. The young man—Birmingham,

Alabama, native Lee Edmundson—had his arm broken during the arrest.[17] Other reports suggest that the youth continued to resist arrest and kicked one of the officers in the shoulder and another in the face as they tried to pull him off. According to one of the arresting officers, the man yelled, "Fuck you and fuck this country." While five officers filed injury reports, some witnesses claimed that the police got in the better of the licks as along with the broken arm, one officer reportedly struck Edmundson in the groin with a nightstick during the arrest.[18]

Throughout the afternoon, protestors staked out across from the Hilton, calling for the end of the war, and listening to Mobe speakers, including David Dellinger. Emerging from their hotels at 6:30 P.M., some of the delegates stopped to listen before heading off to the amphitheater for the first night of the convention; to the north, protestors gathered in Lincoln Park to hold rallies and wait for nightfall and the impending 11:00 P.M. curfew. According to several former cops, the rule was to keep the demonstrators from claiming the streets. "The kids where to be in the park until 11:00 P.M., and after a thirty-minute reprieve, they were to disassemble peacefully and break apart, not congregating in groups, not marching on the delegates' hotels nor to the convention site," says Tom Freeborn. "When they left the park to march, we were told to block them, disperse them, and, if needed, to make arrests. It was only the first day [of the convention], and we were not going to let them take over. And we had *wide latitude* in keeping them from doing that."[19] Another officer says that it looked like the city was preparing for "one hell of a battle." Indeed, on that Monday, the military airlifted 6,000 regular army troops complete in full battle gear—rifles, flamethrowers, and bazookas—onto the streets to deal with any possible scenario.[20]

On that first day it appeared that just about anything was possible. That evening, as Hubert Humphrey arrived at the Hilton, someone threw a stink bomb into the hotel's lobby; with the fumes traveling upward, a *Sun-Times* reporter could detect the strong smell of rotten eggs on the seventeenth floor. Humphrey, who was having his shoes shined at the time, was hustled up to his suite on the twenty-forth floor by Secret Service agents.[21] Whereas the situation on the streets was tense, the atmosphere at the convention center where delegates gathered to hear the first night of speakers was not much better; a "gloomy" mood pervaded the barbwire-encased center near the stockyards on the city's South Side, which the press dubbed "Fort Daley."

Inside the Amphitheater

"The place stunk like a hippie's armpit," recalls former officer Carl Moore. Indeed, the smell from the massive hog slaughtering operation next door permeated the amphitheater site throughout the week, adding to an already sour mood. The venue was inhospitable to be sure, with a 472-member security detail that included a plainclothes policewoman in each ladies' washroom and sixty plainclothes officers working the convention floor under the command of the Secret Service. Ex-cop Ken O'Connor joked that the mood on the convention floor resembled a prison exercise yard, with delegates treated like inmates while Daley's security men played the part of prison guards. Indeed, the mayor planned to keep demonstrators and dissent suppressed not only outside the hall, but inside as well. Daley severely restricted press passes, and security officers made it difficult to reach the floor, while other officers watched closely for signs of delegate demonstrations, roughing up anyone who spoke too loud on the wrong subject and intimidating antiwar delegates, relegated to the back of the hall, into silence. This intimidation bordered on the ridiculous as security even initially refused entry to New York delegate Allard Lowenstein because he held a copy of the hated *New York Times,* which he planned to quote from that evening.[22] As he did during the April peace march, the mayor sent out the message that dissenters had "no right to express their views."

Most absent from the amphitheater was any photo of the sitting president. Johnson understood that his presence, in body or likeness, would do more harm than good given the mood in Chicago. Fearing boos from the galleries, the president decided to stay away. In many ways, however, Johnson still controlled the floor; with his men holding the key positions, there was little evidence that change was in the cards, as Daley's men were not going to turn the convention floor over to antiwar voices.[23] It was a disheartening reality to the supporters of Senator Eugene McCarthy, as they knew that their man had little chance of overcoming the party bosses' intention to crown Humphrey with the party's leadership.

There were also distinct rumblings from the McCarthyites that if it were to become clear that their candidate was going to lose, they would join the protestors on the street.[24] The vice president's supporters, however, could take little comfort in an impending victory as a recent Gallup poll showed that Humphrey had little chance of defeating Republican Richard Nixon in November.[25] Indeed, as the convention opened, Daley, too, was slow to back Humphrey's candidacy. With the little-known McGovern and antiwar candidate McCarthy static in the polls, Daley initially supported a plan to draft Massachusetts Senator Edward Kennedy. In fact, Humphrey was Daley's fourth choice after Johnson, Bobby Kennedy, and finally Teddy Kennedy. The attempt to lever the last Kennedy brother into the fight, however, went nowhere Monday night.[26]

With the youngest Kennedy out of the picture, Daley threw his belated support to the vice president, and Daley's support was seen as important to whichever candidate hoped to lead the party. Publicly, Daley strongly supported Johnson's polices in Vietnam and the president in general.[27] After Johnson withdrew from the race, Daley indicated support for Robert Kennedy and private concerns over the Asian war. Indeed, Kennedy had told journalist Jimmy Breslin, "He's been very nice to me personally, and he doesn't like the war. You see, there are so many dead starting to come back, it bothers him." Kennedy also knew how important it was to have the backing of Chicago's veteran mayor. "Daley," Kennedy said, "means the ball game."[28]

On the first evening, in a sometimes bitter floor fight, the platform committee backed the majority plank on Vietnam supported by Johnson and Humphrey while Daley's omnipresent security men went about intimidating any coalition that threatened to form against the vice president.[29] Dissident Democrats were not the only ones feeling restricted, as members of the press struggled to cover events. Security restricted reporters' access to the convention floor, while camera crews found their access curtailed. Television networks ABC, NBC, and CBS were each limited to seven floor passes for both radio and TV coverage, which contrasted with twenty each for the Republican National Convention in Miami earlier that month.[30] During his evening address to delegates, Daley set the mood. The mayor stated that the important issues in America and in Chicago would "never be solved in rioting and violence in the streets. And as long as I am mayor, there will be law and order in Chicago."[31]

Outside as darkness chased away the last vestiges of the day over Lake Michigan, disaffected youth took to the streets. The young McCarthy workers were already identifying more with demonstrators than with the Democratic Party. As a crowd of about 1,000 marched around the Hilton, chanting, "Dump the Hump," McCarthy volunteers across the street leaned out of their office windows and waved in solidarity with demonstrators. Those on the street shouted back, "Do it, baby, do it."[32] Signs nearby read, "Welcome to Prague."

Nightfall

"Monday night" wrote Norman Mailer, "the city was washed with the air of battle."[33] The evening started off poorly for police as at 8 P.M., a man squirted an acidic fluid into the eyes of an officer sitting in a cruiser at 2041 Lincoln Park West; the officer required treatment at Henrotin Hospital.[34] Officer Sheldon Bartowski says that Monday night was hell. "It was worse than I thought; people running, yelling, throwing bricks, spitting. We didn't seem to have a grasp on what was going on, and it was impossible to keep control of these ever-shifting crowds. It was like, 'don't let them go here; can't let them march here; keep them away from this building; no, they can't go here. The manager of this hotel doesn't want any longhairs in this hotel; keep them out of here and there'; we were running around completely disorganized. . . . It was *just* impossible."[35]

As it was on Sunday, Old Town turned chaotic as groups of demonstrators of up to 2,000 took to the streets. Whereas some of the marchers behaved peacefully, others harassed passing motorists, sometimes standing on the hoods of cars or throwing rocks and bottles. The mission for police was to prevent disturbances from reaching the downtown area and the delegates' hotels. A police task force moved men and four paddy wagons to Wacker and Michigan avenues. At approximately 8:30 P.M. in the adjacent park, Hoffman was counseling the few hundred or so demonstrators to avoid confrontation, telling them that if the police ask them to leave, they should. It was clear that neither Hoffman nor Allen Ginsberg, with his incessant chant of "Om" nearby, any longer had control of events. As Hoffman tried to direct the crowd and appealed for some calm, another man yelled, "We gotta kill all the cops!" Into this mayhem, police released Tom Hayden with a $1,000 bond and a September 18 court date.[36]

At 9 P.M., the first significant group of marchers moved out of Lincoln Park onto Clark Street, intending to march to the Sherman Hotel, home for the Illinois delegation. Members of the Area 6 Task Force moved quickly to block the intersection of Clark and Schiller with police cruisers. Police then formed a line and moved north in formation toward the marching protestors intending to shove them back into the park. In the first major clash of Monday evening, police appeared intent to do more than push back demonstrators as they set upon those who had nothing to do with the marchers but were caught at the wrong place at the wrong time. In one instance, officers beat a lawyer from a local bank who was riding his motorcycle home with a passenger. "I was shocked and surprised to have been attacked by police, since I feel it was obvious that I was not part of any demonstration going on," the man later told government investigators. "I was not shouting or carrying any signs. I was the first motor vehicle in a line of cars that had been held up by the demonstrators, but at the time of attack, the demonstrators had, for the most part, fled some distance north from my position." What troubled him most was the officers' "uncontrolled behavior," as they issued contradictory orders. His impression was that police appeared unsure of what they were doing.[37] Some officers, including Norm Nelson, dismiss such occurrences out of hand. "There was a bunch of whiners who got suddenly caught in the middle of a protest. What the hell were these people thinking?"[38] Others claimed that these instances were rare and usually the result of minor confusion during crowd control.

Whereas the Clark Street marchers quickly dispersed when faced with the rushing police, another group set out of the park, moving down Wells Street, approximately one thousand strong, chanting antiwar slogans. A few demonstrators threw bottles, breaking some of the windows along the street. At 9:37 P.M., as the crowd turned east onto Division, police moved in to force marchers back onto Wells.[39] As some officers held the middle of the street, blocking it, a squad of about a dozen others knifed into the marchers, batons swinging. To avoid the worst of the police assault, the crowd almost immediately faded into the night. Others, however, were not as lucky, as police charged making arrests in a "vicious" manner.[40] Police arrested forty-six demonstrators, charging most of them with disorderly conduct. During the confrontation, five police officers received minor injuries. One officer had the knuckle on his left hand broken, while a demonstrator wielding a two-by-four cracked his helmet.[41] The majority of the crowd, however, dispersed quickly, most heading back to Lincoln Park where they remained until the 11 P.M. curfew and the next showdown with police.[42] But as demonstrators scattered and the streets temporarily cleared, some members of the press covering the events found themselves licking their wounds.

"A Harmonious Relationship"

As they did on Sunday evening, police appeared to target the media for abuse. When attempting to film clashes on the street, several journalists found themselves on the business end of a police officer's nightstick. The victims Monday evening included a photographer and reporter from the *Chicago Sun-Times,* cameramen for both CBS and NBC, and a correspondent and photographer from *Newsweek.*[43] These attacks came even after police commanders admonished their members to act more professionally with the media. After police clashes with members of the press on Sunday, the department attempted to deal with the growing public relations meltdown. Whereas commanders did not appear overly alarmed about demonstrator complaints of abuse by police, conflict with the press at least received a formal response and a request for restraint.

Early Monday, police superintendent James Conlisk ordered an investigation into his officers' conduct on the streets Sunday night and released an order to be read at all daily police roll calls. The edict reminded officers: "Despite any personal feelings of individuals, department personnel should avoid conflicts with newsmen. It is in the best interest of the department and the City of Chicago that there be a harmonious relationship between the news media representatives and our personnel."[44]

The nature of some of the violence concerning members of the media indicated an acute level of "personal feelings of individuals" when it came to members of the police. During the demonstrations on Wells Street, police allegedly made personal threats against *Sun-Times* reporter Brian Boyer who was covering arrests near Division and Wells. Boyer reported that police were blaming the press for attracting protestors to the city in the hope that they would receive publicity. Boyer also suggested that when a photographer attempted to take a picture of an officer who had removed his name tag, a dozen others surrounded the policeman to shield him. When he questioned their behavior, the journalist said that officers informed him, "Just wait until after dark. We'll get you." The police later arrested Boyer and placed him behind bars. Management for the *Sun-Times* not only intervened to secure his release two hours later, but pulled his byline on stories concerning street disturbances for the remainder of the week.[45]

Meanwhile, *Newsweek* photographer Jeff Lowenthal, who was taking pictures of the action, heard cops nearby say, "Get the cameras" and "Beat the press." While pulling out his press identification, police struck him on his arm and shoulder. Police clubbed several others covering the action, including Claude Lewis of the *Philadelphia Bulletin.* Lewis said that after an officer struck him in the head with a billy club, near Lincoln Park, they confiscated his notebook. Among the more serious of these attacks happened to NBC cameraman James Stricklin, who received blows to the mouth and the kidney. Stricklin checked into the hospital Tuesday morning where he remained for two days. The following morning, *Chicago's American* ran a photo of freelance photographer Dan Morrill, his head and face wet with blood following an attack from a cop wielding a billy club.[46] John Evans of NBC recorded Morrill's nasty encounter with a pair of Chicago police officers concerning the photographer's camera.

Unidentified voice: Give me that.

Dan Morrill: I'm sorry, I apologize, I apologize, please, I apologize.

Unidentified voice: Give me the film.

Dan Morrill: I won't (?) give you the film.

John Evans: Why do you want the film, officer?

Unidentified voice: None of your business.

John Evans: You don't have to surrender that film, sir.

Dan Morrill: No, I'll give it to him.

Unidentified voice: Thank you.

Unidentified voice: Mind your own business.

Unidentified voice: Who are you?

John Evans: NBC News, who are you?

At this point, an officer ripped Evan's microphone off his recorder while another clubbed him in the head, causing a six-stitch laceration to his scalp.[47]

Much of the evidence suggests that police on Monday, as they did Sunday, appeared to go after the media as much because they were taking photos than they were "in the way" or "indistinguishable from hippies." *Business Week* photographer P. Michael O'Sullivan was among several journalists who claimed that police not only knocked him to the ground but searched his pockets, taking a roll of film. As they were trying to seize his camera, one officer threatened, "Give us your film or I'll break your head." O'Sullivan noticed that the police not only refused to give him their names but had apparently removed their name tags. *Washington Post* photographer Stephen Northrup received similar treatment while taking a picture of a cop who was hitting a demonstrator on the ground. Both Northrup and another witness heard the cop yell, "Get him, he's got a camera." Beaten to the ground, the reporter needed five stitches to close a scalp laceration.[48]

Police differ in their accounts of press treatment early in the week. Some believe that media representatives had either gotten themselves too close to the action or were "just like" hippies. Although they disagree on whether or not they singled out members of the press for abuse, few had much sympathy for journalists struck or hurt. Says officer Mel Latanzio, "They [the media] hated us, that's for sure. There was no love lost. Yeah, they got their bonnets beaten a little, but if you want to play the game, ya gotta *play* the game. We had been getting bad press long before the convention, especially for what was going on in the black neighborhoods, so what the hell."[49] Others agree wholeheartedly. "I hated those bastards—they were commies," says Randall Bakker. "Sorry, but they were *always* on our case, and *these* guys would not last a *day* on our beat; they had no idea what we were up against, not just during the convention, but every day. They [the press] drove us crazy for the whole damn decade."[50] Others were even blunter in the way they handled their irritation with the press. Says one officer, "They were in the fucking way; any time I saw press credentials, I swung."[51]

Officers also claimed that the press core deliberately skewed images. "They were trying to make us look as bad as possible," says Ernie Watson. "The press was chasing after us, and when we would subdue someone climbing on a car, or rocking a car, or throwing a bottle, we made a move, and you could see the flashbulbs going off, and that's not fair. They never took photos of those people and what they did. They always got it wrong."[52] Others believed that the press had made up its mind that the police would overreact and any skirmishes between officers and demonstrators would be blamed on the former. Says Sheldon Bartowski. "They [the media] were not only getting in the way, but there was no question whose side they were taking, and that should not happen; they should be objective, but the goddamn media is never that way with us. They tried to make us look as bad as possible, and that's why they became a target."[53] Indeed, on the streets outside the Hilton and near the parks, journalists became easy targets, intended and otherwise, of police batons and mace. "The only time I've run to save my hide was Monday night," wrote *Daily News* columnist Mike Royko. "A group of Chicago police were after me. My crime was watching when they beat somebody who didn't deserve it."[54] Whereas fifteen cops reported injuries after Monday night, twenty journalists required some sort of hospital care. Donning larger credentials to avoid the violence they faced after Sunday only made the media more noticeable and seemingly increasingly subject to police wrath. One local ABC reporter learned firsthand from an officer he knew that the "word is out to get newsmen."[55]

Other officers, while admitting that some members targeted the press for reprisals for what they wrote, thought that the entire "press thing" was blown out of proportion. Says Steven Latz, "Most of the guys could not have given two shits about them; they were just another body on the street to be moved."[56] Indeed, government investigators later found that many police did not attempt to distinguish between demonstrators and the journalists who were covering them. For example, Fred Schnell, who was on assignment for *Time-Life,* was photographing a cop dragging a young girl behind a police line. When an officer turned on him, Schnell held out his identification and stated, "I'm a *Time-Life* photographer." The cop swung his baton at him saying, "I don't care who the hell you are—get out of the street."[57] *Chicago's American* reporter Robert Jackson, who was struck in the head and maced, was told by a cop, "I don't give a fuck who you are with," as he took pains to show his press credentials.[58] As police clubbed NBC cameraman James Stricklin, he told the officer he was with the network. According to Stricklin, the cop stated, "I don't care."[59] As journalists from *Time* pointed out, "No one could accuse the Chicago cops of discrimination. They savagely attacked hippies, yippies, New Leftists, revolutionaries, dissident Democrats, newsmen, photographers, passers-by, clergymen, and at least one cripple."[60]

Barriers

Back in Lincoln Park as the 11 P.M. curfew approached, demonstrators hastily erected a barrier to keep out the police. Using park benches, garbage cans, and scrounging for anything else they could find, protestors erected a fifty-yard long barricade in a feeble attempt to prevent the inevitable clearing of the park.[61] On the other side of the growing barrier, police were marshaling their forces to breach the barricade and remove the hardcore demonstrators who refused to leave or felt that they had nowhere to go. Making matters worse were reports that up to a 1,000 demonstrators were planning to resist eviction from the park. Department intelligence had learned that some protestors had armed themselves with bamboo spears, razor blades, and even a shotgun. Also unsettling to police were rumors that members of a black street gang from the South Side called the Blackstone Rangers would join hardcore demonstrators in a fight to hold the park.[62] As police approached the makeshift barrier after 11 P.M. Monday night, they braced for the worst. As Nancy Zaroulis and Gerald Sullivan suggest, those behind the makeshift barricade were not only "taunting the police" but "inviting attack."[63] Other reports had demonstrators yelling, "Kill the pigs!" and "Fuck the pigs!"[64]

To disperse the crowd without engaging in hand-to-hand combat with thousands of kids in the park, the police used teargas. As cop Warren MacAulay recalls, "People complain about the use of teargas, but it's much better than the alternative. It usually cleared out the majority other than the hardcores who we had to clear out by hand, and that's what the press saw and reported. It would have been a lot worse if we didn't use the gas."[65] Joining the officers at the barricade were eighty members of the Area 6 Task Force, armed with teargas and shotguns. Another 160 district officers stood about 100 feet northeast of the barricade. While police prepared to move in, those in the park threw stones, bottles, and even bathroom tiles across the barricade. Fifteen minutes past curfew, police issued a warning by loudspeaker. "The park is now closed." Officers repeated the warning thirty minutes later at 11:45 P.M. With the decision to clear the park at midnight, officers moved into position, easily outflanking the demonstrators' barricade.[66]

As they would for the rest of the week, officers became edgy while poised at the line. Tom Freeborn recalls, "It was a tense time; you could feel your adrenaline and your blood pressure rise. Even though I recall it was not a particularly hot week, we were all sweating like pigs—oh, pardon the pun . . . because you *knew* what you were about to do, and there is the unknown. Will someone have a knife or worse? You don't assume anything, not in a city like Chicago and especially during that period."[67] Joe Pecoraro agrees. "You don't know what to expect—they were throwing billiard balls. You hope some nut doesn't start shooting. You keep your fingers crossed." Pecoraro, who was in plainclothes that week, knew that several demonstrators were armed with three-inch gas pipes in their pockets for weapons. Undercover officers that infiltrated protestor ranks had learned of plans to take down some high-ranking officers. Says Pecoraro, "Me and my partner were assigned to watch [Commander James] Riordan's back, and that's all we did was stay with him and make sure that nothing happened to him."[68]

At twenty past midnight, events proved some of their fears warranted when a single police cruiser pulled in behind protestors from the rear of the barricade. For the first time during convention week, police came under direct attack from demonstrators. As the car approached with its lights off, people screamed, "Get the police car! Get the police car!"[69] Reporters from *Ramparts* described the scene:

Rocks and bottles pelted the police car. Its rear window and most side windows were kicked in, its roof light and siren broken (eerily, as demonstrators pounded on the car, the siren kept emitting a soft, wounded moan). Through it all the two cops inside sat poker-faced, watching, making no move for long minutes until finally the car lurched forward toward the barricade, backed around, and retreated to the police lines.[70]

As the crowd pelted the car with bricks, an officer near the Task Force line stumbled and fell, bringing cheers from those behind the barricade. Several Task Force officers surged forward before their commander ordered them to stand their ground.[71] Police recall becoming extremely jittery in the moments leading up to the curfew confrontations. Dale Jaeschke, for one, recalls, "I remember shaking as we were about to go in there and get them. My heart began to beat fast. I felt excited and sick to my stomach. My palms would sweat and it would run down the back of my neck making me edgy as hell."[72]

Those in the park also became agitated waiting for the police to come and get them. For some, it was like waiting for an opposing army to come out of the dark. McCarthy volunteer and writer William Styron recalled the tension that night, especially when he heard someone yell, "They'll be here in two minutes." With the others, Styron waited for their certain appearance over the rise. In the months following that summer, Styron wrote the following eerie account.

And suddenly they were here, coming over the brow of the slope fifty yards away, a truly stupefying sight—one hundred or more of the police in a phalanx abreast, clubs at the ready, in helmets and gas masks, just behind them a huge perambulating machine with nozzles, like the type used for spraying insecticide, disgorging clouds of yellowish gas, the whole advancing panoply illuminated by batteries of mobile floodlights . . . because of the helmeted and masked figures—resembling nothing so much as those rubberized wind-up automata from a child's playbox of horrors—I had a quick sense of the medieval in juxtaposition with the twenty-first century or, more exactly, a kind of science fiction fantasy, as if a band of primitive Christians on another planet had suddenly found themselves set upon by mechanized legions from Jupiter.[73]

At 12:30 P.M., the order came by bullhorn to clear the park. "This is the final warning. We have information some persons intend to injure police officers. Move out now." As guru Allen Ginsberg and a small group of his followers stretched the surreal by chanting "Om,"[74] 200 to 250 police officers closed in on the crowd of 2,000 to 3,000 defiant protestors, some with Vaseline and wet cloths covering their faces. The crowd expected regular teargas, but police actually fired a volley of half a dozen military-grade antiriot gas canisters. With the gas exploding in front of them, the officers respendent in gasmasks and riot gear, moved into Lincoln Park. According to some reports, police advanced yelling, "Kill, kill, kill!"[75] Retreating rapidly, the demonstrators were forced into Clark Street, blocking traffic, hands over mouths, choking and coughing, tears running down their faces, bandannas over their mouths, the police on their heels. The cops charged into the crowd swinging billy clubs. *Ramparts* reported that the police "were completely out of control . . . the attack was indiscriminate. Cops climbed porches and even went into houses to grab and beat people; officers clubbed a man in his own backyard. There were repeated cries of 'Pig!' but they were fiercely angry, shouted in frustration." Demonstrators fought back, hurling rocks and bottles at police as they jammed into the tri-corner of Wells, Clark, and LaSalle before moving down Wells Street to get away from the charging police, coughing and cursing as they fled. Police, however, were already blocking exit routes. With some holding riot guns, they moved in on demonstrators.[76]

Officers say that they had learned lessons from the encounters of Saturday and Sunday night. "We were learning fast what their tactics were," says former officer Ernie Bellows, "So this was part of the plan. We would stop them from marching in one direction, and they would simply flee en mass down another street and continue their illegal march with us running to catch up. The idea was to let them have no avenue to reform and block other streets. We had to keep control of the situation."[77]

Meanwhile just to the south, twenty-five demonstrators fled down the slope toward South Pond with the police in close pursuit, shouting, "Kill the mother fuckers." Officers instructed others, "Into the pond, into the pond, get the mother fuckers in the pond." Police threw a young man into the water and then knocked his girlfriend to the ground. Officers dragged her along the embankment while striking her about the head, arms, back, and legs with their batons. The young man attempting to rescue her from the assaulting officers received half a dozen nightstick blows to his head. Two members of the clergy near the pond tried to mediate at the scene; police drove them away but not before striking one of the men in the back. As police pushed them away, they ordered the ministers to "Run, you bastards, run."[78] One of the more publicized examples of police abuse came when a twenty-three-year-old Chicago native who was cycling home was pulled off his bike by officers and thrown into the three-foot deep pond.[79]

Near midnight, Hayden had joined a group of McCarthy staffers heading back to the Hilton Hotel where they were registered guests. Hayden, however, was already a marked man, and the hotel's manager prevented him from entering. Forced back onto the street, plainclothes officers quickly pointed him out to others charged to follow him. A uniform officer, joined by another in plainclothes, grabbed Hayden from behind, driving him to the ground. In front of numerous witnesses, police delivered their quarry a few punches before dragging him to a nearby paddy wagon. An understandably upset Hayden yelled, "What did I do? What did I do?" Hayden was charged with aggravated assault for allegedly spitting at one of the officers. Although it was only the convention's first day, the movement's leader had already been arrested twice. For the next two days, Hayden wore a disguise, including a beard, a long-haired wig, and dark glasses.[80]

Meanwhile police had punched their way through Lincoln Park, methodically clearing the area of protestors; at 12:38 A.M. they declared the park clear. The problem was that by then all the park people were on the street, angry, frustrated, hurt, and looking for revenge. As police lined up on the east side of Clark, the crowd began to level attacks, both verbally and physically. Fistfuls of gravel were thrown into passing cruisers; others spat and screamed, "Pigs, oink, oink!" A phalanx of police forced demonstrators into Clark Street where the biggest clash of the night occurred. In the street, traffic came to a standstill with the crush of bodies. A witness described the violent scene:

Cars were stopped, the horns began to honk, people couldn't move, people got gassed inside their cars, people got stoned inside their cars, police were the objects of stones, and taunts, mostly taunts. . . . But there were stones being thrown and of course the police were responding with teargas and clubs and every time they could get near enough to a demonstrator they hit him.[81]

The violence had a cumulative effect. When passing motorists saw the ensuing carnage, many heckled police and, inadvertently or deliberately, drew police attention their way. Officers began to turn their frustration on motorists. In one instance, "four [police officers] surrounded two young and short-haired men in a Corvette and pounded them for thirty seconds."[82] Police also began to rush into the crowd, chasing those who had thrown rocks or bottles at them and initiating another series of violent exchanges. As police swung away at offenders, both real and imagined, other officers at times tried to restrain their comrades. Officer Murray Sheppard agrees that such events took place. "Two or three times that first night I pulled guys off who had worked themselves into a lather. It was hard to control your emotions—people were so against us; you just wanted to hit them. It wasn't right; we needed to let it just roll off our backs. It is easier said than done."[83] Others say that the choice was to control people at the source of the conflict or have the situation slip out of control.

Police, however, appeared to be no longer distinguishing between controlling demonstrators and using force against those who were legitimately using the public streets. Several officers chased an attorney and his wife, striking both with nightsticks; the wife took a blow to the head. According to another witness, police also began slashing car tires and breaking windows belonging to suspected demonstrators and McCarthy supporters. One of the witnesses, an assistant U.S. attorney, said, "It appeared that the officers had either slashed or released the air from the tire." He also noticed several other cars in the area with flattened tires.

The carnage continued as police pushed the crowd until it reached Wells Street and North Avenue. The crowd dispersed, rushing in different directions with police, many of them no longer wearing ID tags, pursuing them, nightsticks held over their heads like swords. "The police were completely out of control," wrote *Ramparts* reporters. "They burst into bars—some hippie bars and some the sort of swinging places where young attorneys meet airline stewardesses between trips—and indiscriminately hurled patrons into the streets, ordering the proprietors to close shop. Once on the street, patrons risked attack for being at large. One middle-aged man, escorting two old women home, was felled from behind by a rifle butt."

Journalists again faced police violence. While taking pictures of officers struggling to subdue a male demonstrator, a photographer was struck in the back with the butt end of a shotgun. The officers then searched him for his film. Side streets were flooded with wild and angry faces—confusion and desperation on some, glee on others. On Wisconsin Street, demonstrators stoned an NBC truck and a police car. The second wave of police smashed cameras and destroyed film. With windows breaking and reports of shots fired, the streets were bedlam. Demonstrators fled into alleys, walkways, hallways, and even into restaurants and bars, with cops on their heels. Onlookers often became unwitting victims.[84]

Former officers have little sympathy for those who found themselves caught in the middle of a riot that had all the telltale signs of erupting for hours. Says Henry Nostbakken, "There were people from the first night out who came to see the action, to gawk and to make our job of crowd control that much harder, and then they complain when they get their tails ruffled when things turn rough." Others say that people should not expect police to "read minds." Recalls Fred Jeffery, "I know for a fact that some guys went over the edge a bit and some innocents were hit or sprayed, but look, things are moving fast, it's at night, you have thousands of people on the street in the middle of a near riot situation, and things are not going to be perfect."[85] Officer Kurt O'Grady defends his fellow officers who continued to pursue protestors into business establishments. "We did leave the street on occasion, because some of these marchers who had thrown shit and pop cans full of sand at us had tried to duck into bars and restaurants, and when they went in these places, they were going to get hauled out. Sometimes it was hard to separate people from others in those hyped-up situations, and you do what you can."[86] Sheldon Bartowski says that officers had little choice: "Well, clearing the streets means clearing the streets; you have these 'onlookers' who should know better, and if they get in the way, then too bad. They knew what was going on, yet they put themselves in the middle of the trouble."[87]

After midnight, protestors and innocent onlookers, found few places to run to avoid the cops. Police formed lines on Wells and Schiller and moved south on Wells from Old Town. When the crowd moved toward LaSalle, another line of police advanced, blocking virtually every means of escape, contradicting a repeated claim by police that their aim was crowd dispersal. Demonstrators panicked and fled in all directions. Police cruisers darted into the fleeing masses, doors flung open, officers jumping out, batons slicing through the air, cracking against skin and bone. Again, police attention seemed directed against anyone who happened to be on the scene, even those who were trying to help them. A doctor who stepped out of his car to draw police attention to some "hippies" who were damaging cars was told by police, "Listen, you goddamn motherfucker, get this car out of here." As the doctor tried again to explain, the cop yelled, "Listen, you son-of-a-bitch, didn't you hear me the first time?" and then struck the man's car with his baton.[88] Police maintain, however, that they not only had a job to do, but faced danger from a crowd that "had turned against them." Some officers began to dread what was awaiting them, and thoughts turned toward home. "I just wanted the shift to end," says Fred Jeffery, "but it was going to be hours of hell before I saw my front door again."[89]

On the streets, the long night of violence raged. Streetlights were broken, car windows were smashed, police cars were stoned, and an officer driving his cruiser on Clark Street had his driver's side door impaled by what he thought was a pickaxe. The cop suffered abrasions to his forearm.[90] By 1 A.M., many of the officers had been on duty for more than fifteen hours. Most were exhausted and, by many accounts, they admitted to losing their tempers. "There were times when I could not have given two shits about anything," recalls Kurt O'Grady. "I couldn't think straight. I remember being so fucking sore. My damn back was killing me."[91] Several officers say that by the end of their shift, they were no longer overly concerned with the subtleties of police work. Their feelings about those they were charged to control also came to the fore. The following exchange from a department radio log speaks to this attitude:

Police Operator: 1814, get a wagon over at 1436. We've got an injured hippie.

Voice: 1436 North Wells?

Operator: North Wells.

The police radio log then records the following comments from five other units listening in.

That's no emergency.

Let him take a bus.

Kick the fucker.

Knock his teeth out.

Throw him in the wastepaper basket.[92]

Officer Milt Brower, however, dismisses the radio log. "That's taking one incident when guys are beaking off, pissed off, tired, and trying to make us seem all the same. It wasn't all of us."[93] Although some officers were careful about voicing what they really thought about the generation they faced on the streets, they uniformly detested those in the movement, a feeling that came out repeatedly in their treatment of demonstrators as the week went on and the confrontations heated up.

Some cops admit that they could not stop themselves from "beating the long-hairs." Says Herbert Bile, "I had seen too much, you could say; it was just such a stinking rotten generation, and after the first night, I knew it was going to be a long week. Let's face it, we hated each other." Others believed that they tried to keep order and blamed the trouble on demonstrators. Says Ronald Adler, "We did our best, I thought, as the convention began, as I remember, but the antiwar crowd was having none of it. We were doing our best to keep the peace. And we were not going to pull any punches, why would we, we didn't owe them anything—treating them with kid gloves while they pissed on everything normal and decent in our nation. They must have been dreaming. When they stepped on our streets, they had to know what was going to happen. Believe me, they wanted to give as good as we gave 'em. But in the end, if they would have cooperated, we would have been able to keep the peace. That's what we wanted to do."[94]

If police genuinely intended to keep the peace on Monday night—a trend they planned to set for the remainder of the week—they failed miserably. As the streets cleared and the city became quiet in the early hours of Tuesday morning, police actions also raised serious questions as to what their orders were prior to convention week. Not only had police failed to keep the peace, but through their actions, they managed to alienate those whose only intention was to voice their opposition to the war in Vietnam. Among the walking wounded that Monday night was a teenage girl with a patch covering one of her eyes, the result, she claimed of a police beating the night before. Her experience left her bitter and looking for revenge. "Those cops don't realize that I didn't want violence," said the teenager, "but now that I've been clubbed, I can't wait to get my hands on them."

TUESDAY, AUGUST 27

As day broke over Lake Michigan, the city winced from a violent hangover. Partly eaten food, broken glass, human waste, cigarette butts, and papers plates and cups covered portions of Lincoln and Grant parks. Stitched up journalists, demonstrators, and police nursing injured heads and wounded prides limped out of hospitals and treatment centers. People with yawning, scruffy faces drank coffee and smoked; bags under their eyes told the previous night's story. The city's papers, as well as the national press, contained sharp reminders of Monday's disturbances. The *Chicago Sun-Times* and the *New York Times* were anything but kind to Daley's police. The *Sun-Times'* page 5 headline read, "Probe Police Beating of Newsmen: Another Photog Clubbed by Police," while the *Daily News* front page stated, "Cops Assault 17 Newsmen." A front-page photo taken by *Sun-Times* photographer Bob Black depicts an officer struggling with a demonstrator. While Black took the photo, two other officers attacked him from behind. An officer swung his baton at Black's head, striking his camera that he used to shield himself from the blow. Black then received another blow to his safety helmet from another officer who approached from behind. The impact spun him around, where he took another strike to the face, cutting his lip. The alleged police threat to Brian Boyer the night before also made it into the story, along with additional allegations of police removing their name tags to shield their identities.[95] The *Sun-Times* editorial blasted the police for the attacks on journalists. "There is a breakdown of police authority and police chain of command when individual policemen can violate Conlisk's own instructions. They should be identified and punished." The editorial also criticized the practice of police removing their identification tags, suggesting that it can only allow them to behave like "bullying anonymous thugs," while the *Daily News* cautioned, "all citizens should be law-abiding, including the cops."[96]

Daley, however, blamed journalists for refusing to follow police instructions. "We ask that the newsmen follow the orders of police, too," the mayor told the press on Tuesday morning. "There is no exception . . . with all of this running and rushing of photographers, the Police Department deserves cooperation, too. These men [police] are working 12 hours a day. If they ask a newsman and a photographer to move, they should move as well as anyone else." Daley was stinging from formal complaints lodged against him and superintendent Conlisk by the *Tribune*, the *Sun-Times*, and the *Daily News*, as well as television networks over the police attacks. The Chicago Newspaper Guild complained that if Conlisk "cannot control his men he should resign."[97] *Newsweek* editor Hal Bruno joined a chorus of media complainants, issuing a telegram to Daley at 5 A.M. Tuesday.

Newsweek Magazine hereby informs you that for the second night in a row our reporters and photographers were subject to unprovoked attacks by Chicago policemen. Three of our men were injured and we have evidence that individual policemen are deliberately assaulting newsmen. We can identify men and units and are anxious to cooperate with you so that immediate measures can be taken to safeguard newsmen in the performance of their duty.

While Conlisk promised to "investigate deviations" of individual officers, it appears that little of any consequence was done to curtail police on press violence.[98] His boss suggested that there was little difference between the media and demonstrators. Daley wondered aloud, "How can they tell the difference?"[99] The *Tribune's* coverage was slightly more sympathetic to police, reporting mostly accounts of demonstrators injuring police officers, identifying the weapons used by "hippies," and outlining their destructive behavior. The *Tribune* also reported the injuries to officers George Swagler and Fred Kelleher who were hurt at Division and Wells; a protestor wielding a two-by-four broke Swagler's helmet, and officer Paul Gorgis was temporarily blinded by a demonstrator who shot him in the face with a lye solution.[100] The other *Tribune*-owned paper, *Chicago's American* stated that Monday night constituted a "hippie riot."[101] That morning, the National Council of Churches issued a statement condemning police action. "We vigorously protest police violence last night against accredited newsmen with clearly visible white armbands, who were performing duties of a free press in covering demonstrations in Lincoln Park."[102]

Several officers that morning were in a surly mood. "I felt like warmed over shit," recalls Will Gerald. "I didn't sleep well, really didn't see my family, took a shower, and went back in. It's the way it was all week. If the mood was bad Monday, Tuesday was even worse. People glared at us no matter where we were. Not regular people, but any of those in the antiwar crowd in the morning and in the afternoon. They were quiet, but you could see the anger just seething under the surface. I knew that as soon as there was the slightest provocation, things were going to turn ugly."[103] Officers who attempted to call in sick were told bluntly to get their "big fat white butts" down to their district. There were also a few near fistfights among some of the members as they tried to berate others for going too far with members of the media the night before, leading to the bad press. Says Don Holtz, "It was no big thing, a bit of yelling, a punch thrown; hell, we were men in a tense situation, not all of us agreed all the time—we weren't machines."[104] Officer Reg Novak says that he knew that there were some heated disagreements at shift changes. "There was swearing, all right, lots of cussing, some of it directed at the press, the hippies—it sounds *so* strange to say that word now—and even at fellow officers. I heard one guy say, 'if you want to beat on something, wait 'til you get home and beat on your meat.' I don't know, it wasn't fun. For a while we weren't crying about the Cubs."[105]

One group that wished to avoid a replay of the previous night's violence was area clergymen. The clerics met with residents of the community at the Church of the Three Crosses to form a Lincoln Park emergency citizens committee. The committee's first order of business was to draft a statement requesting police to allow demonstrators to sleep in Lincoln Park. The committee wanted to ensure police and the city administration that demonstrators were not a threat to the nearby community of Old Town and that forcing the kids onto the streets after 11 P.M. created more problems than the action was trying to prevent. The statement in part read: "the best interests of the community would be served by the withdrawal of the massive police forces from Lincoln Park and the surrounding community." At 4 P.M., a committee delegation met with the police commander from the 18th District police command center in Lincoln Park. The commander only agreed to relay the committee's request to superintendent James Conlisk without comment.[106]

Around 3 P.M., a sound truck drove through the area near Lincoln Park, asking residents to let protestors sleep the night if police once again enforced the curfew. Indeed, the issue of adequate overnight housing had arisen before convention week, with the National Mobilization advising travelers to "bring sleeping bags" for outdoor camping or calling on area relatives to take people in off the streets. "When you get to Chicago," organizers had suggested, "call your aunt, uncle, etc., and ask them for sleeping space."[107] The trouble over where to sleep had become a serious issue following U.S. District Court Judge William J. Lynch's denial of Mobe permits for rallies and marchers. Mobe had sought permission to allow demonstrators to sleep in city parks during the convention. "Providing sleeping accommodations for persons desiring to visit the city," said Lynch, "is not a city responsibility."[108]

The afternoon gatherings in the parks were largely uneventful. The only near altercation between protestors and police occurred near 3 P.M., when a group of protestors yelling, "Pigs! Pigs!" surrounded about ten police officers patrolling the park. Thirty cops were called in quickly to rescue them; forming a wedge, the police moved through the irate crowd without using force. Nearby, Allen Ginsberg held court, chanting along with a group of peaceful followers.[109]

That evening, the business of dissent began once again as 3,500 protestors held an antibirthday party for President Lyndon Johnson at the Coliseum, a few blocks from the Conrad Hilton. While burning draft cards, the crowd listened to David Dellinger speak about the importance of the movement and William Burroughs and Jean Genet opine about police atrocities. While rock bands blasted, Paul Krassner gave a photo of Johnson the finger. The crowd then sang "Happy Birthday" to the president with the lyrics, "Fuck you, Lyndon Johnson, happy fucking birthday to you."[110] Following LBJ's unauthorized birthday bash, organizers planned to divide the crowd into small groups and then gather near the edge of Grant Park, across from the Hilton, to greet the delegates upon their return from the amphitheater. The plan, according to Rennie Davis, was to make a show in front of television cameras.[111]

North in Lincoln Park, Jerry Rubin and Black Panther Bobby Seale spoke to the crowd. Seale tried to engage the mostly white demonstrators by referring to what happened to some of them the night before at the hands of police. "Black people know what police brutality is," said Seale, "and you white people who have been asking whether it's real found out last night." Seale urged the crowd to form into small groups of fewer than five people and "be armed and spread out so we can 'stuckle' these pigs." Rubin, who once stated, "A movement that isn't willing to risk injuries, even deaths, isn't worth shit," told the crowd that everyone should take "the same risks as blacks take."[112]

Whereas there were indeed some risk takers among the demonstrators' ranks, as the week began, police were taking few risks with their service revolvers. One of the few times when a police officer allegedly fired a weapon occurred at about 7:45 P.M. when a group of between 500 and 1,000 left Lincoln Park and marched south on Clark Street. As the marchers reached the intersection of Clark and Burton, and following an altercation between demonstrators and police in a squad car, several officers arrived on the scene, accompanied by a plainclothes man wearing a helmet. The officer stood in the middle of Burton Street and attempted to direct the crowd. According to witnesses, he then pulled out a revolver and fired three times. Demonstrators fled, some of them screaming, as twenty officers pursued them with nightsticks. No injuries were reported during the altercation.[113] Police officers seemed unaware that any of their members fired shots. Others thought that on a couple of occasions, people claimed that police fired into the air to disperse a crowd, fearing they would be overrun. All officers flatly deny that police fired any shots during that week other than teargas canisters.[114]

At 10:30 P.M., 1,000 demonstrators left the park for a peaceful march down to Grant Park. There were no arrests. Back in Lincoln Park, the community clergymen who had earlier tried to intercede to allow protestors to remain in the park after curfew staged a vigil to prevent another night of violence. As the curfew approached, the group, joined by 1,500 others, sang the "Battle Hymn of the Republic." At 11:30 P.M., police once again announced the closing of the park.

The clergymen instructed the crowd that if it wanted to avoid being beaten, teargassed, and arrested, it should leave now. Everyone else should sit in silent vigil and wait for the police. The remaining demonstrators donned wet handkerchiefs, applied Vaseline to protect against the teargas, and sang "America the Beautiful."[115]

While a crowd of about 500 dug in, a sanitation truck moved into position in the center of the Task Force line. The bed of the truck held a teargas dispenser and a large nozzle for dispensing the gas—all requisitioned from the army. Two police officers manned the nozzle.[116] After issuing several more warnings to clear the park, police fired volleys of teargas at the remaining demonstrators. Officers in gas masks then moved into the park in formation, forcing the crowd onto neighboring streets. As they fled, protesters threw rocks, bricks, and bottles at the truck and at the advancing police. A brick struck one officer in the chest.[117] Two police car windows were shattered in the barrage. There were numerous skirmishes as police followed the crowd, trying to disperse it by club and mace. Youths threw bottles at police from passing cars, and officers retaliated on whoever was nearby or deemed to be in their way. Complicating issues was teargas drifting into the eyes of nearby motorists, causing stalled traffic and blocked roads.[118]

The violence on both sides was sometimes vicious: an officer dragged a young man by the hair, struck him with his nightstick, and kicked him in the head. At the Eugenie Triangle, fifteen demonstrators brandishing metal trash cans and rocks trapped two patrol cars, smashing the windows out of both. Two U.S. attorneys who witnessed the attack said that the officers lay on the seats to avoid the barrage until a break in traffic allowed them to escape. Moments later, however, another patrol car was also stoned as it moved south on Clark Street. With all the windows smashed in, demonstrators advanced on the stalled cruiser. The attorneys told investigators, "the crowd moved alongside the car and threw stones and bottles with all their might through the shattered windows at the officers." One of the officers fled the patrol car and ran into a passageway where he was stoned as he stood pinned against the wall of a building. His fellow officer rushed to his rescue; he drew his service revolver and the crowd finally dispersed. The officer did not fire his weapon.[119]

Demonstrators poured in from the park stoning cars and police before moving south toward Grant Park where a massive standoff had already ensued. During the melee, police made thirty-nine arrests, most for disorderly conduct. Seven officers reported injuries, and nine patrol cars sustained damage.[120] During one of the encounters, police officers accused photojournalists of deliberately trying to blind them with strobe lights, making them a target for bottles and rocks.[121] Among the journalists arrested that night was Barton Silverman of the *New York Times*. Police dragged him off to jail moments after he photographed a police sergeant preparing to strike him with his baton. He was released without charge two hours later; his film was not taken.[122] Meanwhile, a long-time reporter for the *Chicago Daily News* stated that when officers charged out of the park swinging their batons, they chanted "Kill, kill, kill." Delos Hall, a cameraman for CBS, said he was clubbed from behind, knocked to the ground, and then attacked by several more policemen while he was filming their actions. Police beat James C. Jones of *Newsweek*'s Detroit bureau on his head and kicked him in the ribs.[123] A reporter for the *Tribune* reported that police threatened that he would get "his head busted" if he continued to stay near the demonstration.[124] The assistant managing editor for *Chicago's American,* Jack Mabley, was near Lincoln Park when he heard the cops behind him. "I ran like hell."[125]

A few blocks south, tension grew as police lined both sides of the street in front of the Conrad Hilton. Protestors thrown out of Lincoln Park had arrived, casting a jaundiced eye at police while they waited for the crowd from the coliseum in the south to arrive. Meanwhile, plainclothes officers mingled through the crowd, complaining of the smell of unwashed clothes and bodies.[126] Says Orrest Hupka, "It was bad, let me tell you. After Monday, you needed a bath after arresting one of those bastards." Ronald Adler agrees: "They stunk to high heaven, and I think they knew it and liked that we were bothered by it." Former officer Lyall Zedowski is amused by some of his fellow officers' complaints. "Well, some of our guys, believe me, didn't smell any better than the hippies."[127] Body odor, teargas, and the constant stench emanating from the stockyards and slaughterhouses provided an unpleasant backdrop. As one journalist recalled many years later, there was "an amazing Satanic smell, a Yippie genius brew that simulated vomit, decomposing flesh, death, cloaca and kindred flavors. It was what evil would smell like if it were available in an aerosol can—bad enough to make the South Side stockyards, next door to the convention, smell almost wholesome. This exotic moral stink had drifted halfway around the world, after all, from Vietnam."[128]

One man who came halfway around the world only to be roughed up by the Chicago police was twenty-seven-year-old correspondent for the *London Evening News,* Winston Churchill, grandson of the late war-time British prime minister. As Churchill attempted to enter his hotel, police intercepted him and began to drag him to a paddy wagon until he produced a room key. Finding his identification unacceptable, the police forced the issue inside his hotel.

I was frogmarched by two policemen to the desk of the hotel where they set about inquiring if I were in fact registered. Meanwhile, a very aggressive police sergeant demanded an identity card from me. I told them I had none. Whereupon he laid his hands on me and proceeded to frisk me in a rough manner. I pushed the man away, and saw his hand reach for his club. But fortunately, just at that moment, the reception clerk reappeared and confirmed that I was, indeed, staying in the hotel. Whereupon the police sergeant let go of me. I cannot help thinking how lucky we are with our police force in Britain.[129]

Also on the wrong end of police attention was *Playboy* magazine founder and publisher Hugh Hefner. Even the dapper and recognizable Hefner, out for a break from his playboy mansion, had his backside struck while watching police beat Yippies. Hefner went out for a stroll with cartoonist Jules Feiffer and newspaper columnist Max Lerner to see the Yippies. Unfortunately for Heff, he got his bunny tail too close to the action and got in trouble. Police got out of a cruiser and ordered Heff and his partners to "Move it!" before paddling his backside. Heff called a news conference the following day and claimed that his experience made him want to become more active in *causes*.[130]

Meanwhile Tom Hayden lurked in the gathering crowd in disguise, trying to keep one step ahead of his police tails, while listening to police radio transmissions.[131] As the crowd moved up from the coliseum, buses arrived with police reinforcements, joining those already standing on the sidewalk two deep. While police helicopters hovered ominously overhead, the crowd began to chant: "Fuck you, LBJ!" "Fuck you, Daley!"[132] and "Pig! Pig! Pig! Pig!" "Hell, No, We Won't Go!" "Fascist Pigs!"[133] Those already at the hotel had heard over the radios monitoring police action that the officers had once again used force to clear Lincoln Park to the north.

With the crowds converging from both the north and the south, police beefed up their reinforcements by the Hilton, standing five deep on some places along the street. As buses carrying delegates back from the convention site arrived, the awaiting crowd yelled, "Peace now!"[134] But peace was certainly not on the minds of some demonstrators as they began to throw bags and balloons full of urine and feces. A reporter from Utah noticed that some of the material was thrown from the upper floors of the Hilton. On the street in front of the hotel, the verbal taunts of those in uniform continued unabated. Police faced incessant calls of "Pig! Pig! Pig!" As party delegates from seven states made the short trek across the street into Grant Park to offer demonstrators their support, one protestor yelled at officers, "We're fucking your wives and daughters while you guys are protecting your city."[135]

The crowd, which the Secret Service estimated to be between 1,000 and 1,500, faced police across Michigan Avenue, many engaging in a sit-down in Grant Park. Several other reports suggested the number of protesters was as high as 5,000.[136] Many in the crowd hurled verbal assaults as well as rocks and bottles, and kicked officers if they came within range. At 1:15 A.M., Conlisk's deputy superintendent James Rochford grabbed a bullhorn and announced that the crowd could stay in the park overnight providing they remained peaceful. The crowd greeted his words with the only cheer police received all week.[137]

The cops that were there, however, were exhausted, some of them on their feet long past the end of their shift. Even though they had been on twelve-hour rotations since Saturday, some, by Tuesday night, had been on duty between fifteen and seventeen hours.[138] Ray Mihalicz recalls the struggle: "It was not good; it's hard to think clearly when you've been at it for that long; and it does not do wonders for your temper, maybe some of your judgment slips. I'm not saying that's what happened, but it can have an effect."[139] According to some reports, the police did show signs of losing control of their emotions that night. "It was clear that the Chicago police had 'had it,'" reported a journalist for the *Washington Post*. "Up to this point they have been fairly calm but now they were showing visible signs of the strain they had been under. The kids knew this full well, and they knew they had made them 'lose their cool.'"[140]

Shortly past 2 A.M., the Chicago Police Department made a formal request for a reprieve from the National Guard. At 3 A.M., the first units of the Illinois National Guard rolled in. The surprised crowd reacted immediately and angrily, as jeeps containing 600 guardsmen pulled in, M-I rifles in hand, bearing gas masks and full battle gear. Calm since the police announcement, the crowd became incensed at the sudden provocative appearance of the troops; they yelled obscenities, some subjecting the guardsmen to what observers called extreme abuse. The young soldiers, by most accounts, remained calm, and refused to be baited.[141] An assistant Guard leader gave government investigators the following account of demonstrator invective and guardsmen detachment.

There was a man walking up and back in front of our line whom I will never forget. He wore black slacks, a white shirt and had long, greasy blond hair and a pock-marked face. Walking by the line, he would spit at us, flick cigarette ashes and lighted cigarette ashes at us. He would pick out the Jewish boys from their nameplates and make anti-Semitic remarks to them. He called me a kike. I turned to a Polish boy standing next to me and asked him who the guy reminded him of. He answered, "A Nazi storm trooper." But there was no reaction from the men as far as I could see.[142]

There was some fear that the National Guard may not be able to put up with the same level of abuse as officers had, especially given their age and their firepower. "I tell you who we were worried about, when they brought in the Guard," says Joe Pecoraro. "These were kids with a rifle in their hands, the National Guard, we thought, holy Christ, I hope they don't start shooting anybody. They got a warning, but I don't even know if their rifles were loaded. I thought they might start a real war, but they did a good job, we just used them as a fence. They had them all shoulder to shoulder."[143]

The Guard's arrival was a welcome reprieve for weary cops. "The police," according to one guardsman, "seemed happy and relieved to see us." The Guard units took up position on the sidewalks in front of the Hilton as the police fell back. As officers marched away in squads, the crowd provided an "oink, oink, oink" cadence for their footfalls. Guard commander Brigadier General Dunn instructed all guardsmen to remove any loaded magazines from their weapons and then ordered them not to interfere with demonstrators "unless they became violent."[144]

Perhaps the best move that police made all of convention week was the decision by police deputy superintendent James Rochford to allow protestors to remain in Grant Park. The discretionary move came as a welcome relief to police at the end of a very long shift. Says Gord Stensill, "I remember that there were two things that worked well and saved one hell of a lot of 7 A.M. paperwork—the arrival of the National Guard and letting that group stay in the park after 11 P.M. one of those nights, I think it was on the second day." Carl Moore, who can't recall the evening distinctly, recalls the arrival of the Guard and his relief. "We were ready for mayhem, you could feel it building; I mean, the protestors were more violent than ever; they had really gotten a lot more militant since Sunday, and they were itching for an awful fight. The more you hit them, the harder they came back. And then it all went away, they could stay, that means no breaking heads, and we got to go home." Near 4:30 A.M., an embattled Tom Hayden reappeared briefly to speak to the crowd, telling them that he was going underground.[145] The streets slowly grew quiet. By 5 A.M., the crowd, once pegged as high as 5,000, dwindled to less than two hundred.

In quiet, tree-lined neighborhoods free from violence, headlights flashed into the driveways of silent houses as police officers arrived home. Some showered and slipped quietly into beds beside their sleeping wives; others passed out on couches, shoes still clinging to throbbing feet. Several cops recall dragging home bits of the stressful night. They had difficulty erasing the violent images from their minds. Says Randall Bakker, "I remember one morning, the room spun in my head as I lay down, even when I closed my eyes, the room still spun, flashes of the night played over and over in my head—half sleeping, half dreaming."[146] Eddie Kelso recalls his trouble sleeping: "I actually dreamed of pigs, and school-yard chants, and I was being taunted in the school-yard, I was a kid and I had on a cop uniform, and the taunts went on, 'Pig! Pig! Pig!'—yelling, screaming children, they yelled and taunted me, they wouldn't stop and I was crying and crying, and then I looked down and it held a gun, and I pointed it and began to shoot; kids were screaming, 'The pig is shooting!' and then I was awake, shaking, soaked."[147]

As the first pale light broke on the eastern horizon, a few remaining souls gathered around small fires in Grant Park, talking quietly, the dew heavy in the grass. Little did anyone know that the worst day of violence was only hours away.

WEDNESDAY, AUGUST 28

Under a warm mid-morning sun, the police took over for guardsmen in front of the Conrad Hilton. By 1 P.M., the Guard set up a command post on the roof of the Field Museum, situated just south of Grant Park on the lakefront and overlooking the band shell. The 2nd Battalion of the 127th Artillery was stationed on the east side of the museum, while the 129th Infantry manned the west side. The city granted Mobe its only permit of the week to hold a rally in the park from 1 to 4 P.M. The crowd swelled from a low of 1,000, to between 8,000 and 10,000. The gathering included hippies and Yippies, young McCarthy supporters, a number of Vietnam Veterans for Peace, and curious onlookers. Also mingling in the crowd were poorly disguised members of the Chicago Police Department, wearing casual "hippie-like" clothing or clean-cut in plainclothes. They made their appearance more conspicuous by what a Chicago attorney said, "was their manner of traveling in a pack and constantly barging through groups of protestors, bumping into them, making cracks, and achieving, if nothing else, the escalation of tempers and hostility."[148]

Questioned about the practice, officers say that given the size and hostility of the crowds, they chose not to send members in alone. Officer Kelly Fredrickson recalls, "It would have been suicide. If our plainclothes guys were as obvious as everyone seems to think, then sending them into an angry crowd—a guy would have gotten beaten or stoned to death before any of us would have known what was going on."[149] Other officers admit that in breaking up fights and clearing crowds, they sometimes hit their own guys. Says Dennis Kaminski, "Yes, they would end up getting the teargas—and a shot or two. In the heat of the battle, it's hard to tell one from the other, and teargas doesn't play favorites."[150]

Plainclothes officers joined their uniformed colleagues and the National Guard in a massive show of force in and around Grant Park. The police boxed in the demonstrators from three sides, as they lined up along the west side of Lake Shore Drive on the eastern side of the park, the west side of Columbus Drive (a thoroughfare that runs north-south and divides the park, running west of the band shell area), and Roosevelt Drive on the park's southern boundary. Police worked through the crowd handing out leaflets stating that the gathering was sanctioned, but no march or activity would be allowed outside the park or at the amphitheater. Police warned those in the park that any such action would result in their arrest.[151]

The afternoon largely passed peacefully; numerous speakers, including William Burroughs, Dick Gregory, and Norman Mailer, spoke to the growing crowd. But with police and the National Guard virtually surrounding the park, helicopters crisscrossing overhead, seething anger from the crowd, instigators on both sides, and the crowd's stated intention to march on the amphitheater, an eruption in violence was only a matter of time. The spark Wednesday came from the lowering of an American flag.

Fighting for Old Glory

During a speech against the draft, a man wearing an army helmet climbed the flagpole to the left of the band shell and began to lower the American flag.[152] There are conflicting reports on both the man's intention and what the crowd yelled. Some accounts suggest the crowd encouraged him to "Tear down the flag!"; others claim that the crowd encouraged him to lower it half-mast. There were suggestions that those on the band shell stage encouraged the man to leave the flag alone. According to a police lieutenant, Dellinger took the microphone and told the man to lower it to half-mast in honor of the wounded demonstrators. As officers, both uniformed and plainclothes, moved in to arrest the man, some in the crowd began to scream, "Pigs! Pigs! Kill the pigs!"[153] As police hauled the man off, the crowd turned on officers near the site and threw chunks of concrete, bricks, sticks, cans, bags and balloons filled with paint and urine, eggs, tomatoes, and seemingly anything else they could get their hands on. A police sergeant reported being struck in the stomach by a "large brick," and a lieutenant was hit in the leg with pieces of concrete and a brick. Speakers on stage implored the crowd to stop throwing objects as they were hitting their own people, while portions of the crowd chanted, "Sit down, sit down." Accounts differ on just what a group of young men tried to run up the flagpole. Witness

Norman Mailer wrote that the man was attempting to replace the Stars and Stripes with some sort of rebel flag; other accounts suggested it was little more than a red cloth or a girl's red slip.[154]

As approximately thirty officers rushed in to seize the flag raisers, Rennie Davis yelled into the microphone, "Here come the blue bonnets." The crowd immediately surrounded the small squad, chanting, "Fuck the pigs!" and "Dirty pigs" while throwing bottles and rocks. One demonstrator tried to grab an officer's gun as he fell to the ground. Police fought back, batons swinging in wide arcs. As Davis went to quiet demonstrators near the flagpole, the police, according to one report, yelled, "Get Davis!" Ironically, as police charged him, Davis was pleading with the crowd to sit down and be calm. Officers struck him from behind, creating a large gash in his scalp, and knocking him unconscious.[155] While the police attacked, the crowd raged, "Pigs are whores!" and "Pigs eat shit!"[156]

Meanwhile, as police arrested the flag raisers, the crowd pelted the officers with bricks and chunks of concrete. Angry for the coverage of their alleged abuses over the past few days, the police began to shout at nearby reporters. "Take a picture of those bastards," yelled one incredulous officer. "Show people what they are doing." During the melee, someone in the crowd struck an assistant U.S. attorney with a bag of urine. Demonstrator violence became so intense that police retreated for cover under fire of flaming rags, shoes, sticks, and a bag of what was thought to be bloody sanitary napkins. A nearby police car was pelted with bags of human excrement. On stage, pacifist David Dellinger looked on, aghast. "Be calm!" he pleaded with the crowd. "Don't be violent." As if to prove to Dellinger the hopelessness of his words, someone in the crowd yelled out, "We have two more days to burn Chicago."[157]

In an effort to repel the crowd, officers fired smoke bombs into the sea of bodies. When a demonstrator threw back the canister into the police line, officers lobbed several more into the crowd and prepared to move in.[158] "It was war, then," recalls one officer, who says his heart was beating wildly in his chest. Another remembers yelling, "Let's get the motherfuckers." Police adjusted their helmets and visors, took practice swings with their batons,[159] and moved in with force, knocking over picnic tables, striking people were they stood, sat or fell.[160] Police recall rising anger. "The guys were damn mad about the flag and some red commie rag going up; that really upset guys," recalls Dale Jaeschke. Another remembers with disgust the communist flags. "They carried around these fucking commie North Vietnam flags. Christ, they were supposed to be Americans, but they were actually traitors."[161]

Police did not appear to single out anyone as most reports indicate they swung their batons at anyone in their way. A young attorney later told government investigators that police "hit and shoved whoever was in their path—men, women, clergymen, newsmen. . . . Some were beaten and clubbed while on the ground." Others stated that the officers' expressions indicated that they "wanted to kill."[162] By the time the police fought their way into the center of the seating era, most of the crowd had scattered, leaving overturned benches and the grass littered with rocks and bottles. While medics moved in to treat scalp lacerations and other minor injuries, cries of "Fuck the pigs!" "Death to the pigs!" and "Fascist bastards!" continued. Thirty police officers reported injuries after the intense skirmish, including cuts and contusions to the body and head. At the end, someone from the stage stated, "We won it, baby!"[163]

At 4:30 P.M., Dellinger, who was clearly disheartened over the ugly spectacle, announced that there would be an attempt to march on the amphitheater, a demonstration that he hoped would be nonviolent and nonconfrontational. But with the city already expressly denying that the event would be allowed to take place, Dellinger's plan had little chance of success. Additionally Hayden, following the unprovoked attack on his friend Rennie Davis, was furious. He no longer wanted to hear about the virtues of nonviolence. Hayden was looking for revenge.[164] On stage, Dellinger, the long-time peace activist, soon found himself surrounded. Dellinger recalled:

Hayden tried to remove me, physically, from the platform. . . . Tom said that I had been immoral, that the police had charged and Rennie Davis was knocked out, and that I had told people to sit down and not to fight back. . . . That I had betrayed Mobe. And that they were taking the microphone away from me. . . . I said "Fuck you, Tom Hayden! . . . That's not the way we operate. If you think that I'm doing it wrong, we're a coalition, and there's a little bit of difference in views."[165]

Hayden, however, seemed beyond peaceful protest. He told the crowd: "Rennie has been taken to the hospital, and we have to avenge him. We must move out of this park in groups throughout the city and turn this overheated military machine against itself. Let us make sure that if blood flows, it will flow all over this city."[166]

Although Dellinger tried to negotiate with Deputy Superintendent James Rochford, it was clear that the veteran activist was not going to get what he wanted. "There was no way this side of hell that we were going to allow them to march on the delegates," says cop Paul Juravinski. "Rochford wasn't any idiot. Not a chance."[167] Police warned over bullhorns that those who were gathering for a march faced arrest. The department's alternative was to allow them to remain in the park the entire night to demonstrate if they wished, or demonstrators could move up to Lincoln Park. Dellinger insisted that they would have their march.[168]

Meanwhile, those trapped inside the park began to look with increasing urgency for any unblocked exit. Those who attempted to move out of the park found their points of exit manned by police or units of the National Guard that blocked the bridges with machine guns. As word circulated that police were allowing clusters of two and three—not entire groups—to leave, many began to break into small units. Soon a crowd of close to 2,000 had congregated in front of the Hilton, with another 5,000 to 6,000 pressed against the amassed forces circling Grant Park. The tension, according to several officers, was nearly unbearable. Carl Moore recalls, "You could smell the violence in the air, like rotting cloying meat."[169] Others remember that there was no way to keep a crowd that size and temperament hemmed in. "They were single-minded," says Frank

Froese. "They were going to find a way out, and when they did, there was going to be trouble."[170] Some demonstrators began to dash in small groups past startled guardsmen; others found back ways, sneaked through with "straights," or simply beat their way through one or two at a time. The bulk of the hemmed-in marchers, however, pressed up against the main line of guardsmen that was preventing their access to Michigan Avenue.[171]

As the crowd became more aggressive, guardsmen used the butt ends of their rifles to keep people at bay. The sudden rush of demonstrators, however, caused a ripple of panic. The National Guard used modified flamethrowers to fire volleys of teargas into the surging, frantic crowd. People ran, choking, some vomiting. Aided by a strong breeze off Lake Michigan, the stinging gas filled the park and drifted across Michigan Avenue in waves powerful enough to bother Vice President Hubert Humphrey in his shower at the Hilton.[172]

People became frantic to flee the park and the stinging gas. Moving north, the crowd found an avenue of escape. The Jackson Boulevard Bridge was wide open. Aided by bullhorn announcements, the word went out: "Two blocks north, there's an open bridge, no gas." As dusk fell, hundreds rushed over the small bridge onto Michigan Avenue.[173] Todd Gitlin recalls the anxious scene:

Eyes burning, lungs filling with this corrosive stuff, throats feeling as though we had swallowed steel filings, hundreds of demonstrators streamed north until we found a blessedly unguarded bridge and crossed over onto Michigan Ave., where the gas was still thick but at least it was possible to run, who knew where, run as fast as you could, hoping to reach some hypothetical safety. I stopped at a water fountain to dab at my eyes, soaked my handkerchief, wrapped it around my nose.[174]

Police generally supported the use of teargas for crowd control. But there were times when some thought that it created more problems than it solved. "On Wednesday when the Guard units used the gas, well, that whole thing was a problem," remembers Brian Ramsey. "There was the biggest crowd yet, they were planning to march on the delegates [at the amphitheater] and that was *not* going to happen, they were getting fired up, and then a couple of our members were attacked preventing some hippies from taking down the American flag and putting up the communist flag. After that we had a problem because they were not going to be peaceful, but the gas, I don't know, it created a real problem." Others disagree. "There was no choice, they got through our lines and the National Guard anyway and went straight for the Hilton where the VP of the United States is," recalls Steve Nowakowski. "Nor were we gonna let them down to the amphitheater. We had to stop them."[175]

The crowd, however, was building fast in the streets, closing in on the Hilton. At the corner of Michigan and Balbo, two lines of police faced the more tenacious of the marchers who had made it through the teargas and the first line of defense. "I remember thinking, 'oh shit,'" says cop Walter Jorgenson, "here they come again."[176] Police also lined two blocks of Grant Park opposite the hotel, while another police line stood on the Hilton's east side. Police also formed a diagonal line across Michigan at Balbo to prevent the new arrivals from the street into the park. Officers were equipped with riot helmets, mace, teargas, and the ubiquitous nightsticks. The demonstrators came equipped with helmets and gas masks; some carried rocks, bottles, and sticks.[177] Hardcore demonstrators came ready for battle, armed with javelins made from snow fence slats, aerosol cans filled with caustic oven-cleaning fluids, bricks, ice picks, bottles, clay tiles sharpened to deadly points, and golf balls studded with spikes.[178]

As the two sides faced each other down, two mobile network TV units moved into position to capture the unfolding drama. The crowd filled the intersection at Balbo and Michigan, overflowing into the adjacent streets. Traffic ceased to move. Teargas hung in the air. At 7 P.M., some officers tried to get people off the streets by ordering them to the curbs. According to witnesses on the scene—one of them a history professor—police would periodically force the crowd back or break it up and move out of the intersection and onto the sidewalks before returning to their lines in front of the hotel. Each time they retreated, the crowd reclaimed their turf. As the Secret Service received a death threat against Humphrey who had not yet left the hotel, a young hippie girl approached a cop, lifted her shirt, and said, "You haven't had a piece in a long time."[179]

Nightfall

As darkness fell Wednesday, the unnatural glow of television and police lights illuminated the chaotic scene. The crowd pushed into the intersection of Balbo and Michigan. TV network lights picked up the crowd, cheering, chanting, burning draft cards, and flashing the "V" sign for the cameras. At just past 7:30 P.M., a portion of the crowd assembled to march on the amphitheater, yelling, "One, two, three, four; stop this damn war"; "Dump the Hump"; "Daley must go"; "Prague, Prague, Prague!"; and "The streets belong to the people, the streets belong to the people."[180] Police began delivering demonstrators a series of warnings, telling them to disperse, to move onto the sidewalks, or to return to the park to "have your peaceful demonstration and speechmaking there." The crowd screamed obscenities in return. A large police unit then moved east on Balbo toward Michigan Avenue. As the crowd saw the advancing police, they shouted, "Pigs! Pigs! Pigs!" As demonstrators threw rocks, bottles, and eggs, police drove in on them in formation to clear the intersection. Knifing into the core of the crowd, police swung their batons with force. Glasses flew from a man's face; another, shielding his face from potential blows, ran into a traffic sign. The tough-talking crowd now fell back in panic, falling over each other to get away from the police onslaught. As the officers advanced, one shouted at the crowd, "Move! I said, move, goddamn it! Move you bastards!" and "Move your fucking ass!" At this point, a member of the American Civil Liberties Union (ACLU) as well as a reporter for the *Chicago Daily News* report police shouting, "Kill, kill, kill, kill, kill."[181]

The crowd had nowhere safe to go as they were pushed into a second line of police on the south side of the Michigan-Balbo intersection. At that point, police began to give orders that contradicted those from police on other lines. "It was fucking mayhem," recalls officer Harold Pancik. "The crowd was so big and unruly, and some were panicking. It is very difficult to move a crowd of this size. It's like moving sheep with diarrhea; they are running every which way, and we were trying to get them back into the park and out of the streets." Some officers speak about the futility of operating in any formation in a pitched battle in the middle of a street. "You're not smiling, locking arms, and doing Las Vegas kicks when you are in a street fight."[182]

At three minutes to eight, with the crowd screaming, "The whole world is watching, the whole world is watching," the Chicago police swept in from opposite directions, slicing into demonstrators and journalists alike, batons swinging. Seemingly, everyone became a target: demonstrators, both long haired and McCarthy kids, women, journalists, and innocent bystanders. Police struck people from behind as they ran and as they fell. Some witnesses described police as beyond angry. Their anger was "deep, expressive, and personal."[183] A reporter from the *Milwaukee Journal* described the police action.

When the police managed to break up groups of protestors they pursued individuals and beat them with clubs. Some police pursued individual demonstrators as far as a block . . . and beat them. . . . In many cases it appeared to me that when police had finished beating the protestors they were pursuing, they then attacked, indiscriminately, any civilian who happened to be standing nearby.[184]

Police counter that their use of force was not indiscriminate. "The bastards always ran the wrong way after we broke them up," says cop Kurt O'Grady. "They ran in circles like chickens with their heads gone and they refused orders to disperse. In the middle of a hippie riot, you don't ask people for their identification." Others blamed the press in these situations for always getting the story wrong. "The damn press, they always saw what they wanted to see," recalls Mel Latanzio bitterly. "But never us getting kicked in the balls when we were making an arrest—there was a reason we were chasing some of those SOBs." Officer Sam McMaster concurs. "Many of those so-called people standing there watching *were* the press, getting in the way and then getting the story of what actually was happening all wrong the next day."[185]

Other cops say that commentators misconstrued what happened next as police officers losing control and refusing to obey their commanders on the scene. But according to some officers, in the confusion, there were conflicting orders. Recalls Terry Novicki, "You had to choose which orders to follow, because I, for one, heard two or more orders that contradicted each other within a few seconds." Others said that their mission was to clear the streets, but with crisscrossing lines, broken lines, and scattering protestors, there was no longer any coherent direction as to where to clear their quarry. As Sam Ivanchenko points out, "It had gotten totally fucked up and it was not our fault."[186] Indeed, an independent observer from the Los Angeles Police Department stated, "The leadership at the point of conflict did little to prevent such contact and the direct control of officers by first-line supervisors was virtually non-existent."[187]

As the clock inched toward 8 P.M., journalists ran to capture the action, television camera lights illuminated the crowded sidewalks, and motorists trapped in traffic tried in vain to escape the rapidly growing chaos. As an evening wind off Lake Michigan swayed the trees in adjacent Grant Park, police and demonstrators battled into position in front of the Conrad Hilton Hotel.

"Seventeen Straight Minutes"

Although the police strong-arm tactics were an attempt to prevent a reenactment of what took place in the wake of Martin Luther King's assassination in April, few could have wished for the spectacle that ensued at the Hilton at 8 P.M.[188] In the confusion that resulted from multiple police formations battling with demonstrators, a group of about 400 became wedged near the front of the Hilton, thrust there by a line of police pushing from the north in a futile effort to clear the intersection while officers pushed another group into the area from the opposite direction. The pincer movement trapped a portion of the crowd against the side of the Hilton and the glass front of the Haymarket Bar. With panicking people pressed up against the glass, officers inexplicably moved in, spraying mace liberally into the trapped crowd. "Oh no, not mace," one woman cried out in fear, while others pleaded with officers to tell them where they should go. On both ends, however, police cut off avenues of escape. Some tried in vain to regroup and push their way out; each time, police moved in and broke them into smaller groups, where they were set upon and beat with batons. Some screamed in terror, while others yelled for help. With no avenue of escape, police advanced, blinding people with mace as they tried to cover their faces with their arms; officers then lashed out, and beat people about the body with their nightsticks. From his nineteenth-floor room at the Hilton, Norman Mailer described the scene unfolding below:

The police attacked . . . like a scythe through grass, lines of twenty and thirty policemen striking out in an ark, their clubs beating, demonstrators fleeing. Seen from overhead, from the nineteenth floor, it was like a wind blowing dust, or the edge of waves riding foam on the shore. . . . They cut through the intersection at Michigan and Balbo like a razor cutting a channel through a head of hair. . . . The action went on for ten minutes, fifteen minutes, with the absolute ferocity of a tropical storm.[189]

As the trapped crowd struggled against a barrage of mace and stinging baton strikes, the weight of their panicking bodies exploded though the Haymarket's plate glass window. "An atmosphere of unreality pervaded the scene," wrote *Sun-Times* reporter Hugh Hough. Some in the crowd, blood streaming from their heads, managed to flee into the hotel lobby where police pursued them on the run. Terrified bodies crashed into the bar, knocking over tables and chairs; blood flowing from baton blows and chards of broken glass, they fled as police continued to chase demonstrators through the hole in the glass persuing their quarry through the bar's inner entrance and into the hotel's lobby. One of the patrons in the bar was activist Terry Southern, who watched the scene in disbelief. "The cops rushed in after them. 'Get the hell outta here!' a cop was yelling, which they were trying to do as fast as possible. But something was wrong with one of them, a thin, blond boy about seventeen. 'I can't walk,' he said. 'You'll walk outta here, you little son of a bitch!' said the cop and clubbed him across the side of the head with his stick. Two of the others seized him by the shirt and started dragging him across the floor of the bar and through the lobby."[190] The desperate protestors, however, ran directly into thirty cops who had raced in from the street. A police captain on the scene yelled, "Clear the lobby," and the officers went to work knocking seven people to the lobby's plush red carpet, now stained with blood. Police made no arrests inside the lobby. Philip Armstrong, a twenty-one-year-old from Bethesda, Maryland, reportedly suffered a severed artery from broken glass when the crowd was forced through the Haymarket Bar window.[191] During that time, police complained about a barrage of objects thrown at them from the crowd and from the higher floors of the Hilton. Some reported that their face shields were smashed by bricks and rocks.[192]

One injured girl was screaming hysterically, trying to enter the main entrance of the Hilton with the help of a friend. A police officer turned them away, shouting, "Get the hell out of here. What do you think this is, a hospital?"[193] Though it was not a hospital, McCarthy's campaign workers turned his fifteenth-floor McCarthy-for-President headquarters into a triage center for wounded demonstrators. The young workers fashioned bandages from hotel bed sheets. McCarthy himself was on hand to comfort some of the young injured, while his personal physician and friend Dr. William Davidson treated the casualties, mostly for head wounds. In the lobby below, the public address system instructed, "Guests registered in this hotel, please return to your rooms immediately."[194] The entire episode of "bloody action" at the Hilton lasted about twenty minutes, and by 8:17 the police regained the intersection at Balbo and Michigan. The night of violence, however, was still young. As one officer recalls, "We had won round one of an old-fashioned street battle."[195]

In the Amphitheater

Given the drama on the streets, it was sometimes difficult to remember that there was a political convention in progress, a war plank to decide, and a candidate to choose. It had been a heated day as delegates debated the antiwar plank earlier in the afternoon. The party intended to vote on the Vietnam plank on Tuesday, but debate carried on well past midnight. Although the hawks, Mayor Daley among them, wanted an early morning vote before adjourning (while the television audience was low), floor and gallery demonstrators in support of McCarthy and McGovern made it all nearly impossible. The party postponed further debate until Wednesday afternoon. In the end, the majority hawk plank won the day, 1567 to 1041, providing a weak vindication for Johnson's Vietnam policy. While the platform passed, delegations in opposition on the floor began to sing, "We Shall Overcome." Wisconsin and New York delegates stood on their chairs in protest, while those relegated to the back of the hall booed those at the front. Dissidents chanted "Stop the War." The struggle to be heard while drowning out others produced a discordant cacophony of sounds. While New York's delegates sang "We Shall Overcome!" the band struck up "Happy Days Are Here Again."

By evening, the mood was even more divisive as delegates prepared to vote for the presidential and vice-presidential candidates. It was not a banner night for American democracy. With Daley's henchmen patrolling the floor, the mood was decidedly undemocratic. As *New York Times* reporter Russell Baker remarked dryly, "The only people who can possibly feel at ease at this convention are those who have been to a hanging."[196]

Delegates were intimidated for failing to return to their seats on command, or if they spoke out too loud on the wrong subject. This sour atmosphere was glaringly apparent as Daley's security force herded fourteen New York state delegates off the floor over a dispute, among them delegate Alex Rosenberg for ignoring an order to quit speaking. Commenting on his prison yard treatment, an enraged Rosenberg yelled, "I wasn't sentenced and sent here, I was elected!"[197] The intimidation extended to journalists covering on the floor. As security dragged Rosenberg away, journalist Mike Wallace from CBS attempted to get an interview. His effort was cut short when a police captain punched him in the face and tossed him out of the amphitheater. Captain Paul McLaughlin tried to rationalize his actions by insinuating that the encounter with Wallace was "man to man, not police officer to man." The officer also said that Wallace started the altercation by slapping him after refusing to leave the scene of the dispute. "Wallace hit me first," said McLaughlin. "I don't know why. He hit me in the face with an open hand. I hit him back. I did not have a club in my hand." He later called the entire incident a "misunderstanding."[198]

The pressure became so pervasive that journalists complained that because they were being tailed around on the street and in the convention hall, they could no longer do their jobs. NBC's Sander Vanocur told Chet Huntley on air that "We can't work with these gumshoes over our shoulders."[199] The night before, CBS showed floor reporter Dan Rather being roughed up and punched while trying to conduct an on-air interview with a member of the Georgia delegation who was ejected from the floor. Rather was grabbed by a pair of security men, struck in the stomach and the back, and thrown out of the hall. One of the security guards held him while the other threw the punch. After the exchange, Rather reported his experience to CBS news anchor Walter Cronkite in the anchor's booth. "Excuse me for being out of breath but a security man just slugged me in the stomach . . . this is the kind of thing we have been seeing a lot of outside the convention hall, but this is the first instance inside." Watching the floor action, Cronkite complained, "I think we've got a bunch of thugs here, if I may be permitted to say so."[200] The outraged veteran anchor suggested that the treatment of the press in Chicago "makes us want to pack up our cameras and go home."[201]

Tempers were also flaring up in the ABC news booth, as commentators Gore Vidal and William F. Buckley became involved in a terse on camera exchange that in many ways characterized the convention. At one point, Vidal referred to Buckley as a "crypto-Nazi" for supporting Daley and the police. Buckley fired back, "Listen, you queer, stop calling me a crypto-Nazi, or I'll sock you in your goddamn face and you'll stay plastered. Let the author of *Myra Breckinridge* go back to his pornography and stop making any allusions of Nazism to somebody who was in the infantry in the last war." Vidal countered, "You were not in the infantry."[202]

As the verbal fencing went on, delegates continued to vote on the convention floor. The images of Daley's security men and police working to stomp out dissent to the proceedings shocked even reverend Billy Graham, who was in the city for the convention. "The unreality of Chicago was beyond anything I have ever seen before," said Graham. "I never thought a President would have to be elected under these circumstances."[203] Meanwhile on the streets near the Conrad Hilton, the turf battle raged on.

"A Flying Wedge of Blue"

Looking down from his suite in the Hilton, Senator McCarthy bemoaned the scene unfolding below. "Very, very bad," said a dejected McCarthy, as he watched protestors hurl rocks and pieces of glass at police while others sat in the intersection, hands over their heads to ward off baton blows. "It looks like the battle of Canae."[204] With each altercation, the police made new arrests, pushing further away from the hotels and deeper into the park and east on Balbo, before sealing off all entrances to the Hilton.[205] In formation, the police then moved further down Balbo, forcing most of the crowd back into Grant Park, as the National Guard continued to block the Balbo Street Bridge. Police then advanced north on Michigan in an effort to keep the street open and clear of demonstrators. Two hundred National Guard reinforcements called over from Soldier Field, blocked Balbo at Michigan, and stood parallel to the Hilton and Grant Park. With the perimeter secure, about fifty police continued their move north on Michigan Avenue, pushing demonstrators as they went. Chanting, "Pigs eat shit!" and "The streets are for the people," the crowd ran in several directions, some down side streets, some back into Grant Park; others worked their way back toward the Hilton.

It was during the period from approximately 8:20 to 10:20 P.M. that some of the worst violence of the week occurred. Although there was no single altercation similar to the battle at Michigan and Balbo from 8:00 to 8:17 P.M., the next two hours produced a staggering number of violent clashes between police and protestors in the streets and alleys around the Hilton.[206] Journalist Lance Morrow offered the following chilling perspective:

[The cops] moved with surprising speed and a nimble fury like that of a rhinoceros attacking. A flying wedge of blue drove down Balbo into the noisy, ragged flesh on Michigan. The cops bent to their work, avengers at harvest time, chop-swinging clubs with methodical ferocity, a burst-boil rage. And in the midst of it, I began to detect a certain professional satisfaction of the kind a hitter feels sometimes. The cops had found a ghastly sweet spot. The sound that a club makes when it strikes a human skull—in earnest—awakens in the hearer a sickened, fearful amazement. No kidding now: a thunk! resonant through the skull and its wet package of thought and immortal soul.[207]

Protestors continued to pelt police with firecrackers, rocks, and bottles as the officers marched up Michigan. Police officers ducked and jumped as objects whizzed by their heads and crashed at their feet. Some of the more aggressive demonstrators climbed traffic signs and started fires in trash cans. As police reached the crowd from both directions, there were reports of them indiscriminately using mace as well as beating protestors with batons after they had fallen to the ground. A woman described as "well dressed" was watching one of the encounters and made the mistake of complaining to a nearby police captain. As she spoke to the officer, another moved up from behind her and sprayed her in the face with mace. Police clubbed the woman to the ground and dragged her into a nearby paddy wagon.[208] There were additional reports of police on motorcycles chasing and sometimes running people over on the sidewalks. A journalist with *United Press International* witnessed one such attack. The reporter stated that one of the offending officers had "a fanatical look in his eyes, was standing on a three-wheel cycle, shouting, 'Wahoo, wahoo,' and trying to run down people on the sidewalk."[209]

Mere feet away, reporters from *Chicago's American* were covering the action, mobile radios in hand, delivering live action back to their news desk. They recorded the following exchange:

Robert Jackson: I'm at 14th and State streets. . . . There's about 200 demonstrators headed towards me. And here come the boys in blue. Man . . . look at those hippies run!

Gene Rezwin: They want to march. If the police won't let them it's going to get bad.

Dorothy Storck: I'm at the scene. . . . God, it's going to get bloody. The police are wading into them at Michigan avenue and Balbo drive.

Lenord Aaronson: It looks like it might be calming down.

Jack Mabley: No . . . they are all over the Loop. There's a large group heading north in Michigan avenue, towards the river.

Don Sullivan: People are screaming . . . running! The cops are clubbing everything in sight. God . . . they don't care who they slug. Girls, kids . . . anything that moves. There are 250 sitting in the intersection of Michigan and Balbo. Police are wading in. I can hear screams.[210]

On nearby Jackson Avenue, police broke into a full sprint down the street pursuing fleeing demonstrators who, according to witnesses, "were beaten indiscriminately. . . . Two men lay in pools of blood, their heads severely cut by clubs." At times demonstrators ran as fast as they could to keep away from the police swiping at their heels, only to be trapped by crowds in their path. Many were caught and beat or were simply "overrun by the police."[211] A reporter from *Time* described the scene: "Chicago cops are built like beer trucks. They flailed blindly into the crowd of some 3,000, and then ranged onto the sidewalks to attack onlookers."[212] McCarthy volunteer William Styron recalls the following ugly scene. "On a traffic island in the middle of Clark Street a young man was knocked to his knees and beaten senseless. Unsuspecting motorists, caught up in the pandemonium, began to collide with one another up and down the street. The crowd wailed with alarm and split into fragments. I heard the sound of splintering glass as a stone went through the windshield of a police car."[213] Back on Michigan Avenue, five cops chased down a young man. A witness stated, "When they caught him, they began to beat him with their nightsticks until he fell on the pavement. They continued to beat him briefly after he fell. Then they dragged him about thirty feet to a paddy wagon."[214]

The police on Wednesday night were "avenging thugs," writes Todd Gitlin. "They charged, clubbed, gassed, and mauled—demonstrators, bystanders, and reporters . . . in the heat of their fury, the police took little or no trouble to distinguish between provocateurs and bystanders."[215] *Esquire* associate editor John Berendt detailed his view of the frenzied scene: "Up and down the street, gangs of cops raced into groups of fleeing civilians clubbing wildly, darting in and out of cars now deserted by their terrified drivers. A policeman carrying a shotgun ran past us into three boys, lost his balance, and fell on his back. In a rage, he jumped up, grabbed his shotgun by the muzzle, and swung the butt end at them as if it was a baseball bat, narrowly missing their heads. As one of them dashed past him in desperation, he lashed out again, missed, and brought the butt down on the sidewalk with a hideous crack."[216] Elizabeth Hardwick, advisory editor for the *New York Review of Books,* heard a woman ask one of the officers on what grounds he was beating a youth outside the Hilton. The cop yelled back, "coffee grounds."[217] Arthur Miller watched the violence on Michigan Avenue near the Hilton. While he looked on in amazement, a reporter next to him observed, "It [the nation] lasted 200 years. What law says it may not be over? Maybe we've come to the end of the string."[218] Some demonstrators, sensing the true result of the mayhem, yelled with spite and glee, "It's a wake, a funeral for the Democratic Party."[219]

Police officers remember the occurrences quite differently, and argue that the press distorted the events. "I got chased by some newsmen while I was chasing two punks who threw a bottle at one of our officers," says Orrest Hupka. "When I caught up to the little bastard who threw the bottle, the camera guy almost ran into my back; the kid took a swing at me, and the press guy didn't take a picture. When I used my stick to put him on the ground and arrest him, the fucking flash-bulb was going off an inch from my head, and I turned around after I had the cuffs on my guy and gave him [the reporter] a shot. Sorry, but I still don't feel any regret about that. The prick had it coming. He should have kept his distance and tried to be fair—all he was doing was interfering with police business."[220]

"The Fucking Press Were in the Way"

The often-violent confrontations involving the press during the first two days of the convention had a cumulative effect. Journalists decried police tactics, and police complained that the media sided with protestors. This perception, real or imagined, eliminated any residual tolerance officers had for journalists. Police officers felt that there was no mollifying the media. Says Steve Nowakowski, "It didn't matter what we did, anyway, so there was no point in trying to please them; we treated them like every other SOB in the way on the street, because leading up to the convention—the entire fucking year—they were on the com-mie's side. So what was the point about giving them special consideration? And anyway, they got it wrong most of the damn time."[221] Ronald Lardo agrees. "That's always been gotten wrong. When you're breaking up a crowd or making an arrest, the press have to back off, and they can't expect to be in your face with a camera, snapping pictures. And we knew that the reason they were taking pic-tures was to make us look bad, and not to tell the whole story, because they never took shots of us getting kicked and spit on." Joe Pecoraro feels that the press focused on police when there were clashes because they were the most eas-ily recognized. "An action creates a reaction. So if a rioter comes up to me and gives me a shot in the nose I'm going to punch him back, and that's what the press is going to see, me punching him back, because they can identify me, I'm the one in uniform. They can't identify him." Another officer simply states, "The reporters acted like they owned the streets."[222]

Naturally, those manning the television booths felt little sympathy for Chicago's police officers. "Chicago police are going out of their way to injure newsmen, and prevent them from filming or gathering information on what's going on," declared NBC's Chet Huntley. "The news profession in this city is now under assault by the Chicago police." By Wednesday night, the televised images emanat-ing from the streets looked like Huntley was right. But even in the face of con-stant police harassment, many journalists continued to report the unfolding events from the streets, sometimes to their peril. If they were awarding Purple Hearts to reporters for their work during convention week, or at least courage under fire, John Evans of the *Chicago Daily News* would surely have qualified. While covering a police beating of three young women in a convertible, he was struck about the head with batons. Moments after having his head bandaged to stop the bleeding, he went back to work. His valor under fire was captured on film as he interviewed another journalist while blood streamed down his suit jacket.[223]

If police were genuinely concerned about receiving good press, they appeared to do little to win favor among journalists. As Todd Gitlin observed, the police, from the beginning, appeared to be their own worst enemy when it came to receiving fair treatment from the press. "They bashed reporters so devotedly," writes Gitlin, "that they guaranteed themselves a bad press."[224] Indeed, in some cases when journalists witnessed demonstrators attacking police, they felt disinclined to bring it to public attention. "I remember watching, amazed, as kids a year or two younger than me threw rocks and slabs of sidewalks at the police, hoping to provoke reprisals," *Village Voice* reporter Paul Cowan wrote later. Cowan filed a story based on his observations then asked his editor not to run it because of his belief that the police attacked "anyone who happened to be on the streets. In other words, the police riot seemed to me a far greater evil than the fact that some kids had wanted to provoke it."[225]

The *Chicago Tribune*'s editorial page that morning, however, blamed protestors and the media for the encounters. The publication had "no sympathy" for the hippies, Yippies, "young punks," and the other "senseless demonstrators" on the streets. The editorial pointed out that many cops are war veterans and need have little sympathy for protestors. They also blamed journalists covering the events. "Judging from photographs, some of the newsmen looked like hippies, and perhaps they refused to obey police orders to move. If so, the police were justified in using force."[226]

Aware that they were not going to receive completely balanced coverage by the press, some officers decided that they might as well get in some retaliatory hits. Recalls Jim Dziadyk, "When someone calls you a thug long enough, you say, 'Well, if I'm going to get accused of it anyway, I might as well act like it,' because they were against us." Others believed that members of the press were too close in proximity to the crowd to separate properly. Says Marlin Rowden, "It may not have been exactly professional conduct by some members, but you're asked to split hairs with crowd control when some in the crowd are claiming observer status. In other words, 'we're not part of this and you are not supposed to touch us, but we're going to write you guys up in tomorrow's paper, or take selective photos and news film of you.' If that happens, you're just another punk in the way and you don't deserve special treatment. You deserve what you get." Others believed that the press could not perceive the reality of what police faced on the streets. Al Ogilvie recalls, "From the beginning—even before the convention began—the press did not get it, that these 'kids' were not really kids; they were far from those practicing peaceful assembly or innocent bystanders, but dangerous subversive hippies. They threw all kinds of sharp objects and bricks at us. The press didn't tell it that way. That was a sham."[227]

Many of those who traveled to the Windy City were indeed looking for a fight with the Chicago police and arrived prepared for battle. Todd Gitlin admits that although not all people in the park wanted a confrontation, the fighters, or "Park People," were unquestionably militant, while others "threw gas canisters back at the cops (a few brought oven mitts for the purpose), darted through traffic, blocked the streets with trash baskets, trashed police-car windows with bricks and rocks, rocked police cars and paddy wagons and tried to overturn them, got their licks in at isolated cops when they could."[228] And contrary to police assertions, some journalists did report violence by demonstrators, albeit much of it after the fact. *Time* observed demonstrators hurling "bricks, bottles and nail-studded golf balls at the police lines."[229]

Many watching on television at home were horrified, and no more than the police officers' families. "Last night, when I got a minute, I called my wife to tell her that I was all right," said one officer. "She had seen some of that stuff on television, cops being hit with bottles and bricks. Being spit on. She was crying. She asked me to quit and come home. I was all she had, she said."[230] Former officer George Horsley is one of many who had to deal with an upset spouse. "She was really scared, for sure. She begged me to quit and come home. She was home watching the convention on TV and got the hell scared out of her."[231] Joe Pecoraro knew his family was concerned. "When you leave for work, you can see they're scared; sure the families are worried—scared—they don't know what's going to happen." By 9:30 P.M. during Humphrey's nomination the first delayed images of the battles on the streets appeared on TV screens in Chicago neighborhoods and inside the convention hall.[232]

"They're Beating the Kids on the Street"

An uneasy stir rippled through the amphitheater as the violent images flickered on the television screens. On stage was Connecticut Senator Abraham Ribicoff who was in the process of nominating South Dakota senator George McGovern for president; Mayor Daley was sitting directly in front of him. Given the images from the streets, Ribicoff could not contain himself. Breaking from his prepared remarks, the Senator stated, "With George McGovern, we wouldn't have Gestapo tactics on the streets of Chicago. With George McGovern, we wouldn't have a National Guard." While delegates erupted in shock, Daley, according to lip readers who later watched the recorded exchange, rose to his feet, and, shaking a fist and cupping a hand to his mouth, shot back, "Fuck you, you Jew son of a bitch, you lousy motherfucker, go home." Ribicoff smiled and said, "How hard it is to accept the truth. How hard it is."[233] The spectacle had become difficult for many members of the press to accept. CBS's Eric Sevareid called the evening "the most disgraceful night in American political history."[234]

As the networks switched from coverage inside the convention center to taped footage from the street, there were gasps and renewed cries among McCarthy's supporters. Among the assailed was Reverend John Boyle a student chaplain at Yale and an assistant to Reverend William Sloane Coffin. Boyle was coming to the aid of a young McCarthy volunteer when police struck and arrested him. Boyle recalled his street experience:

I saw kids being beaten and dragged by their feet, and I went to the police and said, "You don't have to do that" and they pushed me away. Then I saw a McCarthy girl I knew named Betsey Bingsten being clubbed on the shoulder. I ran over and said "Betsy are you all right?" They had thrown her into the paddy wagon and as I leaned in to ask if she was okay, two cops started beating me with their fists and then threw me into the wagon.[235]

By 10:30 P.M., the National Guard once again moved in to replace the fatigued police in front of the Hilton. Although the worst of the violence had ended by then, the mood was still extremely tense with sporadic violence. The National Guard pointed machine guns mounted on trucks directly at the demonstrators. Guards with their machine guns, bayonets fixed, some sitting in their mesh-covered army jeeps, added to an already strained mood. The crowd, however, began to move off in the face of the overwhelming force. Many drifted back into the park, while around 4,000 sat down across from the Hilton, some singing, "God Bless America." By 12:30 A.M., the crowd had dwindled to 1,500.[236]

Humphrey's nomination, however, was not in doubt. Before midnight, Pennsylvania's delegates put the Hump over the top in a first ballot victory, 1,761 to 146.[237] When Humphrey already had enough delegates to win, Daley finally delivered his state's 118 votes to the vice president. As news reached the crowds, boos resounded throughout the park.[238] Soon, demonstrators got on their feet and re-formed near the hotel to await the return of the delegates. As the tension rose, a busload of police arrived near the Hilton.[239] Many of the McCarthy kids were in tears, their hopes for an end to the war dashed with the senator's defeat in the amphitheater. After midnight, the McCarthy workers began to move downstairs to stand watch outside the doors of the Grand Ballroom where McCarthy was holding a press conference. The kids began to chant, "The Democratic Party is dead," and "Peace now!" As McCarthy arrived, the chant shifted to "Fourth Party, Fourth Party!" Denied access to the press conference, the dejected young workers were forced to listen while a middle-aged woman with a Humphrey button pushed her way by them saying, "You lost, didn't you?"[240]

Who won and who lost was not so clear, as the victor watched his party nominate him with one eye and watched police beat demonstrators on the streets below his hotel room window with the other; demonstrators yelled "Dump the Hump" in anger and defiance. "I don't feel so good tonight, with what's going on down there," said Humphrey, watching two televisions in his twenty-fourth-floor hotel room. The Democratic candidate for president of the United States sat "quiet and glum" as he ate ham and eggs with two friends from

Minneapolis.[241] The vice president had not seen anything on the streets or on the convention floor to give him much cause for optimism.

Earlier that evening, the party had waged a bitter and often fierce fight over the peace plank before voting it down 1,567 to 1,041. "This is the moment of truth for the Democratic Party and for this nation," stated presidential adviser Pierre Salinger during the debate earlier that evening over the plank that decided on the Johnson/Humphrey administration's intention to keep bombing North Vietnam over the dove's call for the immediate cessation. Ted Sorensen, long-time adviser and speechwriter for John F. Kennedy and Lyndon Johnson, was thinking of the kids on the street. "If you can't give the young people and the idealists a candidate they want," Sorensen told delegates, "at least give them this plank to preserve their enthusiasm in the Democratic Party."[242] Indeed, near 1 A.M., the youthful demonstrators near the Hilton made their feelings clear as they booed delegates returning from the amphitheater. "You elected Nixon," they screamed. "You ought to be ashamed of yourself."[243] The only ones who received applause were the defeated McCarthy supporters. The surly crowd saved their invective for Humphrey's supporters. "The party is dead," they yelled at delegates. "You killed the party." "Shame, shame."[244]

Back at the amphitheater, a crowd of delegates comprised largely from the McCarthy and McGovern camps began to organize a candlelight march in silent protest in solidarity with demonstrators. The delegates boarded buses to take them to the corner of Michigan Avenue and Randolph Street, where they were to disembark and march to the Hilton carrying candles. Before the group of delegates began their trek, most of the police had completely left the streets near the Hilton, turning security over to the National Guard. It was nearly 3 A.M. before the candlelight party began its symbolic march to the Hilton, carrying lit candles in Pepsi cups. As the remaining demonstrators near the park and the hotel saw the approaching delegates, they chanted, "The party belongs to the people, as the streets belong to the people." Commanders ordered the guardsmen in line near Michigan and Balbo "at ease." Some in the crowd chanted, "We want Gene!"[245]

Wednesday was finally over.

THURSDAY, AUGUST 29

Weary and battered demonstrators, survivors of an often-brutal night, slept fitfully in Grant Park amid the debris. By late morning, many of the young protestors were already boarding buses bound for homes across the country. The National Guard, while still in place, was reduced in size to one company. The recriminations, however, were building. On NBC's *Today Show,* host Hugh Downs wondered if there was any other word more apt to describe police than "pigs" for what he had witnessed the night before.[246] President of the American Newspaper Guild, William J. Farson, called police action against journalists "unprovoked and brutal."[247] Veteran reporter and columnist Jimmy Breslin wrote, "the performance of the police of Chicago on Michigan Avenue last night was one of the worst I have ever seen."[248] An editorial in the *Daily News* was just as scathing. "Just now the paramount danger is not from hippies, yippies, or other demonstrators; it is from an establishment that has lost sight, temporarily at least, of the right of all the people to their fundamental freedoms."[249] An article in *Chicago's American* suggested that police were waging a personal war on the press. The paper's phone lines, however, were jammed with calls supporting Daley and the police.[250]

Mayor Daley was also firing back that morning: "In the heat of emotion and riot, some policemen may have over-reacted, but to judge the entire department by the alleged action of a few would be just as unfair as to judge our entire younger generation by the actions of a mob." Daley said that the department comprised "good and decent men" who would not "respond with undue violence." Meanwhile, Senator George McGovern called for a probe of police actions. "I saw American youth being savagely beaten by police simply because they were protesting polices about which they have had very little to say."[251] The chaos of Wednesday night brought condemnation from both sides of the political aisle. "There's no question of police brutality," said Republican Representative Donald Rumsfeld of Illinois, who watched the previous night's battles from his window at the Hilton. "The atmosphere for this was created by the mayor. The mayor's comments led to this." Rumsfeld said that the city should have provided the youth with a place to demonstrate.[252]

At noon, Mobe and Yippie leaders set up a public address system across from the Hilton to ask the crowd of approximately 2,000 to join them for a march on the amphitheater later that afternoon. Tom Hayden, who had emerged from his self-imposed underground exile, joined Rennie Davis, Jerry Rubin, and David Dellinger in addressing the crowd. "We should be happy we came here, fought and survived," Hayden said in what sounded like a hollow victory. As singers Peter, Paul, and Mary joined the speakers, there were few incidents of violence.[253]

While Hubert Humphrey accepted the nomination of his party as the Democratic candidate for president of the United States, the political fallout from the previous night continued. Indeed, some were at each other's throats. Representative Donald J. Irwin, who had temporarily yielded his seat on the Connecticut delegation so Ribicoff could make his nomination speech for McGovern, was still outraged. "You are the most contemptible man," Irwin told a surprised Ribicoff. "You were a creep last night. I hope they mace you."[254] At 4 o'clock that afternoon, a 500-strong delegation from Wisconsin began another peace march; as the marchers wound their way through the streets, about 1,500 demonstrators from the park joined the delegates. As they approached 16th and State, ten police officers stood in line on State blocking them. "You can't go on," said one of the patrolmen. "Those are orders." As he spoke, four busloads of police reinforcements arrived on the scene. Deciding that they had made their point, the delegates decided to end their march. Soon after, defeated Senator Eugene McCarthy left the Hilton and crossed the street into the park to speak to demonstrators.[255]

Throughout the afternoon, there was little fight left in the crowd and seemingly little left to fight over. Although never matching the fury of the previous three nights, there were a number of clashes between police and demonstrators that evening. The major clash took place as 3,000 antiwar protestors tried to cross police lines at Michigan Avenue and 18th Street. Police and the National Guard used teargas and rifle butts to repel the crowd. Police made eighty arrests, twenty-five of them delegates. Among those nabbed by police were *New York Post* columnist Murray Kempton and activist and comedian Dick Gregory, who led the march. During the melee, a National Guard commander grabbed a bullhorn and ordered his men to "Use your rifle butts and pull this crowd back." Marchers shouted in return, "hold your ground." Police knocked at least thirty people to the ground, many bleeding from blows. Others were reeling from blasts of teargas fired at close range. One girl was kicked in the ribs, and another was struck in the stomach by a police billy club.[256]

Meanwhile, the fallout from clashes between police and the media continued, as the public information director for the police department, Frank Sullivan, revealed that police had taped all TV broadcasts for their officers viewing, including all commentaries and utterances. "There was some question whether TV did right by the police [during the April riots]," Sullivan said.[257] That afternoon, U.S. Appeals Court Judge Elmer J. Schnackenberg served police superintendent Conlisk with a temporary restraining order to prohibit police from interfering with the media, an action brought about by the ACLU. The order stated that the police must restrain themselves from "interfering by force, violence, and intimidation with the constitutional rights" of members of the media. That evening, Daley appeared on *CBS with Walter Cronkite* and complained that the media never showed wounded and bloodied officers lying on the street, only demonstrators. Daley said the press should show the fifty-one injured policemen.

Indeed, while criticizing the media in front of a veteran television anchor who had referred to police as "thugs" just two days prior, Daley had a receptive audience. Cronkite offered that his network had received numerous telegrams and phone calls in support of the mayor and his police. "I can tell you this, Mr. Daley, that you have a lot of supporters around the country as well as in Chicago." Instead of confronting the mayor over the treatment of his journalistic colleagues, Cronkite appeared to go out of his way to ingratiate himself to the pugnacious city boss, as he commented on the "genuine friendliness of the Chicago Police Department." Daley took the national television opportunity to reveal information regarding an alleged assassination plot, which targeted him and three principal DNC contenders.[258]

Thursday, however, was not quite over, as some officers had a score to settle before the conventioneers left town. Angry over the constant barrage of objects thrown on police from the upper floors of the Hilton during the week, some sought a measure of revenge. Believing that much of the debris had come from the hands of the young McCarthy campaign workers, police paid them a particularly brutal dawn raid. At about 4 A.M. Friday—following reports by guardsmen and police of people dropping beer cans, ashtrays, a cream pitcher, smoked fish, and pennies, as well as a bag of military chemical irritant and a grenade with an intact pin, on the sidewalk outside the Hilton—a squad of officers entered the hotel. Observation teams using riflescopes and binoculars pinpointed the general group of rooms thought to be responsible.

With the help of Hilton staff, they determined that the offending room was 1506-A, used by McCarthy supporters throughout the week. Colonel Robert Strupp of the Guard in command at the scene asked police to intervene. When a police captain and a half dozen officers arrived on the fifteenth floor, they found a party in progress, the room littered with beer cans and cigarette butts. The hotel security officer with the police ordered everyone out and down to the lobby. Many, though, attempted to go up to the twenty-third floor, the head-quarters for the McCarthy campaign. With security insisting that they could not go up to the twenty-third floor and people such as campaign worker George Yumich insisting they could, police officers settled the issue. Officers beat Yumich with batons while others herded shocked partiers into elevators; some girls screamed in fear and confusion. Police removed nearly fifty people by force.

The arrival of the second squad of officers, however, caused the most contro-versy. The officers began to rouse anyone connected with the campaign out of other rooms on the fifteenth floor, some of them asleep. Among the accosted was campaign worker Wendy Wayne, who awoke to police officers dragging her off a couch. Police threw the young woman into an elevator. During the frenzied encounter, an officer broke his baton over the head of John Warren, the coordina-tor of McCarthy's Arkansas campaign, while someone shot hairspray into the eyes of two officers. McCarthy arrived soon afterward to console his remaining staffers. He was outraged. "Maybe some kid threw something out of the hotel. That hap-pens in every hotel, but you don't come up and knock heads for it." Police officers such as Ernie Bellows, disagree. "That's exactly what you do when people are throwing things that can injure from fifteen floors up. An astray can split your head open, and that's assaulting an officer. We went up there and shut 'em down."[259]

Nothing more was thrown from the fifteenth floor of the Conrad Hilton.

"A Glorious Friday"

"On Friday," observed columnist Mike Royko, "the Democratic Party limped out of Chicago." Yippie Abbie Hoffman could not help but gloat. "We had won the battle of Chicago," Hoffman said as he fled the Windy City for the more friendly confines of New York's Lower East Side. "As I watched the acceptance speech of Hump-Free . . . I knew we had smashed the Democrats' chances and destroyed the two-party system in this country and perhaps with it electoral politics."[260] Although Hoffman's prediction concerning the future of the Ameri-can political system was inaccurate, the blow to the Democratic Party in the elec-tion of 1968 was undeniable. The political fallout at the time mattered little to members of the Chicago Police Department or for the people of Chicago as convention week ended. One young engineer, while waiting to board a bus on a downtown street, said with obvious relief, "I'm glad it's over." By the following day, residents described the city as "unbelievably peaceful."[261]

Although police officers knew there would be consequences following the violent week, Friday brought a large measure of relief. "At that moment we didn't care," recalls Marlin Rowden. "It was Friday, the convention was finally over, and the weekend had arrived. That the hippies had left town was the third blessing."[262] After a stressful week, many in uniform just wanted to escape. "My uniform reeked of some geek's piss," recalls Steven Latz. "I just wanted to crawl into my basement and stay there for a week." Officer Hank Peterson says that while it was only a week of twelve-hour shifts, it felt much longer. He, like many officers, were disgusted with what they had seen. "It felt like a month of shit and puke. I thought, 'what the hell is the world coming to?' I remember wondering what they'd become as adults, and I found out—Bill Clinton."[263] For others, however, it was all in a day's work. "It was no biggie," recalls Don Holtz. "We're just busy herding hippies and missed supper and coffee breaks, smoke breaks. Working with the protestors was just like herding sheep, except some of these sheep hit back; we hit harder." Some officers recall dark jokes concerning giving the hippies a parting shot. "There was talk about giving them [antiwar protestors] a twenty-one-gun salute on their way out of town, but not aiming the guns in the air," says Steve Nowakowski. "Some of the guys were so mad they were only half joking."[264]

Relief, however, was the prevailing emotion. "I was so glad it was over," recalls Ronald Lardo. "I lost a few pounds that week, and I think some of my hair. My wife didn't care, she cried with relief when the hippies left town." Cop Tom Freeborn was also one of the many relieved officers. "I played catch with my eight-year-old that Sunday afternoon, and it was funny; he said, 'don't worry, I'll never grow my hair long like those smelly hippies,' or something like that. *That* was a great afternoon."[265] That day, the *Sun-Times* and *Chicago's American* both ran the story of cop Gregory Kyritz, who was in a hospital bed where he was recuperating from an attack Wednesday night. His face was swollen and black from a brick thrown by a demonstrator outside the Hilton. He remembered hearing a "big cheer" before he blacked out. Struck below the eye on his left cheekbone, the twenty-one-year-old officer and army veteran was just happy to know he was going to be okay as his wife, Laurian, was giving birth to their first baby in another hospital.[266] Mayor Daley's wife, Eleanor, was also happy to see the convention end. "I'll be glad when the city gets back to normal."[267]

There were no national reporters or television crews to capture the final demonstration in the city that Sunday afternoon. It was a spontaneous expression by 300 Chicagoans out in the rain to thank police for their convention-week efforts. Cop Harold Pacnik remembers the kind words and believes his fellow citizens joined officers in their delight over watching antiwar protestors leave the city. "There were no tears shed when those SOBs left town," says Pacnik. "I don't remember anyone regretting anything. Not one damn thing."[268]

The Illinois National Guard stare down protestors in Grant Park across from the Conrad Hilton Hotel. Photo: Courtesy the *Peoria Journal Star*.

Debris in Chicago's Grant Park following the Democratic National Convention. Photo: Chicago Police Department.

Chicago Police arrest *New York Times* photographer Barton Silverman during the 1968 Democratic National Convention. Photo: © Fred W. McDarrah.

Amid random fires, National Guardsmen follow a line of Chicago Police officers down Michigan Avenue. Photo: Courtesy *United Press International*.

Protestors attempt to turn over police vehicle during street demonstrations. Photo: Courtesy *United Press International.*

Demonstrators face machine guns on Michigan Avenue during the Democratic National Convention. Photo: Courtesy *United Press International.*

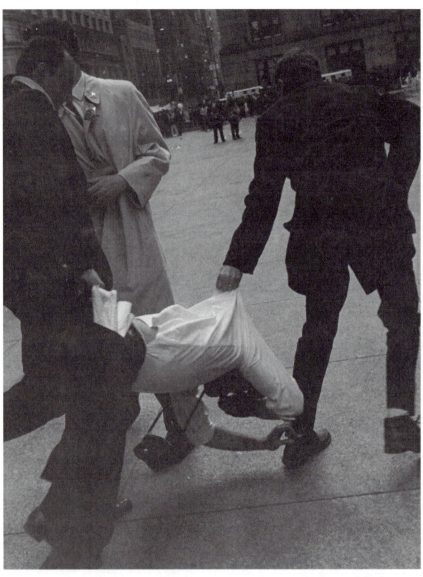

Plainclothes Chicago Police officers haul away demonstrator during the 1968 Democratic National Convention. Photo: Chicago Historical Society, ICHI-36861. Photographer unknown.

Police officers struggle with chained demonstrators. Photo: Chicago Historical Society, ICHI-36860. Photographer unknown.

A group of young protestors march against the Vietnam War during the Democratic National Convention. To many police officers, antiwar demonstrators represented a generation out of control. Photo: Chicago Historical Society, ICHI-36859. Photographer unknown.

Chicago mayor, Richard J. Daley. Photo: Chicago Historical Society, ICHI-25558. Photo: Field Enterprises.

Police guard Chicago streets during the 1968 Democratic National Convention. Photo: Chicago Historical Society, ICHI-20689. Photographer unknown.

Antiwar demonstrators on the streets at night. Photo: Chicago Historical Society, ICHI-18354. Photographer unknown.

Protestors lay claim to the statue of Illinois Civil War major general, Jonathan Logan in Grant Park. Photo: Chicago Historical Society, ICHI-14789. Photographer: Ed Wengen.

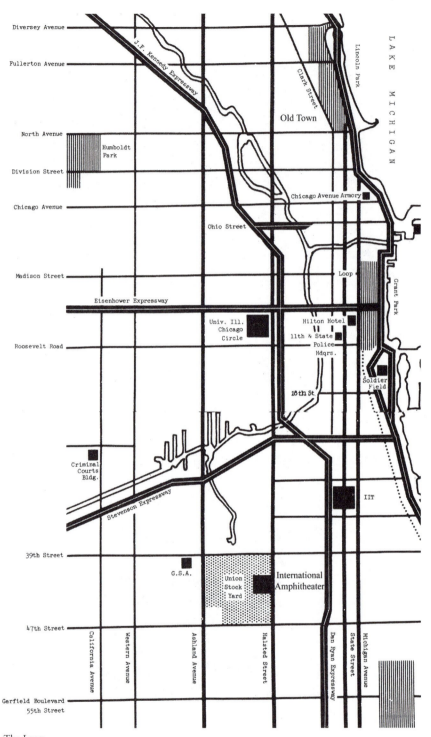

The Loop

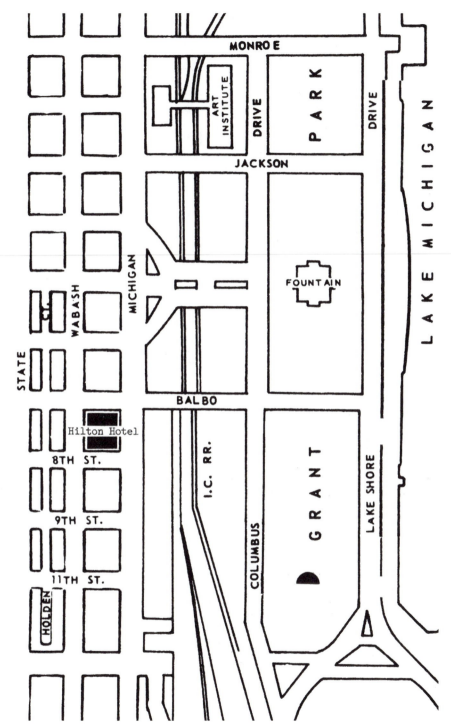

Scene of the most intense street battles: the intersection of Michigan and Balbo, including the Conrad Hilton Hotel, and adjacent Grant Park.

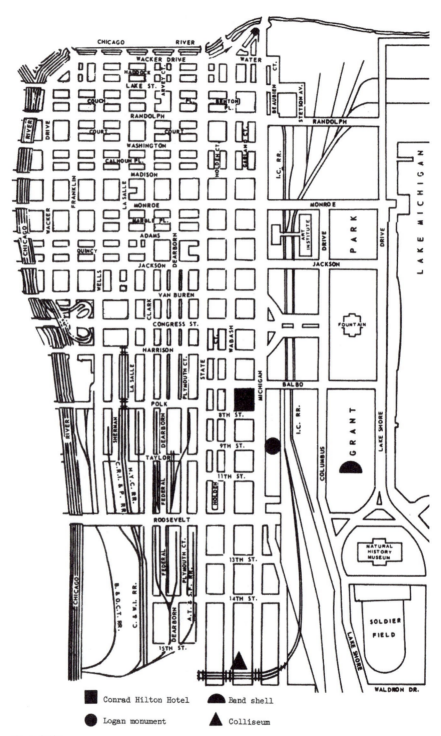

Central Chicago

chapter 6

"Terrorists from Out of Town": Fallout in the Second City

It was a terrible week. It was one of the worst in my eighteen years on the force. My head hurt, my back felt as if I was hit by a two-by-four. My stomach was full of acid. I had someone's spit underneath my collar, sliding down my back. I just wanted to go home and I got a news camera up my ass.[1]

If they're going to handcuff our police and fire departments, we might as well turn the country back to the Indians.[2]

onvention week left few unscathed. Not only was Sir Winston Churchill's grandson and namesake roughed up by Chicago's finest, but British parliamentarian Anne Kerr faced the indignity of a police lockup after getting maced outside the Conrad Hilton.[3] Casualties were everywhere. While the movement emerged battered, fractured, with its hardcore elements more radicalized and dangerous, the real loser was the Democratic Party, emerging from Chicago weak and divided with a federal election only weeks away.[4] Even though the majority of Americans who voiced an opinion approved of police actions that week,[5] an image of disunity and chaos followed the party out of the city and onto the campaign trail. Following the disastrous convention, candidate Hubert Humphrey, sensing the mood in the nation, refused to denounce outright police actions.

In his efforts to avoid the appearance of favoring lawlessness and disorder, however, the vice president inadvertently blamed potential young Democratic voters and confirmed the reservations others held of him. "Goodness me, anybody that sees this sort of thing is sick at heart, and I was," Humphrey told journalist Roger

Mudd after the convention. "But I think the blame ought to be put where it belongs. I think we ought to quit pretending that Mayor Daley did something that was wrong. He didn't condone a thing that was wrong. He tried to protect lives. I know what caused these demonstrations. They were planned, premeditated by certain people in this country that feel all they have to do is riot and they'll get their way. They don't want to work through the peaceful process. I have no time for them."[6] Humphrey lamented a cop stabbed in the face with a broken beer bottle, provocation by demonstrators that was "beyond endurance" and the "filth and manure" demonstrators left on the rugs of the Conrad Hilton while his wife dismissed demonstrators as "noisy and rude."[7] Before leaving Chicago, Humphrey claimed that he had been the target of "an assassination team."[8]

Humphrey emerged from the Windy City looking not like a winner but as a man linked to a foreign policy quagmire and four years of domestic chaos. "It's difficult," the vice president admitted, "to take on the Republicans and fight a guerilla war in your own party at the same time."[9] The implications of the movement's involvement had not yet hit home for some of the more conscientious of its leaders. "We came off well in Chicago," said David Dellinger at the time. "It was a clear cut victory because the police acted abominably and our people showed courage, aggressiveness and a proper sense of values."[10] These "values," however, were not playing well in the city of Chicago and, indeed, throughout much of the nation.

Chicago City Hall was flooded with thousands of calls and 2,400 letters immediately following the convention, the vast majority supporting Daley and the police. The American Legion of Illinois also extended its support. The mayor, the Legion suggested, was "excellent" in "keeping the peace and maintaining law and order in the city of Chicago. . . . We especially commend the members of the Chicago Police Department for the action they took against those who would dare desecrate our flag and attempt to fly the flag of a foreign nation instead." Hugh Hough of the *Sun-Times* wrote that "scores of persons called this newspaper to repeat the same words: 'The hippies got what was coming to them.'"[11] Most callers to the *Tribune* also praised Daley and the police. One female caller suggested that the city "ship all hippies, yippies, or whatever they call themselves to Russia."[12] But amid the applause, critics emerged with numerous calls for investigations from both sides of the political aisle. Stung by criticism of his officers and to the image of his city, Daley went on the offensive to control the fallout and explain "the untold story."

"IMPORTED REVOLUTION"

The veteran Chicago boss wasted little time entering the unfolding public relations battle. Indeed, before the convention ended, Daley was vigorously defending his police and justifying his decision to be tough on demonstrators. Speaking in ominous terms, Daley said that it was clear that in the weeks and months leading up to the convention, there was a strategy by "terrorists" to disrupt the convention and harm the city of Chicago. The testy mayor blamed agitators from outside the state for the bulk of the trouble.

The intention of these terrorists was openly displayed. They repeatedly said and stated they came to Chicago to disrupt the national political convention and to paralyze our city. They came equipped with caustics [lye], helmets and their own brigade of medics. They had maps locating the hotels and the routes of buses for the guidance of terrorists from out of town. . . . The newspapers stated specifically that the terrorists were planning to use those who were opposed to the present Vietnam policy as a front for their violence. It was also pointed out that they would attempt to assault, harass and taunt the police into reacting before television cameras. Fifty-one policemen were injured. Sixty percent of those arrested did not live in Illinois.[13]

Daley's fears, real or imagined, did not play well in editorial rooms in or outside the city of Chicago. Daley, wrote the *New York Times,* "has brought shame to the city, embarrassment to the country and has gravely accentuated the divisions within the Democratic Party." These acts, the *Times* suggested, not only "damaged the party" but also "shocked the nation."[14] Overseas, the *London Times* called Daley's "regime" a "disgrace to the United States. This violence in Chicago is paralleled by the increasing violence in American life."[15] The *Sun-Times'* editorial that Friday put the blame on Daley and the police. "Mayor Daley must share the responsibility because of his failure to distinguish between those who wish to make legitimate protest and those whose avowed intention was anarchy." The editorial also criticized the mayor for undermining the department's independence since April and for showing little concern for police attacks on journalists and other innocent people. They called for an investigation into police action during convention week.[16] The *Daily News* was somewhat sympathetic to the police, suggesting that although they may have "overreacted," radicals "had declared war" on the city. Nevertheless, it suggested that Daley beared much of the blame for the disturbances.[17]

The *Tribune* was the exception. On Friday as delegates and demonstrators left the city, the paper ran a front-page editorial praising the police and blasting protestors. "For ensuring law and order, Mayor Daley and the police deserve congratulations rather than criticism. . . . The rabble has begun to clear out for its purpose has been defeated. Chicago cannot get rid of imported revolution too soon. Shortly calm will return to the city and the orderly life we know will be resumed." The *Tribune* also published the names of the 309 demonstrators arrested by police on Wednesday. One hundred and thirty-six of the arrestees were from outside the city.[18]

In an effort to portray his city and police department in the best possible light, Daley ordered his own internal inquiry and requested national television time to explain the city's side of the story and, more specifically, the "truth" of what "actually happened." Daley was emboldened by civic support; by September 3, his office had received 20,000 letters and 8,000 calls, with 50 to 1 in favor of his work and that of his police. It was no surprise that among the early support came encouraging words from Joseph LeFevour, president of the Chicago Fraternal Order of Police. "I'm sure that when the full picture is shown to the public, the police will be vindicated." Like Daley, LeFevour admitted that some officers may have "overreacted," but he explained that it was understandable given that the actions of protestors presented an affront to their patriotism. "[T]hey are Americans. When they saw people tear down the flag and run up the Viet Cong flag, well, they're red-blooded Americans."[19]

The department also received letters of support, and in the days following convention week, it was common for citizens to approach officers on the street and shake their hands. "It was like homecoming for a while," says cop Brian Ramsey. "There was some free coffee and pie here and there." Another officer concurres, adding, "Yes, there were even some kisses . . . from *women,* of course, and it wasn't a bad fringe benefit; hell, it was a lot better than people spitting on you." LeFevour extended his personal thank you to the mayor "for his support of policemen."[20] Illinois attorney general William Clark gave police a 95 percent grade for their work. "When I was in school, that was a pretty good grade."[21]

For those opposed to what took place on the streets during convention week, the city's official "white paper" report released just days later was less than satisfying, as many saw it as a blanket endorsement of police action. The report, titled the "Strategy of Confrontation" and published on September 6, outlined how police had worked in conjunction with the Secret Service and the FBI on collecting intelligence data prior to the convention, including supposed assassination plots against the mayor and Democratic Party leaders. An Intelligence Division report of August 20 implicated Davis and Hayden as radicals intent on disrupting the convention.

The report strongly supported Daley's stance and blamed the violence on agitators and "some overreaction" to events. In essence, the report found police had behaved "far beyond the call to duty," and showed restraint as, according to the report, police did not fire their weapons. The report touched on the violence directed toward members of the media, suggesting only that some reporters were "arrested for violating the park curfew." Indeed, the report blamed the media. "Any success the revolutionaries achieved in their ultimate objectives . . . was in large part attributable to the almost totally sympathetic coverage extended [by] reporters to the revolutionary leaders." It described instead the actions of the "mob," including the assault on Assistant U.S. Attorney John Simon with a bag filled with paint and urine. It described how protestors were the aggressors in front of the Hilton on Wednesday night and listed the names of the 198 officers injured during the convention.[22] The city-generated document pointed a finger of blame for the disturbances at who it considered to be the principal radical leaders: Tom Hayden, Rennie Davis, Jerry Rubin, and David Dellinger. Indeed, the report blamed adults, not young student activists, for the violence. "An overwhelming majority of the persons arrested were not youngsters, were not students, and were not Chicagoans. They were adult troublemakers who came into the city of Chicago for the avowed purpose of a hostile confrontation with law enforcement." Conlisk produced arrest records to indicate that 279 of the arrestees were under the age of twenty-one, and 362 were over the age of twenty-one. Five hundred and sixty-five were males and seventy-six were females.

Although the Chicago *Sun-Times* praised the city's report for putting the violence into "perspective," it added that it would not be the "last word" on the disturbances during the convention. Less than a week later, the House Un-American Activities Committee once again reared its head looking into subversive acts during convention week and began to focus on the actions of the same cast of characters.[23] On September 15, the same day the ACLU took out a full-page ad in the *Sun-Times* calling for the "full story," Daley's city-produced television program hit the airwaves on 142 stations across the nation. The hour-long program showed none of the clubbings and selected nine officers who told tales of provocations. The narrator read a script that downplayed the violence, stressing that not only were there no deaths, but "few spent even a night in a hospital."

Many critics viewed the program, "What Trees Do They Plant?" produced by California-born filmmaker Henry Ushijima, as a thin whitewash. Ushijima pieced together hours of television footage, scenes of confiscated weapons and injured police officers. One of the weapons was a Louisville Slugger with "cops are pigs" written on one side and "love" written on the other. The program outlined plots against government and city officials hatched by hippies, Yippies, and "terrorists." Whereas Daley strategically limited his televised participation to two brief appearances, the program avoided any references to police removing their name tags and showed no film of police beating demonstrators after they had fallen to the ground. "The force used was the force that was necessary," offered Superintendent James Conlisk with a straight face. Conlisk wanted people to remember that whereas no protesters were killed or sustained permanent harm, 192 of his officers received injuries.[24]

At the time, most police officers felt that they didn't need any help in the image department. As one officer told the *New York Times,* "This is the best police force in the world. We don't have to defend ourselves. And besides, the Mayor doesn't like us to shoot off our mouths."[25] Daley was capable of that all by himself and explained why there was a need for tougher action. "I would like to say here and now that this administration, our administration, and the people of Chicago have never condoned brutality at any time but they will never permit a lawless group of terrorists to menace the lives of millions of people, destroy the purpose of this national convention, and take over the streets of Chicago."[26]

Who or what took over the streets of Chicago quickly became a public and legal matter; a twenty-three member federal grand jury, reporting directly to Federal Judge William J. Campbell, convened soon after the end of the convention to investigate the source of the violence. Convention week also became a target of an official federal government investigation, one that differed markedly in both tone and conclusion to Daley's "whitewash."

"A Communist Rag"

The Walker Report, as it became known, was a document that presented the findings of the Chicago Study Team, headed by Chicagoan Daniel Walker for the National Commission on the Causes and Prevention of Violence, which President Johnson created following the assassination of Robert Kennedy. The report, released to great media interest on December 1, 1968, was based on 3,437 individual accounts, 20,000 pages of witness statements, 180 hours of television film, and more than 12,000 photos. Among the study's major findings were that Mayor Daley had led his officers to believe that violence "would be condoned by city officials" and that police had "singled out" members of the media for assault and "deliberately" damaged photographers' equipment. Although the report outlined a high level of provocations by demonstrators, it blamed the police for their "unrestrained" and "indiscriminate" response. The report said that police violence was often misdirected against "persons who had broken no law, disobeyed no order, made no threat. These included peaceful demonstrators, onlookers, and large numbers of residents who were simply passing through or happened to live in the areas where confrontations were occurring." The actions by law enforcement, the study found, constituted a "police riot."[27]

Walker, then president of the Chicago Crime Commission, concluded that "individual policemen, and many of them," were involved in this "riot," where "some policemen lost control of themselves under exceedingly provocative circumstances." The team found that the climate of violence stemmed from Daley's rebuke of superintendent of police James Conlisk for the restraint police used in the riots following Martin Luther King's assassination. "While it was later modified, his widely disseminated 'shoot to kill arsonists and shoot to maim looters' order undoubtedly had its effect." Walker's report suggested that the shaping of this climate dated back to the April 27 peace march when police officers attacked demonstrators. The report concluded that when the city administration chose to ignore the violence, police officers believed that there would be no consequences if they used violence against protestors during convention week.

Movement leaders including Carl Oglesby received the report well. The veteran dissenter said that the report represented a victory for the proponents of "cool" over "hot" and "Yankee" over "cowboy," with Mayor Daley as the "chief cowboy."[28] Daley himself initially welcomed the bulk of the report, saving his criticism for the document's summary. Reading a brief statement to the press, Daley announced that eight officers were suspended for removing their badges, while a sergeant and three other patrolmen faced dismissal for the use of excessive force. Daley said that he was "pleased" the report found that only a minority of officers participated in the violence. "I'm proud of them," said Daley, "and so, I am sure, are the people of Chicago."[29] Indeed, throughout December, letters to the editor in the *Sun-Times* and the *Tribune* indicated strong support for the actions of police.

From the beginning, however, the report had vocal critics. Among them, many police officers who saw the lengthy document as a personal attack. "We are being piled on," one officer told the *Daily News*. "As far as I'm concerned, we saved the city from anarchists." One watch commander who overlooked 135 officers assigned to the corner of Balbo and Michigan on August 27 thought little of the report's findings. "I led my men in formation," said Ronald Nash. "They were beautiful. They conducted themselves as professional policemen."[30] Donald Yabush of the *Tribune* spoke to several unhappy officers following the report's release. "While most district commanders spoke freely, many policemen declined to comment unless their names were withheld," wrote Yabush. "The majority of these said the Walker report appeared to have been written by members of the United States Supreme Court or Communists."[31] Cop Ernie Watson read and hated the report. "It was a piece of garbage. They must have paid a lot of people to lie or slant the truth. It was a communist rag."[32] Joe Pecoraro, who was working in plainclothes in front of the Hilton during convention week, wonders how the commission managed to reach such a conclusion. "I don't know how they came to that. We didn't start it. They're the ones who came here and invaded our territory and started all the riots and stuff. We were only here to quiet it down—so how could you call it a police riot? . . . It was our duty, if I'm not going to do it, who's going to do it?" Even Tom Hayden thought the report was too hard on Chicago's police. "Unfair abuse has been heaped on Chicago police," Hayden would later tell the House Committee on Un-American Activities. "They shouldn't be blamed. They were acting on orders of Mayor Daley."[33]

The account also touched off a local political battle. Whereas some lauded the study as an accurate portrayal of events, many others thought it was unfair to those who wore the uniform. Chicago city Alderman Vito Marzullo blasted the report. "I think it stinks," said the pro-Daley councillor. "If they're going to handcuff our police and fire departments, we might as well turn the country back to the Indians."[34]

Walker staunchly defended his report, challenging critics by suggesting that the department needed to do more than suspend or dismiss "a handful of policemen. . . . The blue curtain cannot be permitted to fall. The responsibility to root them out and punish them belongs to the police."[35] Walker complained that more than three months had passed since the end of the convention, and no police officers had yet faced disciplinary action. In late November, the police Internal Inspections Division recommended the dismissal of four officers for the excessive use of force; the department had previously suspended nine officers; one other officer resigned rather than accept a suspension.[36] Walker also defended his use of the term, "police riot." He told members of the press that "If a group of demonstrators engaged in the kind of violence the police did, then it would be a riot. The fact that it was the police doing it doesn't change that."[37] The *Sun-Times* and the *Daily News* came out in favor of the document, the former hailing it as a "honest, unemotional account of the violence and provocation on both sides of the police lines" and a "record" of events. The *Daily News* wanted the department to weed out the bad officers, but added that the rank-and-file had "tacit sanction" to do what they did. The editorial saved the bulk of its criticism for police spokesperson Frank Sullivan. Calling him the "whitewash man" for the force, the paper called for his resignation.[38]

The pro-Daley *Tribune,* however, came out against the report, stating that there was no reason for onlookers and bystanders to be watching police quell disturbances; police were justified in any action they took and were the "victims" of convention week.[39] While the papers debated the report's merits, the *Sun-Times* directed the most criticism against the mayor, rebuking Daley for interfering with the police department and for denying permits to march and use city parks.[40]

A day after the *Sun-Times* editorial appeared, Daley and Superintendent Conlisk came out strongly against Walker's study. Whereas Conlisk stated that his officers' decisions were the "correct ones for dealing with law violators," Daley wanted the witnesses quoted in the report to be named. "I think it is the duty of Walker to come forward with identification and substantiation." An insightful cartoon in the *Washington Post* captured the city's increasingly defensive tone. The sketch depicted a burly Chicago cop ripping apart a copy of the Walker study while Daley stood behind holding a placard that read, "It's an excellent study—except for what it says about our police." Daley's only concession was his admittance that there had been "excesses on both sides."[41]

When paperback versions of the Walker Report went on sale in the Windy City on December 5, 1968, Chicagoans quickly snapped them up.[42] The thought of their fellow citizens reading the report bothered some in the department. "I think they're going to be hurt by it . . . internally," said Chicago lodge president of the Fraternal Order of Police, Joseph J. LeFevour. He added that the report would "hurt" the "feelings" of police. "It's our feeling that the police were almost as much victims as the dissenters." But though he defended the police, he blamed the mayor for setting his fellow officers up for a fall during convention week. "The police were put up to this by the city—Mayor Daley—and they got predictably out of control. That inference is clear in the report."[43] However, federal judge William J. Campbell, who was presiding over the grand jury investigation into convention week disorders, virtually dismissed the report as "personal opinions," suggesting also that the report's release may have been timed to influence the grand jury's findings.[44]

State treasurer Adlai Stevenson III, however, agreed with Walker's assessment of events. Stevenson said the real cause of the violence during convention week was that "the city refused to realistically accommodate peaceful assembly and protest. It closed the doors to participation, and then it had to cope with violent assembly and protest."[45] Although Stevenson agreed that the administration's policy led to the violence, pointing a finger of blame at Daley, he saved his sharpest criticism for police, calling them "storm troopers in blue"—men who had rioted and become "Chicago's shame."[46]

Police officers, whatever their perspective, naturally take exception to any characterization of them as unthinking thugs. Stung by the report's tone, some officers claim it not only portrayed them as aggressors, but that its conclusion did not reflect the body of the text. Officers say that in most cases they were defending themselves and their fellow officers from violence and lawlessness. They maintain that the real story of convention week has not been told. That is the one of unprecedented demonstrator provocation.

"They Were Throwing Bags of Shit at Us"

Without question, police put up with a level of abuse perhaps unsurpassed by law enforcement in the decade. Although officers stop short of calling the provocations "terrorism," many admit that their careers had not prepared them for the mistreatment heaped upon them during convention week. They also insist that more than a few protestors were involved in the behavior. Officers report that they were routinely spit on and were the targets of urine and excrement attacks. They take extreme issue with the charge that such reports are no more than urban legends or the retelling of the same event. Indeed, there are numerous independent reports apart from several credible police complaints of such abuse. Walker investigators quoted a U.S. attorney as saying that demonstrators used "the vilest conceivable language . . . by both men and women" and there were numerous "incidents of demonstrators spitting on police."[47] Along with spitting, officers faced balloons full of urine, excrement, and paint; other objects included sharpened boards, pieces of concrete and tile, rocks, bottles, bricks, eggs, and golf balls studded with nails. On a few occasions, officers were sprayed with corrosive liquids. Even Carl Oglesby recalled such incidents. "There were plenty of times when the cops were getting mad. Kids throwing bags of shit, screaming 'Pig! Pig! Pig!' "[48] Vice President Hubert Humphrey called them "hard core trained agitators."[49]

One of the provocations that police speak of with such vehemence was that protestors spit and swore at them. Steve Nowakowski remembers the incidents bitterly. "Put yourself in our position. Being spat on, being harassed and harangued, being shoved and pushed, have people charge at you and somebody get hurts. . . . Is it any wonder that the police had to take action?" Whereas police became accustomed to the almost generic "pig" insults, it was the personal attacks that made them feel that they had a right to do more than simply arrest unruly demonstrators. As Officer Herbert Bile vividly recalls, "Yes, I thought that we were ordered to prevent these people from controlling the streets and we were gonna use force to stop them, but we went to work on them when they crossed the line and they did that a lot. Some longhair told me that he'd like to fuck my daughter up the ass and I snapped. I grabbed him by the back of the neck and shoved my stick into his mouth. A couple of his teeth came out, half broken, and he was gurgling at me, making this sick, mewing noise, and someone grabbed me from behind, and I almost took a swing at him, but it was one of my own guys but he looked scared and confused—a rookie. I let the creep in my hands roll into the gutter and shoved the cherry officer ahead of me on to deal with the next pile of spitting and swearing scum. It just makes me want to hit something remembering it."[50] Other officers tried to remember the "Golden Rule," and tried their best to ignore the taunts. Says Terry Novicki,

We really just had to take it—we were warned all the time that they would say things to provoke us and to just forget it, it doesn't mean anything, pretend they're children, you know, "sticks and stones will break my bones but names will never hurt me." Well, easy to say, hard to do. And some guys lost it. I came close, and I just gritted my teeth, but imagine some punk yelling to you that they'd like to screw your wife; it's all you can do not to kick their brains in. And some of these punks, I'm sure, were drunk, or didn't have any brains, because you don't talk to a cop in Chicago or anywhere like that when he's got a gun and a stick in his hand, with the power to arrest your ass. Some guys [police] crossed the line, though, and that is never right. I'm not making excuses, but it's a little understandable, isn't it?[51]

Other officers cannot understand why they would need to put up with the level of abuse they faced that week. "What do you expect?" wonders former officer Grant Brown. "There's a point where it just doesn't make any damn sense; I didn't sign up to get shit thrown at me. And when bottles are thrown at your head, and those of your fellow officers, you have to act—you can't stand there with a finger up your ass hoping it will all go away."[52] Joe Pecoraro agrees. "We took abuse. One of the officers I knew—in fact, he was my nephew—they threw a paper bag filled with human defecation into his face. What was he supposed to do? Take it? That's abuse we took. But I think that we handled it well, though. We never got any big credit for it, though. We never got any battle medals for it. . . . It was a battleground."[53]

Given the violent circumstances and the threats they had received in the weeks leading up to the convention, many officers agreed that their acts of retaliation were reasonable. Says Jack Ochosky,

It is easy for some commentators and members of the media to come in after and say we acted like Nazis, and we started the trouble. Well, hell, they were marching, three or four thousand on the hotels, and we all knew what they said they were going to do when they got there. We knew of the threats against the delegates and the water supply, and the food, and their wives, and if you saw some of those people up close, like we had all summer and, hell, for the past couple of years, and the kinds of things they did in public, and the kinds of things that they felt about our country and our authority and our government. It was an insurrection waiting to happen. We believed what they said they were going to do, because we knew that they were capable of that and much more.[54]

Ochosky was certainly not alone in believing that the worst was possible. Sam McMaster recalls,

The reports leading up to convention week were taken seriously because of some of the trouble that took place in Oakland and Washington. We knew they were not coming in to have a love-in, like that Ginsbeal guy who was dressed up like the maharachi and chanting "Om" in the park. Those were just harmless idiots and faggots. Those people, if it had been only them, we would have left them alone, even to smoke their pot and all of that shit. But that motherfucker Hayden, and *Hoffman*—that Jew bastard, and these other fuckers; who's that guy, Jerry [Rubin] somebody or other, *those* bastards were up to no good before the convention week began. They set up shop here and were recruiting local kids to do their shit because they knew the city. That, let me tell you, got under the guys' skin. There were some who would have killed those bastards had they the chance, but a guy doesn't want to lose his pension over something like that.[55]

Even though police officers themselves admit they used harsh measures against demonstrators, they believed they could have done much more. "I think that we showed amazing restraint under the circumstances," says Mariln Rowden. "I mean, there could have been some very serious injuries, but we used mace to clear the crowds a lot more than we used batons." It is because of this that many police have always been stung by the type of criticism leveled at them by Adlai Stevenson. Says Steve Nowakowski, "That's the typical bullshit from the uninformed. People should know better than to make us into caricatures in those types of large crowd control situations. What do people expect? We are going to say, 'please, you nice young kids. Will you please not block traffic, hurl garbage cans, accost motorists, threaten to overrun police lines and hotel lobbies.' "[56]

The consensus among the police is that demonstrators were "looking for trouble." Says Harold Pacnik:

Look, they *knew* before they got here that at 11 P.M., that was it. They had no right to stay in the park after eleven. We gave them grace time to get out, as I remember. We didn't go in there with trumpets blasting at 11:01. At midnight they were all still there, getting pumped up, looking for trouble. And they could have dispersed in three of four different directions and went to where they were staying, but they didn't. It was strange that each time they left the park they had this funny way of heading right for the delegates' hotels, or to block the main streets, or march toward the amphitheater. I think that's the key and the focal point of trouble that week. They wanted to disrupt the convention more than they wanted to engage in peaceful protest. We had little choice than to wade in and get them separated as quickly as possible or, as I believe still, it would have been a hell of a lot worse than it was.[57]

Officer Norm Nelson agrees. "They started running away from us, sure, but after they got sneaky and tried to get past us to the Hilton, where there were rumors that they were going to burn the place to the ground, and toward the amphitheater. When we finally had to clear the streets, they start running and screaming and yelling police brutality—my *ass* it was. It was crowd control and there were thousands of those freaks."[58] Most uniformed Chicago police officers maintain that they were not singling out particular people for abuse but treated everyone the same way, despite charges that officers failed to discriminate between "troublemakers" and "innocent bystanders." They claim, however, that charges that they were trying to silence the leaders of the movement are baseless.

Henry Nostbakken remembers, "I mean, no way. Most guys who wore a uniform couldn't tell a Yippie from a cob of corn. We were not targeting anyone. Maybe the suits [plainclothes officers] were; I think they had their orders to follow particular people and hassle them, but your rank-and-file guy was on patrol doing his job and didn't give a damn about politics." Indeed, most observers have always claimed that cops treated everyone the same. As activist Dick Gregory pointed out, "If you were in the streets, and if you moved, you were a Yippie."[59]

Officers claim that their primary concern was protecting the city and "traditional American" values. Marlin Rowden recalls, "We didn't want any commies taking down the American flag, and personal insults were hard to take, but we have been given much too much credit for caring about the antiwar movement. It was not a conspiracy to shut them down. I think if there was some deliberate provocations it didn't come from us; look to those hardcore guys and others on the street during that week." Officer Dennis Pierson agrees. "It was fucked up from the beginning, and I think that some of those agitators hoped that there would be trouble. I heard after that they were laughing that we took the bait and that we made ourselves look like fools. It wasn't just the kids causing trouble out there—there were some real committed activists that were stirring people up— these adult agitators and maybe some of those government intelligence guys— God knows what their aim was. All I know was that there were a lot of agitators on the streets that summer."[60]

AGENT PROVOCATEURS

In the wake of the convention, it became apparent that not all of the agitators came from the demonstrators' ranks. Indeed, some of the agitator's were none other than members of the Chicago Police Department. Among the most visible demonstrators on the street during convention week was a long-haired biker with a long beard and a bellicose attitude named Big Bob Lavin. His intimidating demeanor was so impressive that Jerry Rubin decided to hire the native Chicagoan to protect him from police during the convention. While "protecting" Rubin, Lavin hurled both bottles and insults during numerous confrontations with police as he was being hit with tear gas and beaten with batons. When police arrested Rubin and Lavin, Rubin's bodyguard turned over the Yippie leader's tactical diary. Rubin's biker-bodyguard turned out to be thirty-five-year-old Chicago police officer Robert Pierson. Rubin appeared unfazed by the news. After posting $2,500 in bail, he remarked, "Well, at least he was a good bodyguard."[61] Pierson, who was assigned to the Sixth District Tactical Unit, worked as an undercover investigator for Cook County's state's attorney's office.

During convention week, Pierson passed information by getting the attention of one of the Chicago police intelligence personnel. "I would wad up the note, throw it on the ground, and they would come and pick it up," Pierson said. "On other occasions I would go down in the washroom in the field house and leave notes after again getting the attention of one of the intelligence personnel and leave the note behind the plumbing facilities down there." Pierson reported to deputy superintendent of police James Rochford. Pierson steadfastly denied that he had orders to shout or throw anything at police, and he denied any involvement in the infamous flag lowering incident that took place that Wednesday—a move that sparked an episode of intense violence. Pierson later told government investigators that he was the only infiltrator of which he was aware.[62]

Pierson wasn't alone, however. William Frapolly was a student at Northeastern Illinois State College and a member of the Northeastern Illinois State College Peace Council, the Chicago Peace Council, Student Mobilization, National Mobilization, and a member of SDS. He was also a patrolman in the Chicago Police Department. Frapolly grew long sideburns and hair as well as a goatee and a mustache, and he fit right in. Frapolly later testified during the conspiracy trial that members of the movement were planning to firebomb the Grant Park garage. Former police officers say that Pierson and Frapolly were simply two of dozens from their ranks embedded in the movement during the 1960s, and several members were "deep sixed" within various radical groups before and during convention week. Because of this, officers were aware that during confrontations on the street, they might inadvertently rough up some of their own. Mel Latanzio recalls, "It undoubtedly happened, because if you were good—and we *were* good—it made it practically impossible to tell who was who. But guys were smart, they knew how to sidestep the worst of the conflicts, but as far as looks, these guys played it to the hilt." Officers say, however, that they could not let themselves become too distracted looking for their undercover counterparts within the crowds. "We couldn't worry about that," recalls officer Ronald Adler. "Guys had a job to do, and they were there to gain and pass information and tell us what to expect and to let command know if they were planning to do damage or start fires, poisoning food and water—that kind of thing. They helped us a lot in anticipating events."[63]

Critics charged that undercover officers were doing much more than simply anticipating events, suggesting that undercover operatives helped to incite the crowds. The use of undercover cops to infiltrate protest groups has drawn sharp criticism with the charge that police deliberately helped to increase the level of street violence. Says activist Terry Southern:

[O]ne of the most insidious aspects of the entire police operation was the use of "confrontation provocateurs." These were cops dressed like hippies whose job it was to incite the crowd to acts of violence which would justify police intervention or, failing that, to commit such acts themselves. It is curiously significant that their artfully dressed undercover men were so flagrantly conspicuous as to be impossible to miss, not due to their appearance, which was indiscernible from the rest of the crowd, even the fact that they were encouraging violence, but due completely to the loud, lewd, tasteless stupidity that characterized their every remark and gesture.[64]

Police officers wholeheartedly disagree with such charges of deliberate provocation. Former officer Sash Sadowski speaks to a similar refrain. "Nothing could be further from the truth. Our guys weren't trying to make our job worse, or trying to get us to beat the crowd; a few guys can't do that, anyway. They [undercover cops] had to make it look good so they looked like the real McCoy, but that's it." Ray Mihalicz agrees. "Some are to have us believe that we put our own guys on the street to fight us, to rile us up so we would have an excuse to fight back and beat the movement. If that was the plan for police to do this, then why did we have to have our own guys to rile us up? Why wouldn't we just do what we wanted, because these provocateurs are still us." Still others concur. Says Tom Freeborn, "Is the argument that the violence was restricted to just a few people? Just how many undercover guys do they think we had? The people in the movement have always laughed at our undercover guys, that they could tell who we were right off from how we looked and spoke. If this is the case, then why in the hell do they think they can accuse us of instigating violence? Everyone would have known, laughed, or took photos of these people—and there would have been tons of media accounts of what these people did and said, but there is not any of this evidence. It's all been a farce." Steve Nowakowski, for one, has never been able to understand "all the fuss" over undercover officers, chalking it up to police routine. "It's just a way for our critics to blame us for their behavior and ours. Let's face it, every police unit in all times infiltrates the other side—it is as standard a police practice as a speeding ticket."[65] Indeed, this practice was part of standard police practice in Chicago, one that began well before the 1968 convention.

The Red Squad

The infamous Subversive Activities Unit, or "Red Squad," was part of the Chicago Police Department's intelligence division dating back to the 1920s when the department began spying on suspected communists and other dissidents. Over the years, the squad employed hundreds and perhaps thousands of spies and collected thousands of dossiers on Chicago organizations and citizens, much in clear violation of the First Amendment. These investigations, which infiltrated community and activist organizations, did not stop at simply monitoring dissident activities but included actual sabotage. The Red Squad collected "subversive" dossiers on a host of groups including the League of Women Voters, the United Methodist Church, the Catholic Interracial Council, Planned Parenthood Association, the Chicago Council on Foreign Relations, Jewish War Veterans, the National Association for Advancement of Colored People (NAACP), and the National Council of Churches. Political activists had their phones illegally wiretapped, and others found their files burglarized.[66]

It was no secret that the subversive unit watched members of the antiwar movement in Chicago throughout the 1960s and stepped up their surveillance during convention week. Officers infiltrated and monitored organizations and their leadership. One example of this infiltration emerged during the Chicago Seven trial, when Chicago police officer Irwin Bock admitted infiltrating the movement while assigned to the subversive unit. Bock managed to get close to the movement's core leadership after he successfully joined the Chicago chapter for the Veterans for Peace, sitting on the executive committee; he also became a member of the executive board of the Chicago Peace Council; and sat on the steering committee of the New Mobilization. During the trial, Bock testified against Tom Hayden and Rennie Davis, detailing the activists' plans for diversionary tactics to aid the march to the amphitheater. These tactics, Bock told the jury, included breaking windows, pulling fire alarms, and setting small fires to divide police and force them to either "watch the demonstrators or put down the disturbances." Bock testified that Tom Hayden hoped the city's South and West sides would rise up as they did in the April riots following King's assassination, causing trouble for the police.

The Chicago police, however, were not alone in working undercover and plainclothes operations during convention week. FBI director J. Edgar Hoover used the resources of the bureau's large Chicago office to place extra agents on the street. There was also additional members of the Secret Service in town to provide extra security for the vice president and other top Democrats. Officer Norm Nelson recalls, "We did it. The FBI was out there in large numbers before, that's no secret, Secret Service agents because of the party leaders and the VP in town, during and after convention week, and God knows who else."[67]

The "who else" has led to a great deal of speculation. A CBS Television News special broadcast in 1978, attributed to unnamed army sources, claimed that during convention week "about one demonstrator in six was an undercover agent."[68] Furthermore, CBS contends that on Wednesday night, at least 200 of those that blocked traffic and skirmished with police along Michigan Avenue were undercover agents. The revelation prompted Todd Gitlin to ask, "Just who wanted blood to flow in Chicago, and why?"[69]

Former officers scoff at such an allocation of resources by any government agency, especially the numbers attributed to CBS. Says Randall Bakker, "That doesn't make any sense—there were six to ten thousand punks on the streets doing battle during that time. If that report is right, there would have been 1,000 to 2,000 agents, at least, dressed in hippie garb fighting us outside the Hilton." Orrest Hupka agrees, "It's absolute nonsense," says the officer who worked in plainclothes near the Hilton the entire week. "People say that these phantoms were there to fight us so we would fight them back and kill the movement? How does that work? Force our hand against thousands of cops and undercover agents. These conspiracy theorists." Police suggest that such a level of cooperation with government agents from Washington would have been difficult, as they would not have been able to differentiate between a real protestor and a government agent. "There were rumors that some of the hippies were actually federal agents," says cop Steve Nowakowski. "This made some of the guys swing harder at the crowd."[70]

Although other officers also doubted the numbers, some members who worked in the department's intelligence division suggest that it was no secret that the department and military intelligence worked together closely before and during convention week. Furthermore, there are suggestions that some of those who infiltrated the movement may have been operating with their "own agenda." Intelligence agents were spotted on numerous occasions prior to and during convention week, monitoring the movement. On convention eve, while Hoffman was with the young men putting on a *wash-oi* show in Lincoln Park for the press and watching police, the Yippie leader suggested that there were military intelligence agents in the area. While on trial for conspiracy, Hoffman told the court in an offhanded manner that "The exciting part was when the police arrested two army intelligence officers in the trees."

Though most reports suggest that such agents were only undertaking "routine" surveillance, there are indications that the efforts went deeper. As far back as 1970, the *Washington Star* reported, "plainclothes military intelligence agents played a questionable—and still secret—surveillance role at the 1968 conventions." The *Star* indicated that the U.S. Secret Service borrowed agents from the 113th Intelligence Group based in Illinois that were engaged in intelligence operations on the streets of Chicago. Furthermore, there are suggestions that this sharing of domestic intelligence officers included a constant exchange of information between the 113th group and members of Chicago's Red Squad.[71] George O'Toole, a former chief of the CIA's Problems Analysis Branch, maintains that this contact was more than peripheral.

The Red Squad was in daily contact with the army's 113th Military Intelligence Group during the late 1960s and early 1970s, passing along intelligence reports and receiving a variety of technical assistance. The 113th also provided money, tear-gas bombs, MACE, and electronic surveillance equipment to the Legion of Justice thugs whom the Chicago Red Squad turned loose on local anti-war groups.[72]

In the aftermath of the clash between police and the peace marchers at the civic center in April, army intelligence officers, along with members of the subversive unit, were reportedly in the Chicago Police Department's central district lockup looking over arrestees, supposedly seeking "soldiers absent without leave and known Communists and Communist sympathizers."[73]

Although some officers may wish to play down the number of government agents on the streets that summer, the level of surveillance would have at least matched what is already known to have taken place during those years and certainly during a national party convention with the conversion of known radicals into the city. During that period, the FBI's Cointelpro program had agents hunting for "subversive elements" fulltime. There is now a significant record detailing the bureau's program, which kept both legal and illegal tabs on various groups dating back to the 1920s. Cointelpro, the FBI's secret counterintelligence program, which was designed to target and eliminate "radical" and "subversive" domestic political opposition, became public in 1971 with the release of secret files garnered through freedom of information suits, legal action, and the confessions of former agents. During the program, the bureau instructed its field offices to "misdirect, discredit, disrupt, and otherwise neutralize" targeted groups and individuals. During the 1960s, Cointelpro targeted socialist, communist, and leftist groups, and everyone from the Black Panthers to Martin Luther King Jr. As opposition to the Vietnam War intensified, the program monitored activist leaders, including Abbie Hoffman and David Dellinger.

Such connections between the Chicago Police Department's intelligence division and the FBI's large Chicago field office are understandable as their targets were often the same. There was no secret that the FBI placed numerous agents on the streets of Chicago investigating activities of suspected subversives, including those the bureau believed were planning to disrupt the convention. Cointelpro infiltrations were not only information-gathering strategies but efforts to breed dissension within the leadership of the movement against the war—specifically, between Mobe leader David Dellinger and SDS—with anonymous mailings that criticized movement tactics. The bureau was also watching the movements of Allen Ginsberg in Grant Park during convention week.[74]

Though the FBI was known for its skill in intelligence gathering, some officers and other commentators downplay the effect of the Red Squad during convention week, especially given its reputation for haphazard intelligence gathering. "The Red Squad, as far as I know, was paranoid about what the lefties and radicals were up to," recalls Orrest Hupka. "And some of their activities were over the top and civil liberties were trampled upon, that's for sure. But they were in no way trying to bring some of this stuff off just so uniforms could beat people up. That's totally ridiculous. They were up these guys asses with a tape recorder and trying to get dirt on them to prosecute them; they were not trying to help these guys just to raise a uniform crackdown. The Red Squad was what it was, nothing else."[75] Much of it was also an illusion. According to columnist Mike Royko, the Red Squad was often little more than a rumor mill. "The police Red Squad was snatching up every silly rumor as fact, passing it on to the *Tribune* papers, which printed them, and the city and rank-and-file policemen read them and became even more fearful." Royko suggested that the *Daily News* and the *Sun-Times* dismissed most of the threats.[76] The intelligence division's expertise in information gathering not only had its doubters, but lacked the ability to distinguish between legitimate dissenters and hard-core radicals. Members of the Red Squad, wrote Royko, were unable to "differentiate between a housewife marching for peace and a member of the radical Weathermen. Anything to the left of their neighborhood American Legion is a radical-revolutionary-Red."[77]

Police officers in general believe that too much has been made of the effectiveness of agitators used by government and law enforcement agencies during convention week. They believe such activity would have completely defeated the purpose of maintaining "iron control" that week. "I think it's stupid to think that Daley or the department would have put resources on the street to cause trouble," says Edward Nochowny. "He was looking to close down the demonstrations not inflame them and make them worse. Why do you think they had 5,000 National Guardsmen and other military, let alone put us all on twelve-hour shifts? That doesn't make any sense. I think that if people want someone to blame, look to those demonstrators who if there was a under-cover officer talking tough and talked about taking down the city, well, hell, they took them in with open arms."[78] It's a point taken by some in the move-ment. "Provocateurs by themselves cannot explain everything," wrote Todd Gitlin. "Provocateurs must move in a movement that tolerates their wild talk and wild action. The movement's own incendiaries, rhetorical and actual, colluded in a self-defeating system of rising rhetoric, rising militancy and the-atrics, rising publicity, rising government repression, and presumably rising provocation."[79]

Surveillance activities during the convention, however, gathered enough information not only to launch investigations and grand juries but to motivate some on Capitol Hill looking for the fingerprints of subversion. In late Septem-ber 1968, the House Un-American Activities Committee once again emerged, this time to investigate subversive involvement during convention week. The committee subpoenaed Tom Hayden, David Dellinger, and Rennie Davis. Among those providing testimony was undercover cop, and Rubin bodyguard, Robert Pierson. The Chicago police officer delivered the goods on the move-ment, accusing some of its members of conspiring to disrupt the convention, to embarrass the mayor, and to win support from the press by forcing confronta-tions with police. Pierson also testified that Rubin wanted to isolate a couple of police officers and kill them. Pierson suggested that SDS, Mobe, the Black Panthers, and the Yippies shared the goal of overthrowing the U.S. government.[80]

During his House testimony, Hayden tried to distance himself from some of his more provocative preconvention violent rhetoric. "I believe that violence should never be ruled out as a method of change; especially, I believe that a country that is burning up Vietnam has no right to lecture people to be nonvio-lent," said Hayden. "However, I believe also, *I always believed,* that Chicago was no place for a violent confrontation. . . . It became a violent situation because of the Chicago Police Department, of which this committee is, I believe, an extension."[81] When confronted with his inflammatory words in the weeks lead-ing up to the convention, and especially following the beating of his friend Ren-nie Davis on Wednesday of convention week, Hayden admitted that it was how he felt in the heat of the moment. "I stand by it."[82] Chairman and Representa-tive Richard H. Ichord from Missouri inadvertently revealed the tortured logic behind the committee's investigation when he expressed the body's tightrope act in trying to separate dissent from subterfuge. "Where," asked Ichord, "does legit-imate dissent end, and where does criminal disobedience begin?"[83] There were those who believed they knew the difference as the alleged criminal acts by movement leaders were put on display in one of the first show trials in American history.

"We Couldn't Agree on Lunch"

The conspiracy trials for the Chicago Eight, later becoming the Chicago Seven, were the result of indictments handed down in March 1969 under the 1968 antiriot act—crossing state lines with the intent to riot. The eight indicted demonstrators included Abbie Hoffman, Jerry Rubin, David Dellinger, Tom Hayden, Rennie Davis, John Froines, Lee Weiner, and Bobby Seale. Before the case went to the jury, police arrested Seale for the murder of Panther recruit Alex Rackley. Seale was already subject to four years in jail for contempt at midtrial. The case was separated from the others turning it into the Chicago Seven. In many ways, the trial was a farce of yelling, shouting, battles between lawyers and Judge Julius Hoffman, and repeated outbursts from both defense lawyers and defendants including the colorful Abbie Hoffman. The key charge against the accused was that they had entered into a criminal conspiracy to disrupt the convention.[84]

The testimony of undercover Chicago police officers, Irwin Bock, William Frappolly, and Robert Pierson proved to be the foundation of the government's case. The witnesses told the jury of plots ranging from disrupting traffic and sabotaging restrooms to "hit-and-run guerilla tactics." Pierson told the court of his first meeting with Abbie Hoffman, saying that the Yippie leader intended to "Fuck up the pigs and the convention." Pierson also implicated Rubin, accusing him of conspiring with others to pit police against protestors. The undercover cop testified that Rubin wanted to incite the crowd by forcing the police into a fight. "One of the ways to get this would be to start fires in the Loop that would cause the armed forces and police to come out in force, and it would show the people all over the country that we are living in a police state."

Pierson also charged that the Yippie leader incited the crowd to harm officers during the flag lowering incident in Grant Park:

Rubin began to yell, "Kill the pigs! Kill the cops!" The police car finally got out of the crowd and got over to in front of the flagpole. Rubin continued to scream, "Kill the pigs! Kill the cops!" The crowd pelted the officers with various objects as they got out of the car. On another occasion, Rubin began yelling "Kill the pigs! Kill the cops!" And the crowd picked up the chant and hollered the same thing.

Plainclothes officers also testified against Rubin. Chicago police sergeant Robert Murray, dressed in casual clothes, testified that on Sunday night, convention eve, he overheard Rubin utter, "Tonight, we're not going to give up the park. We have to fight them. We have to meet violence with violence. . . . The pigs are armed with guns and clubs and mace, so we have to arm ourselves [with any kind of weapon they could get]." Making matters worse for defendants was Judge Hoffman's decision to allow the inflammatory speeches made by defendants in the weeks and months leading up to the convention. The decision forced the defense to explain that Yippie threats, such as lacing the city's water supply with LSD, were only jokes.

There was little doubt that Hoffman, Hayden, Davis, and Rubin wanted to disrupt the convention. What became obvious during the trial was how unorganized their efforts to bring down the convention actually were. In the months leading up to Chicago, Mobe was plagued with disorganization, competing visions, and egos. The idea of a coherent, organized conspiracy emerging from this cast of characters appears unlikely. In the end, leaders were not able to decide on much as the movement headed to Chicago divided and disorganized. Defense witness Norman Mailer spoke to this reality. "Left-wingers are incapable of conspiracy," said Mailer, "because they're all egomaniacs." One memorable exchange managed to characterize the lack of strategy the movement employed for the Chicago convention. "Abbie Hoffman," asked a government attorney, "prior to coming to Chicago, from April 1968 on to the week of the Convention, did you enter into an agreement with David Dellinger, John Froines, Tom Hayden, Jerry Rubin, Lee Weiner, or Rennie Davis to come to the city of Chicago for the purpose of encouraging and promoting violence during the Convention week?" Hoffman was bemused. "An agreement? . . . We couldn't agree on lunch."

The court found all seven defendants guilty, sentencing them to prison terms for 159 counts of criminal contempt for their courtroom behavior, which included referring to the court and prosecution witnesses as "liars," "hypocrites," and "fascist dogs." The Seventh Circuit Court of Appeals later reversed their convictions. On February 18, 1970, the jury acquitted all defendants on charges of conspiracy, but found five defendants guilty for the intent to incite a riot while crossing state lines, violating the Anti-Riot Act of 1968. Each were sentenced to five years in jail and a $5,000 fine. The Seventh Circuit Court of Appeals also reversed these decisions in November 1972. The reversals were based primarily on the trial judge's "deprecatory and often antagonistic attitude toward the defense." The court also considered the troubling reality that the FBI had bugged defense attorneys' offices with the knowledge of both Judge Hoffman and the prosecutors.[85]

Despite the reversals, Rubin knew that the question of their innocence was a different matter. "We wanted exactly what happened. We wanted the tear gas to get so heavy that the reality was tear gas. We wanted to create a situation in which the Chicago police and the Daley administration and the federal government and the United States would self-destruct. We wanted to show that America wasn't a democracy, that the convention wasn't politics. The message of the week was of an America ruled by force. This was a big victory."[86] In the end, the veteran activist admitted, "We were guilty as hell."[87]

chapter 7

"Half the Power of God": Chicago in '68 Revisited

Some said that we lost control—that we overreacted, that we played judge, jury, and executioner. I don't think that's fair. Most of these critics weren't there. They don't know what really happened. We were threatened verbally, physically, psychologically. I don't think we lost *anything*. I think we won and turned back what was looking more and more like an insurrection—a revolution if you will. We stood on that wall, did our jobs, and the country today is a better place because of what we did even though that is difficult for some to accept. In the end, we did what we *were expected to do*. If we really had lost control of ourselves, there would have been a lot of dead hippies.[1]

For the protestors, the press, the politicians, and the police, the images of the summer of 1968 are entrenched in memory. While movement leaders wrote books, politicians published memoirs, and the media wrote and rewrote their accounts in news articles and editorialized in print and on television, the cops returned to work and licked their wounds. Since 1968, the police officers that served during convention week have been likened to the brown shirts of Germany in the 1930s—stereotypical thugs and malcontents. Indeed, the lasting image of these men is that they were henchmen or "storm troopers in blue"—representations promulgated in high school classrooms, college textbooks, and hardwired in the language. They are known as 12,000 police officers who literally went "berserk" on the streets of Chicago.[2] Given the complete absence of lost lives or permanent injuries, the term's use begs examination and explanation. Although media accounts and government investigators concluded that police actions during convention week were "unrestrained," the evidence suggests otherwise. As will become evident, police misdeeds and their fierce response to scrutiny created an image that, while incomplete and inexact, was one for which they were largely responsible.

"SPECIFIC INSTRUCTIONS"

Although the consensus has been that a "large minority" of officers "lost control" of themselves during that week, police apologists claim that at worst, a handful of officers "may have overreacted" in their efforts to protect delegates and party leaders from demonstrators. When pressed with evidence, however, several former officers acknowledge that, in fact, neither picture is true. They admit that something much more "uniform" took place that summer on the streets of the Windy City. "Let's face it; we knew we were supposed to thump the crap out of them, to teach them not to mess with 'Daley's city,'" says former cop Marlin Rowden. "We did it right across the board—evenly, a good whacking, but just short of causing lasting damage, so none of us would lose our pensions. I know this; lots of guys know this but won't admit it. And you know, so many of the guys hated those long-haired kids, they jumped at the chance to get at them." Officer Tim Markosky agrees, adding, "That's why there were few commanders telling the members to stop. Only those who began to realize how bad it would look under the glare of TV lights were telling members to back off. The rest were letting it happen. It was controlled and sanctioned mayhem."[3] These officers are certainly not alone in expressing this view. Says Hank Peterson:

I think that this was planned from the beginning. I don't want to point a finger at anyone directly, and not necessarily any commanders, but it was no secret that the city—I mean, boss Daley—wanted to see a situation where we were going to beat the hell out of demonstrators. He wanted it to happen, I was sure of it then, and thirty years later, I'm still sure. Although I can't prove it, people in power wanted it to happen just like it did.[4]

There is no question in the minds of cops such as Edward Nochowny that they were strongly encouraged to be ruthless with protestors and not let them disrupt convention proceedings. They also knew that they were not following normally approved police procedure. "We were supposed to hit them. . . . We broke the rules. One of our rules was always allowing people to have an avenue of escape, to disperse, and we didn't always do that, so that was clearly wrong. It was certainly the case outside the Hilton when the window caved in. Before that, the guys used mace pretty freely, and that broke another rule; we had them trapped, and we punished them. It's drilled into us that punishment is decided by courts not cops. So we failed there, but it's a bit understandable, I think, given the circumstances. We knew what we had to do. And that was to knock them around every chance we had."[5]

The "circumstances" came in the form of considerable pressure from city hall. Daley had lobbied hard in late 1967 to host the convention, maintaining that he would be able to control the demonstrations that everyone expected. The feisty city boss knew he could use the department to keep antiwar protestors in line and, if need be, teach the radicals, whom he loathed, a lesson. In October of 1967, Daley stated, "No thousands will come to our city and take over our streets, our city, and our convention." Aware of these circumstances, some officers claim that Daley used them as pawns so he could feel in control of his city during difficult times. Indeed, the veteran mayor bears a great deal of the responsibility for the excesses by rank-and-file police officers during convention week; his interference shattered the chain of command in the months leading up to the convention. Says Al Ogilvie:

There is no question that boss Daley was calling the shots. He ran the police department like an overlord. I mean everyone knew that [Superintendent of Police] Conlisk jumped when he called. And when his butt was kicked he kicked butts—and it all came from the top, and that was Daley. His attitude, or will, allowed commanders to let things like the beatings to go unchecked because it was their jobs and careers on the line if they were too soft on hippies, and they were not going to sacrifice that for some longhairs. Daley knew he could handle the fallout of charges of police brutality—he was impervious. The bugger ended up dying in office. He knew how the game was played.[6]

Indeed, according to some officers who knew him well, Conlisk was in a position where he would have to "jump" or resign. During the press conference following the riots after King's assassination, the mayor revealed that he, not his superintendent, was in charge of the police.

I have conferred with the superintendent of police this morning and I gave him the following instructions: I said to him very emphatically and very definitely that an order be issued by him immediately and under his signature to shoot to kill any arsonist or anyone with a Molotov cocktail in his hand because they're potential murderers, and to issue a police order to shoot to maim or cripple anyone looting any stores in our city. Above all, the crime of arson is to me the most hideous and worst crime of any and should be dealt with in this fashion. I was most disappointed to know that every policeman out on his beat was supposed to use his own discretion and this decision was [Conlisk's]. . . . I assumed any superintendent would issue instructions to shoot arsonists on sight and to maim the looters, but I found out this morning that this wasn't so, and therefore gave him specific instructions.[7]

The pressure put on Conlisk transferred down to all of those under his command. It was clear to the men on the street that they were not to behave during convention week as they did during the April riots. Former officer Kelly Fredrickson recalls:

You have to remember how that command to shoot and kill arsonists reverberated through the ranks. Now, I don't mean that we truly believed that he meant that any of us was going to be shooting to kill looters, but he was saying, "You buggers, you do your fucking jobs and don't let these bastards get away with what they did." Now it was given in the context of King's assassination, but it was directed at the force for what lay ahead in the summer—I mean the convention. Everyone knew that. It was no secret.[8]

A city administration official told *Time* magazine that the mayor was out for revenge after the rioting that followed King's assassination. "Daley went crazy. He couldn't believe that his city could do it to him."[9] Officer Will Gerald agrees, recalling that police faced the brunt of criticism—condemnation that led to subsequent police action. "Mayor Daley was pissed in April—that led to what happened during the peace march, and what took place on the streets during the convention. The word was out that officers were gonna get a few free swings—it was good for their jobs to do it, they were getting pressure from their communities, families, commanders, the mayor's office, and all of this played into many of the guys' own sense of hatred of the antiwar movement."[10]

This reality did not sit well with some officers who felt that the mayor's saber-rattling put them in a bad position that August. Not only had the police academy not prepared them for what they faced during convention week, but they felt that they were "set up" to fail because the mayor sought revenge for the carnage following King's assassination. "It was an unbelievable situation, and we just did our jobs under terrible conditions," says Walter Jorgenson. "I think that old Daley was looking for a butt to kick after the King riots, and the convention was a chance to do just that and make us the whipping boy."[11] Indeed, an editorial in the *Daily News* in December of 1968 expressed a similar sentiment. "There is powerful evidence, moreover, that those policemen who misbehaved did so in the confidence that such harsh measures were expected of them in dealing with demonstrators and the news media." The editorial suggested that it was time that Daley let the department govern its own affairs.[12] Soon after the convention ended, *Time* magazine arrived at a similar conclusion:

[T]he Chicago police department responded in a way that could only be characterized as sanctioned mayhem. With billy clubs, tear gas and Mace, the blue-shirted, blue-helmeted cops violated the civil rights of countless innocent citizens and contravened every accepted code of professional police discipline. . . . Had Daley been gifted with either humane imagination or a sense of humor, he would have arranged to welcome the demonstrators, cosset them with amenities like portable toilets, as the Government did during the Washington civil rights march of 1963. Instead, Daley virtually invited violence.[13]

Officer Walter Jorgenson, like others, was unhappy with the circumstances. "The situation was unworkable with the clearing of the parks, and no parades or marches, which goes against civil liberties. We all looked like assholes—I mean no one looked good coming out of Chicago that summer. It was the convention from hell." Many believed that they had been used for political ends and were placed in a position where it was easy to behave at their worst. As Tim Markosky points out, "It seemed clear to me at the time that we were played like a fiddle.

In that frame of mind, how we felt about those kids, anyway, it was easy for us to be rough and knock them around." Walter Jorgenson agrees. "That wasn't police work—we were actors in a city hall farce. It's still embarrassing. I remember thinking that we should have been on *Laugh In* except no one was laughing."[14]

The decision to enforce an 11 P.M. curfew, which prevented demonstrators from sleeping in the park for the first few days of the convention, still has some officers shaking their heads. They maintain that the actions led to several nights of unnecessary violence and made them "look bad." They suggest that by pushing protestors en masse into nearby communities such as Old Town and near the delegates' hotels, they were inviting spontaneous marches. The tactics, they admit, did not lend themselves to orderly crowd dispersal. "I knew—I think it was after Saturday or Sunday night, even before the convention began—that this curfew shit was not going to work," recalls officer Paul Juravinski. "It was impossible to disperse such crowds." Fellow officer Dale Jaeschke agrees. "It was damn near impossible, and every night it was the same thing. Remember, they hated us before we pushed them out of the park at curfew, and then we forced these kids into confrontations with our fellow officers on the street. Where in the hell where they supposed to go? We knew that a lot of them came here with no money and only the clothes on their backs. The kids had no place to go."[15]

Many officers believed they should have allowed protestors to remain and sleep in the park where police could have controlled the bulk of the crowds. "In hindsight, that would have been the easiest way," says Sam Nuberg. "But for some damn reason, Daley seemed to want to make it as hard on these kids as possible. There was no chance that this was going to go well. We should have let them stay in the park, and if they turned to march in great numbers on the convention site or the Hilton, then we should have shut them down, but we forced them, in a sense, to march. . . . I think the mayor was an idiot about some things. Very mule headed." Others believed Daley needed to look strong. "I think he wanted to have us knock them around, believing that was what people who voted for him expected," says Warren MacAulay. "He didn't want to look soft, and because of that, we had to do the dirty business."[16]

In the end, these officers did what they believed was right given the situation that summer. Indeed, Dr. Clifton Rhead of the Chicago Police Psychiatric Board did not blame the officers, but the influence exerted upon them by Daley and a bellicose administration. He believed, in the end, that most police officers still felt that they were right to protect the city. "I would expect that every policeman felt that he was doing his duty," said Rhead. Although there was immense pressure for these officers "to do their duty," by city hall, officers such as Joe Pecoraro were proud to serve under mayor Daley. "He was a great man," says Pecoraro. "I loved him; he stuck up for the policeman all the way. That was a man you wanted to work for. He stuck up for our rights."[17]

Many veteran officers, however, knew that they had to walk a fine line between satisfying some of the pressure they believed they were under and keeping themselves out of trouble. Interestingly, it appears that several officers on the streets that summer were in part going through the motions, getting "in their swings" and doing just enough "to make it look good" for the mayor and others who might have been just as happy with image as substance.

"IT WAS ALL A BIG SHOW"

Other than the numerous eyewitness accounts, the main source of evidence for police violence was the hundreds of photographs. Although there were some well-documented incidents of police confiscating film—some indeed captured by other photographers—there does not appear to have been any concerted effort by police to confiscate and destroy film and cameras. Had there been, officers obviously failed miserably in their task. Indeed, except for a few well-publicized cases, police officers appear to have not made the effort to seize cameras or chase down photographers for their film. Even materials that came into their possession after arresting a photographer were returned upon release. Thousands of photos taken by recognizable and highly visible members of the media easily survived, and hundreds went to press in newspapers and magazines across the nation.

The clearest evidence that police did not systematically confiscate film came during the arrest of *New York Times* photographer Barton Silverman. As officers dragged Silverman with one camera in his hand and another around his neck into a waiting paddy wagon on Tuesday night, photographer Fred W. McDarrah from the *Village Voice* standing only feet away captured his arrest on film. Neither photographers' film was touched, even though Silverman took a photo as a police sergeant was about to strike him with his baton. Police later released Silverman and his film; his photos depicting police violence appeared in the following day's *New York Times*. Indeed, such behavior was the norm, not the exception. Had police intended to bar the media from showing the public what officers were doing on the streets—a constant charge—police only needed to expose the film carried by those they arrested.

Interestingly, journalists did not report police mistreatment after arrest, either inside the paddy wagon or in the lockup, well away from television cameras and outside the view of the crowds. Indeed, all abuse by police took place in front of a maximum number of witnesses under the glare of television lights. Those in the movement also failed to make charges of abuse by officers after arrest. Oddly, Tom Hayden, arrested three times during convention week, agrees that police violence stopped after they were taken into custody. "I mean, a lot of abuse has been heaped on the Chicago police," Hayden said during the House Un-American Activities Committee (HUAC) hearings, "and it is not really their fault. They were obeying the orders of Mayor Daley . . . because when we went to jail, they didn't beat us in jail, they didn't act like irrational monsters in jail."[18]

Some police officers believe that this absence of post-arrest violence should have been obvious all along. As officer Gord Stensill suggests, "Most of what took place that week with arrests was a show for our bosses, not this 'spanking' nonsense. Yes, some guys may have wanted to give these bastards a shot or two—I didn't like them either, and have no sympathy for them—but most of this was just a big show for our bosses, to make them happy so we would not have them coming down on our heads. We needed to look like we were taking no prisoners; that means rough-looking arrests, and lots of them. It had to be obvious for people to see—I mean the city. But after we had them in custody, what's the point?"[19] Joe Pecoraro agrees, adding that officers merely wanted to keep people out of the Loop and out of their face. "We had compassion, we knew what they're doing, [so we told them], 'Damn it, stay off the street, quit making my job hard—you're killing me—you know, lay low. I'm going to keep you here, so here's your coffee, here's your baloney sandwich,' and that's it. That's what it turned out to be. We didn't treat them like they were enemies. Like we were going to kill them. I think that's why I don't think that no one really got hurt bad. We didn't go out there and beat them up like they said we did. If anyone took a lot of beating, we did."[20]

Officer Tom Freeborn is one of many who not only agrees with this view, but who is still at a loss as to why no one has questioned the absence of post-arrest violence—in police cars, paddy wagons, back alleys, or at the district offices.

No one has dealt with this before—why did not one of these people come out of jail claiming they were beaten? Where are all these people who we put the thumbscrews to after we arrested them? Nowhere, that's where, because they don't exist. Nothing happened to them *because it was a show—a sham for Conlisk and Daley* that we were not going to let this generation and the Negroes run free in his city and embarrass *his* city, and many of the guys were happy to oblige, but most of these people were later released and were released outright or with a slap on the wrist.[21]

More interestingly is that often these highly published arrestees not only did *not* receive a "slap on the wrist," they never made it to a Chicago police lockup. While miles of news footage and thousands of still photographs indicate that police hauled away more than 1,000 demonstrators that week, police records indicate that only 668 were logged in from Sunday, August 25, to Friday, August 30, or an average of 111 arrests per day. This average appears well below the obvious numbers of demonstrators thrown into paddy wagons and squad cars throughout the Loop and in Old Town throughout the afternoons and the long violent evenings.[22] Indeed, it appears that it had become a practice during convention week for some officers to "unarrest" demonstrators. "So much of what took place that week was an act," recalls one former officer. "We had a job to do, and that was to disperse the crowds and keep them away from the Hilton and the Sheraton, and that's what we did—we carted them up, drove them out of the Loop, and dropped them off." This practice was not isolated to a few officers, as at least a dozen units operating paddy wagons were involved in this unsanctioned activity. "Who wanted to do the paperwork on these guys? It was easier to kick them out away from the rioters," says another. "It calmed things down and got them out of our hair and saved a hell of a lot of work."

While saving them work, the activity also took the players away from prying eyes, cameras, and away from the scrutiny of the mayor and their bosses. "It looked like we were doing what Daley wanted, you know, making arrests and cleaning the streets, making it look good for the good citizens of Chicago," says one sergeant with twelve years on the streets. Other officers knew that the fight had gone out of their quarry after arrest and they felt no need to do more. "Some of the guys had got their licks in, some may have felt bad or sorry for them, especially the kids, and everything had calmed down a little and we really did not want anything more to do with them. So why bother keeping them in a lockup and writing arrest reports? So we unarrested them."

Other officers, though not participating in such actions themselves, knew that it happened. "Sure it took place; the numbers don't work, because we picked up one hell of a lot more than 600 people that week, let me tell you." Joe Pecoraro, already a sixteen-year veteran of the force in 1968, and president of the Chicago Patrolmen's Association, agrees that such activity took place:

[I]t's just a way to get them away from the crowd; you just fill up a wagon and drive them down a couple of miles and let them off and tell them to go home—get them away from it. You can judge them. You can judge if they're nice people and are caught up in all this stuff, they are all excited, things are happening around them so they get caught up in it; so the wagon would take them out and just tell them to go home. Try to get them away from those people. Try to get them away from the hecklers, because as long as they think they have a crowd behind them, they think they're like Tarzan. But by themselves, they are nothing; they're nobody.[23]

Many officers on the streets shared this sentiment. "There's no question. Look, we weren't monsters, we just needed to get some of these people away from the action; they calmed down, and we just let them go, let them walk back twenty blocks. By that time, it's over. And we were able to clear our heads, too." Another officer admits:

It was easier that way. We did what we were supposed to be doing—clearing the streets. But then what were we supposed to do with these kids? Most of them, we were just going to release anyway or with a charge of disturbing the peace, or on a silly curfew violation—might as well charge them with jay walking or littering. C'mon, we were Chicago police officers, not nursemaids. So we kicked them out on a side street. Some of them actually, we later arrested again. Once they knew we were not going to really hurt them, some of them became even bolder, so I guess some of that backfired on us.

There were a few moments of levity for those in uniform looking at the surprised faces of arrested demonstrators when the paddy wagon doors came open in an alley away from the action and they were told they were free to go. "We'd say, 'Get the hell out of here before we change our minds.' They'd just give us these dumb blank looks for a second before running away—their hair flying out behind them."

The main precaution police took was freeing their arrestees away from prying eyes and ensuring that they had not arrested any journalists. As one officer admits, "We were a bit careful, but no one would have believed it anyway." There's evidence, however, which suggests that the odd journalist may have been "unarrested," in a practice some officers verified as "station adjustments." One such revelation emerged in Daley's official city report on convention week violence. The report stated, "a reporter from *UPI* and a reporter from *Chicago's American* were arrested for violating the park curfew during this incident. This incident resulted in a station adjustment, i.e. no formal charges were filed and the arrestees were released. After being removed from the action situation and placed in the calmness of an office at the police district headquarters, both participants were able to see more clearly each other's point of view." Some officers find the "no formal charges" wording amusing, as arrestees once taken to a district lockup were either charged or released without charge. As Ray Mihalicz recalls, "My thinking is that somebody suspected something, and this was slipped in, in case the story got out; then they could say, 'Sure we knew about it, and we stated it right in our city report.' Someone was trying to cover their ass."[24]

Given the circumstances, the silence from demonstrators on the subject of unarresting should not be a surprise. Protestors would have been disinclined to admit that their arrest following a gallant struggle with Daley's police was not how it appeared, and that the police had actually just let them go free. As one officer points out, "None of these kids said a thing after, as being arrested by the big bad Chicago police during convention week was a badge of honor, a right of passage into the movement, so they were *not* gonna say that they just got kicked back into the street around the corner. Remember, we were *monsters*—that's what the press said. If we suddenly become human beings, well, that just doesn't fit the image some people were trying to portray us as. That's human nature. Things are often not what they seem."

The image that emerged in the wake of the convention, however, was one of police as irrational, "unrestrained" thugs, consumed in their zeal to attack and punish demonstrators and anyone else caught in their sites. This picture was the result of the biggest mistake police officers made during convention week: their decision to treat the nation's news media the same as those who had come to demonstrate their opposition to the Vietnam War. *The Politics of Protest,* a report submitted by the Task Force on Violent Aspects of Protest and Confrontation for Johnson's National Commission on the Causes and Prevention of Violence, pointed out the folly of such behavior given the concentration of media in the Windy City during convention week. "What is truly unique about Chicago, however, is not the occurrence of police violence," stated the report. "Rather, it is the extent and quality of media coverage given to the actual events."[25]

"The Press Were Hippies with Cameras"

During convention week, there was one journalist for every two officers on the street, as 4,000 members of the media from across the country joined with 2,000 local journalists to cover events. These individuals would play a significant role in determining the long-term image of Chicago and its police officers. Such a reality was not lost on the police department as just prior to the convention, Superintendent Conlisk distributed a brochure to the media, welcoming them to the city.

Welcome, newsmen! Welcome to Chicago, the City of "The Front Page," with an outstanding tradition of competitive journalism. Another tradition has been the excellent rapport between the Chicago police and newsmen.[26]

Prior to the convention, district, unit, and Task Force commanders were concerned with how their men would behave toward journalists. Some in the department were indeed nervous. Less than a week before the arrival of the delegates, Conlisk articulated the importance of maintaining good media relations in a message to his officers.

Within the next few days thousands of delegates, newsmen and visitors, will assemble here. Our responsibility is to assure them a safe and pleasant stay. We know what a magnificent city we have, what great people live here and what capable police officers we have. Largely by our conduct, these facts can be replayed to the rest of the world through the news media. To a substantial degree it will be on our actions that the rest of the world will judge Chicago and to some degree our nation itself.[27]

Indeed, Conlisk was more right than even he could have imagined. Though rough treatment of demonstrators was condoned, officers were expected to leave the press alone. It became apparent before the convention's opening day, however, that the media was a target. This was especially evident following the events of Saturday and Sunday. Demonstrators, too, had become aware that they were not the only mark. On Monday night of convention week, while *Newsweek* editor Hal Bruno was covering police chasing down demonstrators, one of the youths running by shouted, "Man, the pigs have gone wild. They're not after us, they're after you."[28] Several officers have long held that the press had made up its mind about the police before the convention began. "Oh, they were bastards!" says cop Eddie Kelso. "They just loved any opportunity to call the brothers 'Nazis' and 'thugs.'"[29]

Attacks on the media were not isolated incidents, but they were quite pervasive on four consecutive nights. Although there is no indication that such attacks were planned, there is much to indicate they were personal. As cop Victor Olafson recalls,

They were liberals who were against us from the beginning. And that was bad, because many of us moonlighted for them as bodyguards when they were doing dangerous stories—that occurred for years. I remember that in the '50s; a guy had a chance to make some extra money for his family. Why not? So we knew them and they knew us, and then they turned on us during the riots—you know, in the black areas and especially the way we handled the Vietnam people. That was personal. They were not loyal.[30]

Police complained that the press had turned against them long before convention week and no longer gave them the benefit of the doubt as they had done in the old days. As Paul Juravinski points out, "I don't know what it was, but they changed; even the old-time columnists who should have known better sounded like they were trying to keep up with the young punk writers coming out of college. Some of them admitted that they were criticized for being hacks and not going after the hard stories. We became the hard stories. That stunk."[31]

The city's officers were stung when their local media outlets gave them "bad press." Although they largely wrote off the national media, local criticism hurt. "They were looking for things to take photos of; trying to make us look bad for two or three years before that time," says Greg Parzanski. "I expected that from those damn liberals from New York and Washington, but not from our local guys. They were traitors to Chicago. To their own people." The national media indeed did ridicule the behavior of Chicago's finest. Tom Wicker of the *New York Times* mocked police concerns about demonstrators. "The Chicago police suggestion that the marchers planned to burn down the Conrad Hilton Hotel is ludicrous," blasted the veteran correspondent. "If you want to burn down a hotel, you don't march on it by the thousands, singing peace songs and holding hands."[32] Journalist Walter Schneir referred to police action as "terrorism."[33]

Former officer Norm Nelson says that the media's attitude shaped their reporting of the street action to serve their own purposes. "They'd zero in on any clash between an officer and a demonstrator and take their pictures. We noticed on Monday and even Tuesday—early in the week, anyway—that they only took certain photos, and they never took ones when shit was being thrown at us, or bricks came flying out of cars, or from the sidewalks." Officer Dennis Kaminski says the practice was deliberate: "It was clear that they were trying to create an impression of us to the world, and in many ways, they succeeded. I'm not saying that some of the members didn't lose their cool once in awhile, it was hard not to, but they [the press] were trying to make us look like it was planned—what's the word, *systematic,* and hell, it wasn't that at all."[34]

Police officers insist that there was no plan to attack members of the media, but their mere presence close to the action became infuriating. Will Gerald recalls, "They got right in there, you know, about an inch away, and we knew how they were going to report things—so no way were they just innocent bystanders." Other officers suggest that in the middle of a street battle, there is little time for people who get in the way. Says Warren MacAulay, "Things on the street happen fast—in the heat of the moment—things are quiet and then all of a sudden, all hell is breaking loose. We got the city, and the delegates, and people's places of businesses to protect, and they are rocking cars. If a reporter wants to stick his big nose right in the middle of the action, he is going to get bitten. It was nothing more than that. No one should try to make it something it's not."[35] Other officers admit that there was good reason to go after the press. "Yup, no question we had men who would have liked nothing better than to have the opportunity to tag a journalist or two after what they wrote about us," recalls Terry Novicki. "But remember, there was *cause;* what they wrote about us went beyond the pale; they were scripting things before they happened and saying why we were going to do what we did—unbelievable. So sure, some guys were gonna get their pound of flesh out there, but there were, as we say, *mitigating* circumstances."[36]

Some of these mitigating circumstances involved the way police felt about aggressive cameramen taking pictures of them while they worked, and how the camera itself became a weapon. Says Carl Moore, "A lot of people don't like getting their picture taken at the best of times, and even if someone you know is persistent and keeps trying to put a flash in your face, it's annoying." Others believed that having a camera flashed next to them was much more than annoying. "Try having that happen at night under pressure in a war zone, adrenaline pumping, rocks and bottles whizzing by your head, wrestling some two-hundred-pound guy to the ground while he's wiggling like an eel, and someone is flashing a strobe light in your face," says Norm Nelson. "When that happens, you take action, and yes, it's not going to be pretty. A flash bulb next to my face feels like an assault."[37]

Although police accused journalists of blinding them with strobe lights and making them easier targets, refusing to obey orders, getting in their way, and taking sides, the most telling complaint was that they could not tell them apart from demonstrators. The argument that officers were unable to distinguish between hippies and members of the press core speaks as much to the officers' attitudes as it does to their eyesight. "They looked and spoke the same, as far as lot of us were concerned," says Eddie Kelso. "The press were hippies with cameras, most of them, anyway, and they were after us." Even Daley used the same argument to defend his officers' treatment of the media, telling Walter Cronkite on Thursday night during convention week that police were not able to tell the difference between journalists and hippies. "They're in the crowd and many of them are hippies themselves in television and radio and everything else. They are part of the movement and some of them are revolutionaries and they want these things to happen."[38] Officers, such as Joe Pecoraro, however, do not believe that officers went after members of the media. "I don't believe that. They [the press] were hiring off-duty policemen to walk with them, to protect them; TV guys, they hired off-duty police. Things are hard, man; if you could make an extra hundred dollars a week for your family, so you give up four hours of the twelve that you were off." He does admit, however, that things had changed in police relations with the media since he came on the force in 1952. "We used to take the press on raids with us, on book joint raids and gaming raids; I had a captain who let one of these guys break a door down; but people change, the press changed, the Vietnam War changed everything. During the riots, [demonstrators] say to the press, 'here, we are going to turn this wagon over,' they were there, saying, 'go ahead, turn the wagon over'; they just wanted to get the picture. They used what they want to use. What sells papers? Bad news sells; they never print the good things police officers do."[39]

The Walker Report suggested, however, that the police had passed around the unofficial word early in the week that reporters were going to be targeted. Says the report, "A newsman was pulled aside on Monday by a detective acquaintance of his who said: 'The word is being passed to get newsmen.' Individual newsmen were warned, 'You take my picture tonight and I'm going to get you.' "[40] While it's clear that officers did not want their photos spread over the third page of the city's daily newspapers, the deeper concern was how the clashes between police and the media were ripe for distortion. As Marlin Rowden suggests, even though both projected stereotypes about the other, one side had the power to communicate images.

I think the whole press thing fit into both political views. To the press, we were the freedom-killing fascists, and to us, they were the liberal, pinko-communists. Boy, when that slimy Rather bugger from CBS got belted by a security guy on the convention floor, they couldn't play that son-of-a-bitchin' clip enough times. I saw Rather's head flopping on the news for nights. They made it look like he got whacked a bunch of times and he only took one little pop.[41]

Indeed, even some in the media realized the almost gleeful "piling on" that had taken place in some news booths while their colleagues were mixing it up with Chicago's finest. As *Time* magazine wrote a week following the convention, "CBS took almost grim delight in replaying in slow motion the decking of Dan Rather, somewhat as if he were Sonny Liston going down for the count."[42] Indeed, there are indications that the exclusive rights to putting on a good show in front of the cameras may not have been solely held by members of the police.

"It Was Only Ketchup"

The accuracy of some of the media accounts has been a nagging question since even before the end of convention week. Several officers complained loudly at the time that the media were helping to stage events with the sole purpose of discrediting police. To be sure, there was controversy concerning some of the action filmed by CBS cameras, following accusations that protestors on occasion faked injuries, ones that were staged with the cameramen's knowledge—a claim denied by the broadcaster. CBS investigated the incidents and found no evidence to substantiate the claims. One of the witnesses to a staged event, however, was U.S. attorney Thomas A. Foran from Chicago.[43] During its investigations, the

Walker Study Team found evidence of not only fudged reporting, but interference with police. Its report noted:

Camera crews on at least two occasions did stage violence and fake injuries. Demonstrators did sometimes step up their activities for the benefit of TV cameras. Newsmen and photographers' blinding lights did get in the way of police clearing streets, sweeping the park and dispersing demonstrators. Newsmen on occasion did disobey legitimate police orders to "move" or "clear the streets." News reporting of events did seem to the police to be anti-Chicago and anti-police.[44]

One police sergeant complained loudly at the time that demonstrators would engage police in conversation then suddenly feign an assault in front of cameramen, while others wore fake bandages around their heads. In one incident, as Senator Gale McGee of Wyoming and his wife walked into Grant Park, they saw a camera crew lead two hippie girls near some National Guard troops. When the cameras began to roll, one of the young women cried out, "Don't beat me. Don't beat me."[45] Joe Pecoraro believes that demonstrators worked in tandem with the media to distort the images from the street.

I worked the Hilton in plainclothes. [Protestors] were throwing those big silver coffee pots out the window. And they would hit the sidewalk and bounce up about 10 to 12 feet, and they were throwing pillows and mattress covers out the window to the people who wanted to sleep in the park. So the management of the hotel asked if a couple of policemen could escort them up to the tenth floor. So my partner and I went up with the manager to the suite . . . there must have been about seventy-five to eighty people in there. So the manager told them they would have to leave, and if they didn't, they'd be put out. . . . We could tell they were smoking pot. We couldn't prove that they were the ones that were throwing the stuff out the window, but we knew that was the room it was coming out from. So we went down and the manager told us we would give them an hour or two to get out. So we reported to the captain what was up there, and about fifteen minutes later these reporters all gathered around the elevator with their flashbulbs and everything and I was wondering what the heck was happening. . . . Then Eugene McCarthy comes out with five or six people, boys and a couple of girls with him, and they were bandaged up . . . blood stained, and one fell on the floor and [McCarthy] started hollering that we went up there and beat these people up and were throwing them out of the hotel and they were his people. We know we didn't do nothing, my partner and I, so I was in plainclothes, so I reached down and grabbed the bandage off one of their heads and I smelled it and it was nothing but ketchup; I threw it away and I walked out of the hotel. That's what it was. A big show with a bunch of reporters around snapping pictures . . . like it was all prearranged or prestaged. Like they notified the press that we are coming in, and "this is what we are going to be doing" and the press is there waiting. The press knew what was going to happen in front of the Hilton a day before it happened, because they were there a day and a half before building these platforms with these cameras. How did they know what was going to happen there? . . . Sometimes I wonder if it was all just a big show. But who suffered the consequences? The police officers.[46]

Issues such as these cause former officers the most resentment. Says Steve Nowakowski, "The real problem with the photographers and why they got some abuse out there was because of how those photos were used the next day in the paper—it could be used falsely, to create a false image, a moment in time that could cost an officer his job." Ken O'Connor made the case for several officers: "The media were not our friends—let's not fool anyone—and these images can skew reality."[47]

The image of Chicago had taken some hits as convention week came to a close; a psychiatric convention that was to be held in the city was canceled, a move that prompted one of its members to complain that the nation had been duped by the media into having a false image of events. Psychiatrist S. I. Hayakawa wrote an open letter to complain abut his colleagues' knee-jerk reaction:

In the same way we learned not to believe everything we read in the newspapers we've got to learn not to believe everything we see on television. It gave the impression that starry-eyed, idealistic youths were being beaten up by the cops without provocation. Actually the leaders were tough, cynical career agitators experienced in utilizing television to their own ends . . . they'd goad the police into violence. They trick the networks into carrying into millions of homes the message that police are public enemies.[48]

Even some commentators who were critical of police behavior realized that television reports were not always capturing an accurate image of street action. Carl T. Rowan, an African-American columnist for the *Chicago Daily News,* knew there was something wrong in what he saw on television.

[C]onscience forces me to report that something of both tyrannies were at work at Chicago. I was an eye witness throughout last Wednesday night's melee around the Conrad Hilton Hotel. I saw the fringe element of the protest groups harangue, curse, spit and make physical forays into the police ranks until they produced the violence they wanted. One protest leader said his group had come to show up the police "as the brutes they are." Adequately provoked, the police obliged them. Television reported incidents that I had seen and I felt TV was misleading in a way that made the cops look beastly and the beaten young people look like harmless and helpless victims of a Nazi storm troopers brigade.[49]

Newspaper journalists also did not always present an accurate image of what took place—one that perhaps owed less to reality than to emotion. Tom Wicker of the *New York Times,* and among the most outspoken in the media, was outraged by police behavior, suggesting that all demonstrators that week were harmless victims. "The truth was these were our children in the streets, and the Chicago police beat them up," Wicker wrote following the convention. However, out of the 668 recorded arrests, only sixty-four were under the age of seventeen; 221 were between the ages of eighteen and twenty, and 378 were over the age of twenty-one.[50] It is a fact that still raises the hackles of police officers. "Cronkite said that we were beating up our children downtown—they weren't children," says Joe Pecoraro. "Why don't you come down and see these children with handcuffs and chains in their hands with these big clubs—was that their children? We weren't beating up nobody; we have children of our own. They tried to make us look like villains, like we're the Gestapo running around beating these kids up. We were just trying to stop them from getting into the neighborhoods where people were living were with their families."[51]

For police, there were reasons to fear what was taking place on the streets of Chicago. By 1968, murders topped 645—an all-time high in the city, up from 390 in 1964 and 330 in 1959. The reality of a rising crime rate and an increase in disturbances involving riots and antiwar protests contributed to the decision in March 1968 to require patrolmen to carry mace on their belts capable of firing forty-five, one-second bursts.[52] Given the circumstances, police saw themselves not as a liability but as protectors of their city, defenders of what they saw as a dangerous movement that was ruining the nation. "Lots of guys really did not only hate them, but there was fear there and we were willing to do Daley's bidding because that generation did everything in their power to destroy our culture and ruin our country," says Mel Latanzio. George Horsley feels similarly: "They were taking over; they were embarrassing us and our city. It was going on for years with the antiwar movement and the drugs, and someone needed to stand up." Many officers felt that if they didn't take a stand, a dangerous subversive culture would take over the nation and their city. "We did step up when they tried to subvert the Democratic Party that week," says Victor Olafson. "They were subverting the entire decade, and the future of the country was at stake, and our city. The country was really going to hell; it was becoming a place that we no longer recognized."[53]

"Drugged-Out Animals"

A week before the convention began, *New York Times* journalist J. Anthony Lukas, in Chicago to cover the convention, referred to the city as "the perfect place for the elemental clash." Lukas, like several of his learned colleagues, predicted "a clash" resulting in "some very nasty violence."[54] The convergence of the Chicago police and the 1960s youth culture, wrote Todd Gitlin, was an explosive "chemical reaction."[55] Indeed, while Yippie Abbie Hoffman carried his "flower in a clenched fist," many police carried their nightsticks with a similar verve.[56] During convention week, it was clear that officers not only detested protestors, but in some cases actually feared their unpredictable behavior. By the summer of 1968, the successive string of altercations between police and antiwar activists was due to not only a generational gulf but a cultural disconnection between those in uniform and the growing throngs of dissenters. Cop Steve Nowakowski recalls his experiences during those years with particular resentment: "Those stinking long-haired bastards; they not only stunk but they were dangerous and they were coming after us right from the beginning. They were not pacifists. There were a lot of lawbreakers, and they were indeed threatening to delegates and to the hotels. And God knows what they're on. Their eyes were wild."[57]

The unpredictable nature of demonstrators had police on edge as the week progressed and the crowds swelled in size and anger. That some in the crowd were high on drugs made officers more than uneasy but colored the way they viewed everyone. Demonstrator behavior played into some of the worst stereotypes police had of the hippie culture. As Henry Nostbakken clearly recalls, "It was scary to get close to those kids. Their faces were flushed; their eyes were glassy. They looked at you, but it was as if they were looking right through you—and up close, you could smell the dope on them. And they were saying just some gibberish sometimes and then yelling insults and taunts, the next." Many officers complained that the constant taunts of "pig" and "killers" came from drug-induced minds. Worse yet, they believed that there were agitators in the crowd that were getting the younger more naive demonstrators high so they would attack police. "There were these hippie pushers who were getting the kids to do drugs and then getting them to attack us," says Lloyd Matthews. "I heard it was going on but never saw any of it directly. But some were just goners, stoned out of their minds as they were rushing us, throwing rocks and spitting on us. It was hairy. There were some real freaks out there." Police often wrote hippies off as a "lost generation." One officer at the time told a reporter for the *New York Times* of his surprise seeing them all together on the streets. "I never saw anything like it. You can't tell the boys from the girls. They wear their hair alike, and they both cuss the same."[58]

Such views led to not only a loathing but a fear of the movement. Brian Ramsey was one of many officers who didn't know what to expect when dealing with antiwar and counterculture crowds. "We were the frontline troops, and they were so drugged out, like they were these drugged-out animals; it was scary." Former officers maintain that it was this fear, in part, that motivated them to move against the crowds and break larger groups into smaller ones on the sidewalks or streets. They believed that they had to prevent demonstrators from moving around in force. Says Kelly Fredrickson, "We didn't want them moving as a group, their eyes were damn scary, and they became mighty brave when they were in a pack. God, you didn't know what the hell they were going to do; so we broke them apart, dispersed them into small groups where they couldn't do much harm." For others, dread was mixed with simple disgust. Says Sheldon Bartowski, "They were ugly, dirty little shits who would hit you when you turned your back, and then they ran like pussies yelling 'police brutality.' " Steve Nowakowski simply states, "I think that many, if not all, of those bastards were fixin' for a fight."[59]

Contributing to the hostility was that officers seldom made distinctions between hardcore agitators and activists and counterculture enthusiasts. Virtually anyone with long hair and sandals was a subversive. The one-dimensional view led to some of the baser stereotyping of anyone on the streets. "Have you ever stared into the eyes of a wild animal?" asks former cop Hank Pacnik. "Have you thought you saw intelligence or the ability to reason, and then thought you were safe? So you slip your fingers between the bars of the cage only to get them bitten. Well, that's the way it was with those SOBs. What we did was swing through those bars to get a piece of them before they got us."[60]

While this is a striking view, it is not uncommon. Indeed, several other officers echo these thoughts, adding that they were involved in a generational and cultural war on the streets. Says officer Eddie Kelso, "They were all into free love and peace, yeah right! That was a crock from the beginning. They cried out against the Vietnam War but were waging their own kind of warfare right here at home. And their enemies were real Americans who worked hard every day to build this country, who paid their taxes, kept their neighborhoods clean, and wanted a better life for their children than they had themselves. Well, the whole stinking generation had declared war on that." Randall Bakker agrees. "They proved they were dangerous, I think history has proved that, even though some thought they looked like peaceful beatniks." Ernie Bellows, for one, thought that it was time to fight back. "We, at least I, knew that they were serious, that given the chance, they would bring us to our knees—sorry, but the prone position is not for me. They were going to do it to the entire country. We were going to fight back."[61] Joe Pecoraro believes that officers had a right in certain circumstances to retaliate, but that it does not mean that the force lost control. "I don't think that the whole group lost control, maybe an individual. One policeman, they threw the bag of human waste right in his face—splattered all over his face—that guy lost control; he broke rank and went after that guy, and boy did he get it. I don't blame him a bit, and maybe the policemen around him helped him, but the whole line didn't go berserk. We're talking two hundred—two hundred and fifty policemen; they didn't all go berserk. But there are certain circumstances where enough is enough."[62]

The street battles at home, combined with a failed war in Southeast Asia led to not only worry for those in uniform, but depression. Believing that things in the nation "were falling apart," some officers had difficulty watching the evening news, as it reminded them too much about what they faced each day. "I couldn't watch Cronkite anymore; it had gotten that bad," says former cop Dennis Pierson. "I saw it on the news and I saw it on the streets every day at work. Then we were shoved into the teeth of that movement [during the convention] and it was like the infantry; we were on the leading edge—the front lines of the war that was taking place at home." George Horsley felt the nation was becoming "a scary place," to the point where he didn't want to get out of bed some mornings. "I wanted no more of it and almost quit, but there was a family to think of. It had seemed that the nation was rapidly losing its moorings." Cops such as Grant Brown, however, knew that they could not give up, as they feared the nation would collapse before the end of the decade. "We were the warriors, the combat troops for domestic warfare, and what we did was necessary. I truly believe that these people were trying to cause an insurrection, and they were trying to bring down the government. They were not all peace and love—far from it." Near the end of the convention, the words of one young black woman managed to encompass police attitude toward the movement. She told the *New York Times* that the police beat demonstrators "because they don't consider them to be white. They think those hippies are another race or something."[63]

"Pigs in Police Uniforms"

Raging stereotypes were not relegated to the police, as journalists and movement leaders often held similar views of those in uniform. The following observation of police by the assistant editor of the *New Left* is as illuminating as it was common. "The Chicago police, with their thick heads, small eyes, and beery jowls, actually resembled pigs," wrote Jack Newfield during convention week. "And they surely behaved like animals in this city famous for its stockyards."[64] Jimmy Breslin's comments, like other members of the media, were not always confined to the officers' police work, but of them as people. "Nobody has ever accused a policeman of being a social genius," wrote Breslin. "A policeman is a working man who takes a job that is essentially a lousy job. The working man takes this job because of the pension. So you have a man working a job simply because he wants to get a pension in twenty years. A man who does this is not happy or imaginative. Police as a rule are poorly read."[65] Breslin's attitude was tame compared to McCarthy volunteer and writer William Styron. "I noticed that Daley, or someone, had allowed them to smoke on duty. Constantly stamping out butts, their great beer guts drooping as they gunned their motorcycles, swatting their swollen thighs with their sticks, they gave me a chill, vulnerable feeling, and I winced at the way their necks went scarlet when the hippies yelled 'Pigs!' "[66] Activist Doug Dowd was disgusted with the cops' "big guts." He likened their behavior to "mad dogs."[67] Jene Genet, a French playwright writing a piece on the convention for *Esquire* wrote, "Chicago has these policemen's bellies which are so fat that one must presume that they live on the slaughterhouses required by the city which resembles three hundred hamburgers piled one on top of the other, and daily consumes three million hamburgers. A policemen's beautiful belly must be seen in profile. . . . Its owner wheedles it, fondles it with both his beautiful but heavy hands. . . . Suddenly we are surrounded by a sea of policemen's bellies barring our entrance into the Democratic Convention."[68] William Burroughs compared police officers to dogs. "The police acted after the manner of their species," said Burroughs. "The point is why were they not controlled by their handlers? Is there not a municipal ordinance requesting that viscous dogs be muzzled and controlled?" Genet told a gathering during the convention that he found it "perfectly natural that dogs wanted to bite and even to eat hippies, students and journalists, and it does not displease me that white Americans find themselves threatened by these dogs who for the past 150 years have done the same thing, with even greater brutality to blacks. It is, therefore, good that American dogs are trying to devour American whites."[69]

To Yippies like Abbie Hoffman, police officers were "fascists." As a result, there was a belief in the movement that activists could say whatever they wanted to officers on the streets. Hoffman was proud that he had his "cop talk" down to a crude art form. "When I get pissed at cops," wrote Hoffman, "it goes something like this: 'You fuckin' fag-ass cocksuckers! You commie pimps! You Jew-bastard fags! You get your fuckin' paws off me, you bunch of cowards! I can kick your fuckin' ass in! I'll bet you fuck each other up the ass. How come you guys never get laid?' That's cop talk. That spooks them."[70] As was seen during convention week, such invective was not specific to Yippie leaders but common to the crowds on the street. The police were reduced to "fascist animals." The only media defender of the Chicago Police Department during and after the convention was the editorial staff of the *Chicago Tribune*. "Chicago did not invite these street fighters to come here in the hope of disgracing the city," said a front-page *Tribune* editorial following the convention. "The movements they represent did not originate here, but in Berkeley and New York. A sick cause mustered by sick people."[71]

Such were the polarized attitudes in the summer of 1968—two competing visions of America—differences seen so vividly and violently during convention week. To Lance Morrow, Chicago represented "the Big Bang of the American culture wars." He added:

In front of the Hilton, on Michigan Avenue two sides of America ground against each other like tectonic plates. Each side cartooned and ridiculed the other so brutally that by now the two seemed to belong almost to two different species. The '60s had a genius for excess and caricature. On one side, the love-it-or-leave-it, proud, Middle American, Okie-from-Muskogee, traditionalist nation of squares who supported the cold war assumptions that took Lyndon Johnson ever deeper into Vietnam. On the other side, the "countercultural" young, either flower children or revolutionaries, and their fellow-traveling adult allies in the antiwar movement, the Eugene McCarthy uprising against L. B. J., people whose hatred of the war in Vietnam led them into ever greater alienation from American society and its figures of authority.[72]

Sun-Times' reporter Hugh Hough observed that there were two "unyielding forces" in Chicago. "In retrospect, it is clear that a confrontation was inevitable between the forces of law and the radical young." To playwright and delegate Arthur Miller "There were two Americas in Chicago, but there always are. One is passionately loyal to the present, whatever the present happens to be; the other is in love with what is not yet."[73] For others, such as columnist Max Lerner, Chicago signified a reality that needed exposure. "This is the America I have seen and come to recognize as I have crisscrossed the nation in the last few years. It is better to have it shown in full glare here in Chicago than have it hidden from view behind contrived public relations veils."[74] The full glare of that reality was difficult for many to accept. Indeed, as Arthur Schlesinger Jr. pointed out, "Americans are today the most frightening people on the planet."[75] This sentiment played directly into the hands of nihilist Yippies like Abbie Hoffman who wanted to turn the system upside down. "Chicago was, as I have stated before, a Perfect Mess. . . . In a Perfect Mess only the System suffers."[76]

During the Democratic National Convention, the lasting image of the system's protectors did indeed suffer. Police abuse of members of the media did more to shape the history of that week than any other event. It was clear that journalists truly believed that police had "lost control" of themselves, and if not, deserved any characterization attributed to them. Walker investigators, who read the hundreds of news stories and other media accounts, agreed. Whereas Superintendent James Conlisk undoubtedly knew what his men had done that week, he also understood that their behavior was far from unrestrained. "To speak of a 'police riot' is to distort the history of those August days," said Conlisk following the convention. "The world knows who the rioters were."[77] To be sure, it was not just a majority of Chicagoans who wholeheartedly backed police, but Americans polled at the time also agreed with the views of Chicago's top cop. Following the convention, the *New York Times* reported that a nationwide poll conducted with 1,000 people overwhelmingly supported the police. Television networks were also inundated with mail condemning the media's coverage and interpretation of the convention. Letters to CBS were eleven-to-one in favor of police action.[78] A Gallup poll two weeks after the convention suggested that Americans supported police fifty-six percent to thirty-one percent.[79]

In a survey conducted by the University of Michigan two months later, 30 percent of respondents believed police used the right amount of force, while 19 percent thought it was too much, 25 percent believed police used too little force, and 24 percent did not know enough to form an opinion.[80] Interestingly, only 36 percent of declared McCarthy supporters thought that police used too much force.[81] The results were not exactly what Yippies such as Abbie Hoffman wanted to achieve. "We want to fuck up their image on TV," Hoffman told Walker investigators. "It's all in terms of disrupting the image, the image of a democratic society being run very peacefully and orderly and everything according to business."[82] It was clear, however, that the image that received the most damage in the eyes of Americans without press credentials was the antiwar movement; the public sided with the police. As Todd Gitlin observed, "As unpopular as the war had become, the antiwar movement was detested still more—the most hated political group in America, disliked even by most of the people who supported immediate withdrawal from Vietnam."[83] Pacifist David Dellinger, in retrospect, was saddened by Chicago. "The Chicago Convention protests were the test and the Movement failed the test."[84] Years later, Jerry Rubin spoke of the folly of the situation. "In the summer of 1968 a group of us went to Chicago to try to get a police permit for a revolution. . . . We didn't get a permit."[85]

The story from that week, however, did not come from the living rooms and the kitchen tables of America but from media images and government reports—results shaped largely by police officers unable or unwilling to cope with the scrutiny necessary in a functioning democracy. Their attacks on the press set in motion a journalistic backlash—a profession that responded to mace and night-sticks with typewriters and television reports. Journalists, understandably upset with their treatment at the hands of police, took a personal approach to the reporting of events, something that colored all subsequent images, descriptions and depictions of Chicago's convention. Some observers at the time wondered what the fuss was about. "We hear a lot about brutality but not one word about the television network brutality," said Lady Bird Johnson's press secretary, Elizabeth Carpenter. "After listening to the wails of anguish these last few days over television from some of my friends in the press about getting shoved about and spoken to roughly, all I have to say is: Try a real combat zone."[86] Thirty years later, police officers are still upset with what they call the "myth of 1968." "The American people watching on TV knew that despite what they were being told by the talking heads on CBS, it was the longhairs on the street that were rioting and we were doing our jobs," says Terry Novicki. "But they wrote it all up like we were these irrational monsters, and that's because they got a few shots on the streets; they told a big fib—the story that we rioted on the streets that summer."[87]

"HALF THE POWER OF GOD"

There was almost a palatable note of relief in Mayor's Daley's voice as the veteran city official uttered the words, "no one was killed" in the wake of convention week. Jimmy Breslin, a contributing editor for *New York Magazine* and an outspoken critic of police that week, was at a loss for why police didn't manage to kill anyone. Believing that the cops had lost complete control of themselves, he remained puzzled. "So these pigs in police uniforms punched and gassed and clubbed and I still don't know why they didn't shoot," wrote Breslin. "Certainly, they wanted to."[88] Such attitudes have former cops shaking their heads. They claim that the press never examined their own perceptions. "So you have these people who write these stores and say that we lost control of our emotions but somehow failed to use our weapons," states an incredulous Steve Nowakowski. "How's that work, exactly?" Indeed, far from losing control, many police insist that they were actually acutely aware of the line they could not cross. Says Carl Moore, "We weren't crazy; nobody wanted to kill somebody and run the risk of losing their pension. We all had families to think of." Officer Tim Markosky agrees. "We knew just what we could get away with short of causing permanent injuries with batons and mace. We understood that we were to teach the antiwar crowd and maybe even a generation a lesson. It's what everyone here wanted us to do. But no one lost control; you could not afford to with a .38 strapped to your hip."[89]

Following the convention, journalists ridiculed police for finding it necessary to take tough action to keep the crowds from harming top Democrats and party delegates. A common editorial comment was that there was no evidence to suggest demonstrators had any nefarious intent. "The odd thing is that the Chicago police took so many of the demonstrators' boasts seriously," suggested *Time*

magazine. "Even now, they fail to understand that if an army of 10,000 genuinely violent 'revolutionaries' had descended on the city, many policemen and
bystanders would have been killed."[90] Although the article's point is sound, it
fails to account for the opposite—if 12,000 police officers on twelve-hour shifts
with guns and nightsticks had actually "lost control" with "unrestrained" actions
during convention week (as government and media accounts repeated again and
again), it would have resulted in the deaths of scores of demonstrators, "onlookers," and journalists. As a former New Orleans police officer put it, a cop carries
"half the power of God" on his hip—the power to take life in a moment. It was
a power an "out of control" and "berserk" Chicago police force neglected to
exercise at anytime during convention week.[91] "If we were the 'goons' that they
said we were, why did no one get badly hurt, let alone killed during convention
week?" asks cop Len Colsky. "People need to remember that if we were what
they said we were, then bodies would have been strewn all over downtown
Chicago."[92] Cop Sheldon Bartowski points out that people never examined the
meaning of the terms they used to describe police officers or Chicago in 1968.
"They [the leaders in the antiwar movement] talked about a 'police state.' Us
being 'Nazis.' My ass, it was. Let me say that they don't know to this day how
lucky they were to leave this city with their peckers intact."[93] Hans Kempski, a
correspondent for a daily newspaper in Munich in Chicago for the convention,
scoffed at the image of Chicago's police officers as fascists and unrestrained thugs.
"People who have seen a real police state know this is far from being one. If it
were, you would see no demonstrators at all. No one would be allowed on the
streets."[94]

Years later, Jerry Rubin found himself in agreement: "But you have to realize
that the violence that took place in Chicago was very symbolic. There were no
permanent injuries, there were no deaths. Somebody was killed a few days before
the convention, but during the demonstration itself there were no deaths. People
were clubbed, but the stitches healed. As Abbie says, 'All the violence of the Sixties put together doesn't add up to a weekend in Beirut.' "[95] Tom Hayden suggested later that the massacre in Beijing's Tiananmen Square made convention
week look like "a Pacifist Tea party."[96]

It seems unlikely that police would have lost control in any event, as
Chicago police officers at the time were among the most carefully screened in
the country prior to being hired onto the force. Recruits were subject to a bat-
tery of psychological examinations designed to test for emotional instability; if
any doubts were raised about a candidate, the applicant had to appear before a
board of three psychiatrists. Nearly 40 percent of applicants were rejected
annually due to the psychological tests or a background check that turned up a
history of instability. As former cop Joe Pecoraro notes, "We didn't go berserk.
If anything we kept our cool real good; I think we were selected from all the
police departments in the country—Chicago was selected—because we had the
best police department money can buy—a good department. I don't want to
put any of the others down, but I know Chicago. I was a policeman for thirty-

five years. And they are good guys. "Yeah, you're going to find a bum here and there, you ain't going to find 13,000 guys all perfect, one or two is going to be a bum."[97]

While feelings of anger and frustration remain among officers, there has also been room for reflection and introspection. Officers are understandably upset with their lot in American history books. They bristle when they read comparisons of them with storm troopers of the Third Reich, a regime that their fathers and uncles helped defeat during the Second World War, or that they stomped on rights protected by the U.S. Constitution. These men suggest that given what they were up against, events that summer could have turned out far worse. "It could have been a disaster," says Will Gerald. "The whole decade could have been *so* much worse. I don't know what happened to us in that decade. I like to watch the old films—the '60s radicals, the flower children, the chanters of eastern faiths, and the age of Aquarius mystics—and they were all Americans, and they seemed so foreign to me then; it was like an alien world, and watching those films brings it all back; it's like I can barely believe it all happened. But I was on the streets during the 1960s, and I *know* it happened."[98]

In the end, many officers blame the war in Vietnam for much of the difficulties police officers faced during the 1960s. "Without the war we would not have had all that trouble," says Paul Juravinski. "Without the bloody Chinese and Russians screwing around in Vietnam and the world, we would not have fought that hot war there in the middle of a cold war and we would have had peace over there and peace at home. Keeping the peace then was damn near impossible. I think that given the circumstances, on balance, we did pretty well." Joe Pecoraro agrees. "Maybe they were right over the Vietnam War, I don't know, but they didn't have to go to those extremes. Tearing our flag down and burning it. That to me was just chicken and they really didn't want to go to war. They were hiding out or going to Canada. If you don't like what your country's doing, then move out. We elect people in this country and figure they are responsible and we are going to do what they tell us to do. It's our country. And we are going to abide by the laws. These people just came here with one intention—to tear up this city. And they did a good job." Some officers wonder why the entire American society didn't implode during the 1960s. "I've thought over the years, that in uniform, we were just flying by the seat of our pants," says Brian Ramsey. "I was there. How we didn't have a second American revolution with lots of deaths is beyond me." Ken O'Connor agrees. "Things that summer looked to me like they were on the verge of total anarchy. What was that song a bit later: 'Where have you gone, ole' Joe DiMaggio? Our nation turns its lonely eyes to you.' That's how we felt. . . . We could have behaved better; we did some things that were wrong. Maybe as bad as some of us behaved, we gave the rotten apples of that otherwise, I think, well-meaning generation a good old spanking and we stopped the meltdown. And maybe we could have been better people, too. Maybe we were just lucky. I don't know. . . . I don't know."[99]

Conclusion

Here in Chicago you see America plain, with no warts missing from the portrait . . . with hippies and Yippies and the New Left, with soldiers and Secret Service and the maddening security tightness, with newsmen and photographers being clubbed by overreacting police squads, but with an unflinching resolve to show and face what America is really like.[1]

Balancing order with dissent is a conundrum that lies at the heart of any free nation. Even in the most open of societies, however, the tolerance for dissent is never absolute. If it were, there would be little protection against anarchy. During the turbulent 1960s, the force used to quell civil disorders by police often appeared excessive, at times, ruthless, with little consideration for the First Amendment rights of citizens. In Chicago during the Democratic National Convention, where dissent was often confused with disloyalty, thousands of photographs, miles of television footage, and hundreds of reliable witnesses reveal that officers meted out summary punishment on the streets. The evidence also clearly suggests that the abuse was not simply the emotional excess of a handful of officers, but the result of the actions of hundreds, and aided, supported, approved, or ignored by thousands of others. The disposition of police uninvolved in extraneous violence did little to dissuade others, even if they were not swinging batons themselves.

Despite crossing the line between protection and punishment, however, the police maintained an internal discipline and a consistent manner when dealing with crowds that week. Rather than acting in the heat of the moment, overall police behaviour was the antithesis of out-of-control and instead was a measured, uniform pattern of force and violence that was tacitly sanctioned by Mayor Daley prior to the convention. A significant number of officers were willing to do the mayor's bidding, relishing the opportunity to "spank" a "spoiled generation," one that they both loathed and feared. There is no question that police officers genuinely believed that demonstrations posed a threat to surrounding neighborhoods. That they managed not to fire on protestors, let alone kill or even permanently injure anyone that week, suggests that they were quite *in* control of their emotions, far from men who had gone "berserk" in the face of demonstrator provocation. Additionally, police did not beat their captors while in custody, and on occasion simply went through the motions, satisfying the pressures to make visible arrests while clearing the streets. Wanting to avoid paperwork and having little interest in charging demonstrators, police officers released scores of arrestees before they reached district stations.

The image of Chicago police as "storm troopers in blue" was in many ways their own making. Viewing the media through the same lens as the counterculture and the antiwar movement led officers to ignore repeated warnings from their commanders to avoid such conflict. It was a line they crossed repeatedly during convention week. Although they believed they were sanctioned to use rough methods against demonstrators, the attacks on the press core created a public relations disaster that Daley and his lieutenants were at pains to explain away all week. The attacks also produced a staggering amount of evidence later used by government investigators to indict police not as individuals who had meted out summary punishment but as rioters. Even though the use of violence to quell demonstrations during the Republican National Convention in Miami was much worse, the actions of Chicago's police were likened to Soviet tanks crushing dissent in Prague; demonstrators' ranks no longer included adult activists, violent agitators, and anarchists, but were simply "children" that were beaten on the streets by "pigs," "thugs," and "goons." Given the unprecedented media coverage in Chicago, police violence on its representatives, though reprehensible, only further distorted the reality of an already polarized political event.

By the summer of 1968, each side had reduced the other to the narrowest stereotypes: Cops were "pigs," demonstrators were "subversives," the media were "sensationalists" or "communists," and politicians were "war mongers." During convention week, a stage was set where these caricatures stuck to the script and played out a drama before a national television audience. Even though the mayhem virtually disappeared as these players left the stage, the reviews of Chicago's long, hot summer were scathing. The word coming out of the convention was that the police in America could not be trusted. Law enforcement's reputation among the young had soured to the point where Rolling Stones' front man Mick Jagger decided to hire the Hells Angels to provide security for a large outdoor rock concert at Altamont, California, the following December. The Angels, stoned on acid, promptly beat and stabbed to death eighteen-year-old concertgoer Meredith Hunter. The one night of violence unfortunately eclipsed anything that took place in Chicago, where the police department didn't manage to kill anyone during an entire week of rioting.

While the days of national strife continued, the federal government issued the final report of the National Commission on the Causes and Prevention of Violence. The commission, launched by President Johnson following the assassination of Robert Kennedy, tried to give the turmoil a silver lining. "There were, alas, the murders of Dr. Martin Luther King, Jr. and Senator Robert Kennedy, the riots in Washington and other cities, the pitched street battles in Chicago during the Democratic National Convention, and the ugly brutalities of the campus disorders and anti-war demonstrations," wrote Louis Heren. "Yet at the end of the year the Presidential election was held, and there was no violence as 69 million Americans went to the polls. The enormous power of the presidency passed peacefully from one man to another."[2]

America, however, was not at peace or in unity following the election of Richard Nixon, with a mere 500,000 votes separating victor from vanquished—a result reflecting the deep divisions so glaringly apparent that August in Chicago. For cops such as Joe Pecoraro, nothing in their careers prepared them for the experience. "That Vietnam stuff and the rioting was all new to us. We couldn't imagine anything like that. We couldn't imagine the American people turning on the American people—and I guess since then it has been going on." Following the convention, *Sun-Times* columnist Flora Lewis struggled with what she witnessed in her city on the banks of Lake Michigan and what it meant to her as an American. Amid the teargas and the screams of anger and frustration, Lewis tried to understand the dissension that plagued the nation and would continue to for much of the next four years. "Inside the convention hall and out, it was a matter of Americans confronting Americans," wrote Lewis. "On each side there were young and old, black and white, rich and struggling, and on each side there was a bewilderment that the sense of common patriotism has been lost in the hostility."[3] For Americans, a "common patriotism" remains elusive. Locked in a perennial and passionate internal quarrel over power versus restraint, freedom versus duty, national purpose versus individual creed, moral persuasion versus the force of arms, and consensus versus dissent, the nation often behaves like an emperor with two discordant heads. Although this embattled sovereign struggles internally for a victor, it is clear that one cannot survive long without the other.

It was raining the Tuesday following the convention as officer Nick Geldon drove to Springfield with his wife and daughter to attend a funeral. The service was for a family member who returned home from Vietnam in a casket shroud in stars and stripes. As an honor guard played "Taps," Geldon stood in his police dress uniform and shook with grief and anger. "He volunteered to serve— twenty-three and he gave the only life he had to give," says Geldon, remembering his cousin, reliving the moment with each word. "So much family standing in a drizzle looking lost, wondering who to blame. There seemed to be so many to blame but no one to take responsibility." Mourning the death of another American, activist Carl Ogelsby also believed there was no one to take responsibility—

that the chance for national redemption was lost following the slaying of Robert Kennedy. "There was no longer anyone to speak for the Democrats and say, 'I'm sorry about racism, I'm sorry about poverty, I'm sorry about Vietnam, and I want to be president in order to help solve these problems.' Such a simple speech. But after the Ambassador Hotel, there was no one to speak it."[4] Standing in a small Illinois cemetery with his family, Geldon believed that no one spoke for them, either. "The world had turned its back on us. The government, everybody. And we had all these people who refused to serve, who laughed and ridiculed our service, and spit on our flag. They seemed to want to rub in our pain, to insult our sacrifice, to treat us like what we did and who we were no longer mattered. It hurt . . . it still does."

Notes

CHAPTER 1

1. Interview with Mel Latanzio, August 9, 1999.

2. Norman Mailer, *Miami and the Siege of Chicago: An Informal History of the American Political Conventions of 1968* (Harmondsworth, England: Penguin Books, 1969), 83.

3. See Robin L. Einhorn, *Property Rules: Political Economy in Chicago, 1833–1872* (Chicago: University of Chicago Press, 1991), 28–60; Bessie Louise Pierce, *A History of Chicago, Volume I* (Chicago: University of Chicago Press, 1937), 32–42; and William Gronon, *Nature's Metropolis: Chicago and the Great West* (New York: W. W. Norton & Company, 1991), 26–92.

4. *Nature's Metropolis*, 97–206, 355–360, 392; Harold M. Mayer and Richard C. Wade, *Chicago: Growth of a Metropolis* (Chicago: University of Chicago Press, 1969), 3–116; *A History of Chicago, Volume I*, 44–74; *Property Rules*, 28–60, 61–103.

5. *Nature's Metropolis*, 207–259; *A History of Chicago, Volume I*, 75–123; and *Volume III*, (1957), 108–144; see also Louise Carroll Wade, *Chicago's Pride: The Stockyards, Packingtown, and Environs in the Nineteenth Century* (Chicago: University of Illinois, 1987).

6. *Miami and the Siege of Chicago*, 87.

7. *Nature's Metropolis*, 207–259; see Lizabeth Cohen, *Making a New Deal: Industrial Workers in Chicago, 1919–1939* (Cambridge: Cambridge University Press, 1990), 12–52, 54–97; and *A History of Chicago, Volume I*, 171–221, and *Volume III*, 20–63.

8. *New York Times*, August 19, 1968, 27.

9. Terkel is quoted in the *New York Times*, August 19, 1968, 27.

10. Henry David, *The History of the Haymarket Affair: A Study in the American Social-Revolutionary and Labor Movements* (New York: Russell & Russell, 1958), 108–232; Paul Avrich, *The Haymarket Tragedy* (Princeton: Princeton University Press, 1984), xi,

160–177, 181–214, 260–354, 401–414, 415–427; Steve Babson, *The Unfinished Struggle: Turning Points in American Labor, 1877–Present* (Lanham, MD: Rowman & Littlefield, 1999), 1–18; Eric L. Hirsch, *Urban Revolt: Ethnic Politics in the Nineteenth-Century Chicago Labor Movement* (Berkeley: University of California Press, 1990), 23–42, 43–85, 117–143; and *A History of Chicago, Volume III,* 234–299.

11. In 1957, following two previous relocations, the statue was moved to the northeast corner of the bridge over the Kennedy Expressway at Randolph Street. In October 1969 and October of 1970, saboteurs blew the statue off its pedestal. In January 1972, the city moved the statue to the lobby of police headquarters at 1121 S. State Street and later to the court-yard of the Police Academy at 1300 W. Jackson Boulevard. As one former officer observed, the "statute is about as restless as the city, as restless of the ghosts of those fallen men."

12. For a look at the Great Chicago Fire, see Ross Miller, *American Apocalypse: The Great Fire and the Myth of Chicago* (Chicago: University of Chicago Press, 1990); and Robert Cromie, *The Great Chicago Fire* (New York: McGraw-Hill, 1963).

13. *Nature's Metropolis,* 345–350; and *Chicago: Growth of a Metropolis,* 117–281.

14. *New York Times,* August 19, 1968, 27.

15. See Steven A. Riess, *Touching Base: Professional Baseball and American Culture in the Progressive Era* (Westport, CT: Greenwood Press, 1980); Eliot Asinof, *Eight Men Out: The Black Sox and the 1919 World Series* (New York: Henry Holt & Company, 2000); and Donald Gropman, *Say It Ain't So, Joe!: The True Story of Shoeless Joe Jackson* (Citadel Trade, 1992).

16. For an extensive look at gangland crime in Chicago and in the nation during this period, see William J. Helmer, *Public Enemies: America's Criminal Past, 1919–1940* (New York: Facts on File, 1998); Humbert S. Nelli, *The Business of Crime: Italians and Syndicate Crime in the United States* (Chicago: University of Chicago Press, 1981); Dennis E. Hoffman, *Scarface Al and the Crime Crusaders: Chicago's Private War against Capone* (Carbondale: Southern Illinois University Press, 1993); and Jesse George Murray, *The Legacy of Al Capone: Portraits and Annals of Chicago's Public Enemies* (New York: Putnam, 1975).

17. Ibid.; See also Dianne M. Pinderhughes, *Race and Ethnicity in Chicago Politics: A Reexamination of Pluralist Theory* (Urbana: University of Illinois Press, 1987), 141–180; and Paul W. Heimel, *Eliot Ness: The Real Story* (Coudersport, PA: Knox Books, 1997).

18. *New York Times,* August 19, 1968, 27.

19. Melvin A. Kahn and Frances J. Majors. *The Winning Ticket: Daley, the Chicago Machine, and Illinois Politics* (New York: Praeger, 1984), 16–19.

20. For a good look at machine politics and capturing the ethnic vote, see Lloyd Wendt and Herman Kogan, *Big Bill of Chicago* (New York: A Bobbs-Merrill Company, 1953), 330–333, 337, 338, 340, 341; Milton L. Rakove, *Don't Make No Waves—Don't Back No Losers: An Insider's Analysis of The Daley Machine* (Bloomington: Indiana University Press, 1975), 31; John M. Allswang, *Bosses, Machines, and Urban Voters: An American Symbiosis* (Port Washington, NY: Kennikat Press, 1977), 108–109; Paul M. Green and Melvin G. Holli, eds., *The Mayors: The Chicago Political Tradition* (Carbondale: Southern Illinois University Press, 1987), 103, 109; and Roger Biles, *Big City Boss in Depression and War: Mayor Edward J. Kelly of Chicago* (DeKalb: Northern Illinois University Press, 1984), 22, 98–101.

21. *Miami and the Siege of Chicago,* 88.

22. *Race and Ethnicity,* 5; Mike Royko, *Boss: Richard J. Daley of Chicago* (New York: E. P. Dutton & Co., 1971), 38; and *Miami and the Siege of Chicago,* 102. Chicagoans reelected Daley in 1959 and in 1963, and in 1967 he became the first Chicago mayor to

be elected for a fourth consecutive four-year term. In April 1969, Daley became the longest serving mayor in the city's history. In 1975, voters granted him his sixth term as mayor of Chicago. He died in office on December 20, 1976.

23. For a complete rundown on the police scandal, see the *Chicago Tribune,* January 19–24, 1960, and March 5, 1960. See also Roger Biles, *Richard J. Daley: Politics, Race, and the Governing of Chicago* (DeKalb: Northern Illinois University Press, 1995), 67.

24. Ibid.

25. *Chicago Tribune,* March 15, 1963, 17; March 22, 1963, 6, and March 31, 1963, 22. See also *Boss,* 111–117, and the *New York Times,* August 19, 1968, 90.

26. See the *Chicago Tribune,* April 5, 1959, 24; April 1, 1959, 2, and March 28, 1959, 12; and *The Making of a President, 1968,* 263, 264.

27. *New York Times,* August 26, 1968, 20.

28. For Nixon's thoughts on the election, see Richard M. Nixon, *RN, the Memoirs of Richard Nixon* (New York: Warner Books, 1979), 274–281.

29. Some counter that the Democrats also stole the election in Texas, where Lyndon Johnson's cronies controlled much of the state's political apparatus. They counter that Nixon could have taken both states giving him the electoral votes necessary to take the presidency.

30. The debate over the election results continues. For a good look at the 1960 election, see Lucy S. Dawidowicz and Leon J. Goldstein, *Politics in a Pluralist Democracy: Studies of Voting in the 1960 Election* (New York: Institute for Human Relations, 1963); Theodore Harold White, *The Making of the President, 1960* (New York: Atheneum, 1961); Christopher J. Matthews, *Kennedy Nixon: The Rivalry That Shaped Postwar America* (New York: Simon & Schuster, 1996); and Louis W. Liebovich, *The Press and the Modern Presidency: Myths and Mindsets from Kennedy to Election 2000,* Rev. 2nd ed. (Westport, CT: Praeger, 2001).

31. *Time,* September 4, 1968, 33.

32. David Halberstam, "Daley of Chicago" *Harper's Magazine,* August 1968, 29.

33. *New York Times,* August 19, 1968, 27.

34. *Boss,* 160, 161.

35. Interview with Joe Pecoraro, October 13, 2003. Pecoraro believes that Conlisk was a "nice man" and a "good superintendent" but he was "low-key." For a look at Wilson's tenure and some of the issues surrounding policing and the city's black community, see William J. Bopp, *O. W. Wilson and the Search for a Police Profession* (Port Washington, NY: Kennikat Press, 1977); Robert M. Fogelson, *Big City Police* (Cambridge, MA: Harvard University Press, 1977), 257; and James Q. Wilson, "Police Morale, Reform and Citizen Respect: The Chicago Case," *The Police* (New York: John Wiley & Sons, 1967), 145.

36. *Boss,* 116, 117, 160–61.

37. *The Winning Ticket,* 99, 114; Adam Cohen and Elizabeth Taylor, *American Pharaoh: Mayor Richard J. Daley: His Battle for Chicago and the Nation* (Boston: Little, Brown, 2000), 7–9; Paul M. Green, ed., et al., *The Mayors: The Chicago Political Tradition* (Carbondale: Southern Illinois University Press, 1987), 153–163; the Chicago *Defender* March 16, 1959, April 1, 1959, and April 2, 1963, and *Boss,* 135. See also James Ralph, *Northern Protest: Martin Luther King Jr., Chicago, and the Civil Rights Movement* (Cambridge, MA: Harvard University Press, 1993); and Arnold R. Hirsch, *Making the Second Ghetto: Race and Housing in Chicago, 1940–1960* (Cambridge, MA: Cambridge University Press, 1983).

38. See Theodore Harold White, *The Making of the President, 1968* (New York: Atheneum Publishers, 1969), 263; and *The Winning Ticket,* 20, 43, 44.

39. Lewis Chester et al., *An American Melodrama: The Presidential Campaign of 1968* (New York: The Viking Press, 1969), 510; and *The Winning Ticket,* 18, 19, 88–90.

40. *The Winning Ticket,* 66.

41. See *The Making of a President, 1968,* 258–264; and *American Pharaoh,* 9.

42. *Boss,* 155–194.

43. *The Winning Ticket,* 85.

44. Police interviewees came from a variety of associations and organizations in communities ranging from Chicago to Las Vegas, Nevada, through contacts with former officers' networks including cultural associations and business networking after retirement. Interviewees also came from throughout the ranks, ranging from rookies to men with more than twenty years on the job. The officers included sergeants and patrolmen, uniformed and plainclothes. All officers in this sample were white; even by 1968, the vast majority of police officers in cites such as Chicago were white—black officers constituted a small minority of officers. Efforts to locate an African-American officer from that summer were unsuccessful.

45. Interview with Greg Parzanski, April 17, 2002. Parzanski went to lengths to explain that his reference to blacks entering his neighborhood was not racist, but more that he was stating a reality. In his view, black families tended to be poorer, thus there was a greater chance that there would be a rise in the neighborhood's rate of crime, as poorer neighborhoods, in his view, always have a higher crime rate. A discussion ensued over visible crime and white-collar crime. He said he had no opinion on "invisible crime."

46. Indeed, even by O. W. Wilson's retirement, only 2 percent of Chicago police officers had a college education. See William W. Turner, *The Police Establishment* (New York: G. P. Putman's Sons, 1968), 110.

47. Officers from the time say that it was common for new recruits to be selected for being "square-jawed" Polish, Irish, and Italian boys from the neighborhoods, especially if they were in good physical condition and had "anything between their ears."

48. Interview with Tom O'Malley, July 27, 2000.

49. Interview with Warren MacAulay, January 17, 2000; Jerry Ewaschuck, September 17, 2000; and Don Holtz, May 20, 2001. See also Richard P. Taub, *Paths of Neighborhood Change: Race and Crime in Urban America* (Chicago: University of Chicago Press, 1984), 1–17, 76–118, 167–194.

50. Interview with Dennis Kaminski, June 27, 2001, and Jack Ochosky, March 12, 2002.

51. Interview with Joe Pecoraro, October 13, 2003.

52. Interview with Ernie Watson, June 17, 1999.

53. Interview with Steven Latz, June 4, 1999, and Tom Freeborn, March 11, 2001.

54. Interview with George Horsley, July 15, 2001.

55. Interview with Grant Brown, October 17, 2002.

56. Interview with Randall Bakker, June 30, 2002, and October 13, 2003, and Brian Ramsey, June 23, 2001.

57. Interview with Steve Nowakowski, November 1, 1999, and October 11, 2003.

58. Interview with Henry Nostbakken, June 12, 2002, and October 10, 2003; Kelly Fredrickson, March 4, 2000; and Orrest Hupka, September 14, 2002.

59. Interview with Paul Juravinski, January 26, 1999; Al Ogilvie, September 21, 1999; and Milt Brower, January 19, 2000. For a discussion of how police felt under siege with the increase in race riots and antiwar protests, see Robert M. Fogelson, *Big City Police* (Cambridge, MA: Harvard University Press, 1977), 239.

60. Interview with Tim Markosky, July 8, 2001, and Joe Pecoraro, October 13, 2003.

61. Interview with Marlin Rowden, June 21, 2000.

62. Interview with Steve Nowakowski, October 11, 2003.

CHAPTER 2

1. See Eldridge Cleaver, *Soul on Ice* (New York: Dell, 1968), 71.

2. Interview with Henry Nostbakken, October 12, 2003.

3. Actually, Johnson was playing for political mileage as his Republican opponent Barry Goldwater had been talking tough new terms for prosecuting the war in Vietnam. Johnson delivered his words in a campaign speech at Akron University in Ohio, October 21, 1964. For more about Johnson's attitude at the time, see *Public Papers of the Presidents of the United States, Lyndon B. Johnson: 1963–64.*

4. Anthony Austin, *The President's War: The Story of the Tonkin Gulf Resolution and How the Nation Was Trapped in Vietnam* (Philadelphia: Lippincott, 1971), 10–46, 161–190; Joseph C. Goulden, *Truth Is the First Casualty: The Gulf of Tonkin Affair—Illusion and Reality* (Chicago: Rand McNally, 1969), 23–78, 100–160, 163–180; and Ezra Y. Siff, *Why the Senate Slept* (Westport, CT: Praeger, 1999), 19–40.

5. From President Johnson's address at John's Hopkins University, April 1965.

6. Todd Gitlin, *The Sixties: Years of Hope, Days of Rage* (New York: Bantam Books, 1987), 242. For a good look at the early days of the movement, see also Nancy Zaroulis and Gerald Sullivan, *Who Spoke Up? American Protest against the War in Vietnam, 1963–1975* (New York: Holt, Rinehart, & Winston, 1985), 7–67.

7. *New York Times,* April 27, 1965, 1.

8. For an interesting discussion of the impact caused by those who were blocking the trains carrying troops, see *U.S. Congressional Record* (Washington, DC: Government Printing Office, October 18, 1965), 27251. For references to protest by self-immobilization, see Marvin E. Gettleman, (ed.); *Vietnam and America: A Documented History* (New York: Grove Press, 1985), 293.

9. See *Vietnam and America,* 302–305.

10. Allen J. Matusow, *The Unraveling of America: A History of Liberalism in the 1960s* (New York: Harper & Row, 1984), 361.

11. *Vietnam and America,* 307–308.

12. *Who Spoke Up?* 129.

13. *The Unraveling of America,* 363.

14. Quoted in Stokely Carmichael and Charles V. Hamilton, *Black Power: The Politics of Liberation in America* (New York: Vintage, 1967), 52–53.

15. The city, in fact, was long a racial boiling point and separation always an issue as white communities feared encroachments by blacks. This racial tension broke in July of 1919, after whites noticed six black teenagers swimming in the "wrong" section of Lake Michigan. A white man on the shore struck and killed one of the swimmers with a rock, and rumors spread on both sides—whites reported that blacks killed a white swimmer and blacks countered that the police helped a mob stone blacks. From July 27 to July 31, the streets ran red. During the riots, white gangs prowled the city's South Side attacking indiscriminately, while black gangs attacked white merchants in black neighborhoods. The rioting took the lives of twenty-three blacks and fifteen whites. See Carl Sandburg, *The Chicago Race Riots, July 1919* (New York: Harcourt, Brace, 1969), 3–16, 31–36, 52–81; and William M. Tuttle Jr., *Race Riot, Chicago in the Red Summer of 1919* (New York: Anteneum, 1972), 3–32, 156–183, 208–239, 242–268.

16. *Black Power,* 152–154.

17. Ibid., 184–185.

18. *Vietnam and America,* 317–318.

19. Eldridge Cleaver, *Soul on Ice* (New York: Dell Publishing, 1968), 60–61, 121.

20. Ibid., 129–130.

21. Interview with Kurt O'Grady, March 22, 2000.

22. Theodore Harold White, *The Making of the President, 1968* (New York: Atheneum Publishers, 1969), 205.

23. *Soul on Ice,* 131; and interview with Len Colsky, July 12, 2000.

24. Eldredge Cleaver, *Post-Prison Writings and Speeches* (New York: Vintage Books, 1969), 38.

25. See Mitchell Goodman, *The Movement Towards a New America: The Beginnings of a Long Revolution* (New York: Knopf, 1970). This 752-page collection of underground and alternative newspaper articles, speeches, fliers, posters, and photos from the 1960s is an excellent source for the movement's political mindset.

26. Interview with Paul Juravinski, January 26, 1999.

27. Interview with Ray Mihalicz, July 8, 1999.

28. Interview with Sheldon Bartowski, July 19, 2000, and Tom Freeborn, March 11, 2001.

29. Interview with Ronald Adler, November 16, 1999. Many police officers were understandably unimpressed with the findings of the Kerner Report, the result of Johnson's National Advisory Commission on Civil Disorders in March of 1968. The report suggested that systematic white racism, including the feelings of some police officers, were, in part, to blame for some of the rioting and discontent in black neighborhoods.

30. Interview with Ronald Lardo, April 12, 2001.

31. Interview with Hank Perterson, February 16, 2001.

32. Interview with Eddie Kelso, December 11, 1999, and Carl Moore, March 5, 2000.

33. Interview with Norm Nelson, April 17, 2000, and Don Holtz, May 20, 2001.

34. Interview with Henry Nostbakken, June 12, 2002, and Sam McMaster, September 18, 2000.

35. Interview with Will Gerald, May 6, 2002, and Herbert Bile, May 12, 2002.

36. Interview with Archie Pasis, August 23, 2001, and Ira Freyling, May 19, 2002.

37. Interview with Terry Novicki, October 15, 2001, and Cal Noonan, March 17, 2002.

38. Interview with Victor Olafson, July 9, 1999.

39. Interview with Fred Jeffery, December 8, 2002, and Steven Latz, June 4, 1999.

40. Interview with Eddie Kelso, December 11, 1999, and Ronald Lardo, April 12, 2001.

41. *The Pentagon Papers* (Gravel ed.), vol. 4, 538–539.

42. Interview with Milt Brower, January 19, 2001, and George Horsley, July 15, 2001.

43. Interview with Orrest Hupka, September 14, 2002, and October 13, 2003. See David Farber's excellent *Chicago '68* for a good discussion of the increasing pressures on police to deal with the combination of racial disturbances and protests from the growing antiwar movement, pages 129–132.

CHAPTER 3

1. Interview with Marlin Rowden, June 21, 2000.

2. *The Sixties,* 286.

3. See Adam M. Garfinkle, *Telltale Hearts: The Origins and Impact of the Vietnam Antiwar Movement* (New York: St. Martin's Press, 1995), 154–160; see also Don Oberdorfer,

Tet!: The Turning Point in the Vietnam War (Baltimore, MD: Johns Hopkins University Press, 2001), 157–196, 238–277.

4. Walter Cronkite on the *CBS Evening News,* January, 1968. Cronkite delivered his editorial comment following his regular evening newscast after returning from a stint in Saigon where he saw firsthand the result of the Tet Offensive.

5. *Tet!: The Turning Point in the Vietnam War,* 157–196, 238–277.

6. Unlike the killings of four white students at Kent State two years later, the shootings of black students at Orangeburg garnered little press coverage. Kent State also easily surpassed the attention paid to the shooting deaths of two black students at Jackson State University by police on May 14, 1970. See Jack Bass and Jack Nelson, *The Orangeburg Massacre* (New York: World Publishing, 1970).

7. Allen J. Matusow, *The Unraveling of America,* 391; and *Who Spoke Up?* 157.

8. See Herbert Y. Schandler, *The Unmaking of a President: Lyndon Johnson and Vietnam* (Princeton, NJ: Princeton University Press, 1977), 290–350; Stanley Karnow, *Vietnam: A History* (New York: The Viking Press, 1983), 561–563; *Telltale Hearts,* 154–160; Tom Wells, *The War Within: America's Battle over Vietnam* (Berkeley: University of California Press, 1994), 240–246; *Who Spoke Up?* 158; and Arthur M. Schlesinger Jr., *Robert Kennedy and His Times, Vol. 11* (Boston: Houghton Mifflin Company, 1978), 896–908.

9. Johnson was talking to Doris Kearns Goodwin. Quoted in *Robert Kennedy and His Times, Vol. 11,* 905–906.

10. See *Public Papers of the President,* Lyndon Baines Johnson 1968, 476; Theodore White, *The Making of the President,* 113–120; for reasons Johnson changed his mind on the war, see Herbert Y. Schandler, *The Unmaking of a President: Lyndon Johnson and Vietnam,* 290–350.

11. *The Unraveling of America,* 394.

12. *Chicago Sun-Times,* April 1, 1968, 3.

13. *Time,* April 12, 1968, 18–19; and *Chicago Sun-Times,* April 5, 1968, 6.

14. *Robert Kennedy and His Times,* 914.

15. *Time,* September 13, 1968, 28.

16. *Chicago Tribune,* April 5, 1968, 1, 3–5, 11; and *Chicago Sun-Times,* April 5, 1968, 2–6, 18, 20, April 6, 1968, 1, 4–9, 11, 12, 14, and April 7, 1968, 3, 6.

17. See *Chicago Tribune,* April 7, 1968, 1, 3, 4–6, 10, 1A6, 1A7; and *Chicago Sun-Times,* April 7, 1968, 4.

18. *Chicago Tribune,* April 8, 1968, 1, 2, and *Chicago Sun-Times,* April 7, 1968, 4. Daley's attitude toward King was ambivalent at best. "He is a religious leader who feels intensely about the causes he espouses and he does a very good job of espousing them," Daley said, in what was not exactly a ringing endorsement of the civil rights leader. Daley once referred to King as a "rabble-rouser, a trouble-maker." The city itself had also not been the friendliest of places for the Memphis native. King had received rough treatment on some of his visits to the Windy City. In August 1966, King was knocked down by a rock on Chicago's Southwest Side during a civil rights march. He got up and continued the march while eggs, rocks, and bottles flew by his head. According to the veteran cop Joe Pecoraro, some in the crowd were throwing billiard balls. During one of his trips to Chicago, an angry crowd chanted, "Go back to Africa. We don't want you here." Some months later, Daley accused King of visiting Chicago to "stir up white-backlash vote." But on the day of the civil rights leader's assassination, Daley praised King for his efforts, adding, "Violence accomplishes nothing." But overall, the Chicago mayor had little kind things to say about MLK, and somewhat cynically renamed South Parkway "Martin Luther King Drive." See *Boss,* 147; the *Chicago Sun-Times,* April 5, 1968, 14, and April 5,

1968, 4; interview with Joe Pecoraro, October 13, 2003; *Fire in the Streets,* 436–437, and *The Unraveling of America,* 205.

19. *Chicago Sun-Times,* April 7, 1968, 12.

20. Ibid., April 7, 1968, 76.

21. Ibid., April 9, 3, 5, 21, 23, 25, and April 10, 3–5, 21, 22, 32.

22. Ibid., April 11, 1968, 3; April 12, 1, 20; and April 15, 4, 38. See also *A Report on Chicago Crime for 1968,* Chicago Crime Commission 1968, 5–7.

23. *Chicago Tribune,* April 11, 1968, 1, 2.

24. Ibid., April 9, 1968, 3.

25. Ibid., April 13, 1968, 6.

26. Ibid., April 16, 1968, 1, 2, 16.

27. *Chicago Sun-Times,* April 16, 1968, 4.

28. *Chicago Tribune,* April 16, 1968, 2.

29. Ibid., April 16, 1968, 2.

30. Ibid., April 17, 1968, 1, 2.

31. Ibid., April 17, 1, 2, and April 18, 1–3.

32. Ibid., April 19, 1968, 10.

33. See the *Chicago Sun-Times,* April 18, 1968, 3, 4, 35.

34. *Chicago Sun-Times,* April 16, 1968, 25.

35. See the *New York Times,* April 18, 1968.

36. Lindsay was quoted in the *Chicago Sun-Times,* April 17, 1968, 3.

37. For a discussion of Columbia's expansion plans, see "The Siege of Columbia," *Ramparts,* June 15, 1968, 27–29. See also *Time,* May 31, 1968, 42.

38. The *New York Times* reported that the city's police commonly used plainclothes officers in such situations, who were often a major part of police deployment. Police officials have explained that these officers are used in tense situations because they are virtually invisible until needed. Police have also acknowledged that there can be more problems controlling their behavior when making arrests and dealing with crowds than arise with uniformed officers. During provocations with antiwar demonstrators, some plainclothes officers apparently prevented bystanders from watching as their fellow officers beat a demonstrator. See the *New York Times,* April 28, 1968, 72.

39. *Who Spoke Up?* 166–167; *Ramparts,* "The Siege of Columbia," 33–39; and *New York Times.*

40. Quotations taken from Tom Hayden, "Two, Three, Many Columbias," *Ramparts,* June 15, 1968.

41. The *Unraveling of America,* 329.

42. Interview with Sam McMaster, September 18, 2000.

43. Interview with Norm Nelson, April 17, 2000.

44. Interview with Sam Ivanchenko, November 14, 1999.

45. See Chapter 4 for the section on the Yippies and Police department communications as well as for Rubin's complaint about New York police questioning him.

46. Riordan is quoted in the *Chicago Sun-Times,* April 28, 1968, 3.

47. *Chicago Sun-Times,* April 28, 1968, 12.

48. *New York Times,* April 28, 73. Although organizers claimed that marchers totaled 12,000, police estimates were closer to 3,000, while the *Tribune* reported the number at 5,000. The same day, similar protest marches took place in San Francisco and Philadelphia with no violence. See also the *Chicago Tribune,* April 28, 1968, 1, 8.

49. Interview with Ernie Bellows, February 10, 2001, and Bob Nurnberger, May 27, 2000.

50. Interview with "Sash" Sadowski, November 1, 1999.

51. Interview with Harold "Ham" Pacnik, June 3, 1999.

52. See *Dissent and Disorder: A Report to the Citizens of Chicago on the April 27 Investigating Commission. April 27 Peace Parade* (Chicago: American Civil Liberties Union, 1968), 30–31. The panel was headed by Dr. Edward Sparling, President Emeritus of Roosevelt University.

53. Interview with Ira Freyling, May 19, 2002, and Cal Noonan, March 17, 2002.

54. Interview with Brian Ramsey, June 23, 2001, and Reg Novak, May 27, 1999.

55. *The Sixties,* 321.

56. *Boss,* 169, 174. Indeed, the coverage in both the *Sun-Times* and the *Tribune* was minimal.

57. Interview with Gord Stensill, October 16, 2001.

58. *New York Times,* April 28, 1968, 1.

59. For a look at Humphrey's personal recollections on the war, see Hubert Humphrey, *The Education of a Public Man: My Life in Politics* (Garden City, NY: Doubleday, 1976), 318–361.

60. See the *Chicago Sun-Times,* April 3, 1968, 30.

61. *New York Times* April 28, 1968, 67; and *Chicago Sun-Times,* August 20, 1968, 5, 11.

62. *Robert Kennedy and His Times,* 939.

63. See Jules Witcover, *85 Days: The Last Campaign of Robert Kennedy,* 1969 (New York: Putnam, 1969), 116. See also Arthur M. Schlesinger Jr., *Robert Kennedy and His Times;* and *Robert Kennedy in His Own Words,* 879–914.

64. For a good discussion of the 1968 election campaign between Kennedy and McCarthy, see William L. O'Neill, *Coming Apart: An Informal History of America in the 1960's* (Chicago: Quadrangle Books, 1971), 360–395.

65. *Newsweek,* June 17, 1968, 22, 29. See also *The Making of a President 1968,* 182, 183; *85 Days,* 264–291; and Edwin O. Guthman, ed., et al., *RFK: Collected Speeches* (New York: Viking, 1993), 400–402.

66. The brief exchange involving Kennedy and the kitchen worker was culled from *Newsweek,* June 17, 1968, 29.

CHAPTER 4

1. Interview with Dennis Pierson, October 12, 2003.

2. *Miami and the Siege of Chicago,* 93, 96. For a description of RFK's funeral train, see *The Making of a President, 1968,* 184; and *85 Days,* 308–318.

3. James Reston, Editorial, the *New York Times,* June 9, 1968, 14E.

4. Oglesby is quoted in *Camelot to Kent State: The Sixties Experience in the Words of Those Who Lived It* (New York: Oxford University Press, 2001), 306.

5. See *The Unraveling of America,* 404; and the *Chicago Sun-Times,* August 13, 2.

6. *Chicago Sun-Times,* August 14, 1968, 20, 29.

7. Hayden's actions taken from *Who Spoke Up?* 171. See also Carl Oglesby, "Chicago 1968: Street-Fightin' Man," in Mary Susannah Robbins, ed., *Against the Vietnam War: Writings by Activists* (Syracuse, NY: Syracuse University Press, 1999), 127–128.

8. *Robert Kennedy and His Times,* 956.

9. "Chicago 1968: Street-Fightin' Man," 128.

10. Ibid., l29.

11. *Rights in Conflict: Chicago's 7 Brutal Days: A Report Submitted by Daniel Walker, Director of the Chicago Study Team, to the National Commission on the Causes and Prevention of Violence,* 25.

12. "Chicago 1968: Street-Fightin' Man," 129.

13. *The Sixties,* 311.

14. *The War Within,* 237.

15. *New York Times,* August 18, 1968, 64. See also *Fire in the Streets,* 446.

16. See Davis and Hayden in the *Records of the Chicago Study Team Investigation, National Commission on the Causes and Prevention of Violence* (NCCPV), Lyndon Baines Johnson Library, A192, Box 7; and *The War Within,* 237–238.

17. *The War Within,* 262–263.

18. *New York Times,* April 18, 1968, 64.

19. *Chicago Sun-Times,* April 2, 1968, 8.

20. *The Unraveling of America,* 412.

21. *The Sixties,* 233.

22. Abbie Hoffman, *Revolution for the Hell of It* (New York: The Dial Press, 1968), 102–108. See also Milton Viorst, *Fire in the Streets* (New York: Simon & Schuster, 1979), 431.

23. *Revolution for the Hell of It,* 90.

24. For a good description of the events in Grand Central Station, see Don McNeill, *Moving through Here* (New York: Knopf, 1970), 224–230; and *Revolution for the Hell of It,* 91.

25. See the *Chicago Sun-Times,* August 15, 1968, 5. *Revolution for the Hell of It,* 102.

26. *Revolution for the Hell of It,* 26.

27. Ibid., 128–130, and *The Sixties,* 233–236, for a discussion on how Hoffman used the media for his own ends.

28. *Revolution for the Hell of It,* 133–134.

29. Abbie Hoffman, *Soon to Be a Major Motion Picture* (New York: Putnam, 1980), 99.

30. *Revolution for the Hell of It,* 26.

31. Ibid., 27.

32. Interview with Ray Mihalicz, July 8, 1999.

33. Interview with Ernie Bellows, February 10, 2001.

34. Officer Mel Latanzio meant the Diggers. Interview of August 9, 1999.

35. *Revolution for the Hell of It,* 53.

36. "The Yippies Are Coming," *Ramparts,* September 28, 1968, 21.

37. Interview with Norm Nelson, April 17, 2000.

38. Interview with Len Colsky July 12, 2000.

39. Interview with Warren MacAulay, January 17, 2000.

40. See the *New York Times,* June 15, 1968, 39.

41. Interview with Marlin Rowden, June 21, 2000.

42. Interview with Kelly Frederickson, March 4, 2000.

43. See Chapter 6 for a discussion of the department's Red Squad.

44. *The Unraveling of America,* 413.

45. *Chicago Sun-Times,* August 22, 1968, 3; and "The Yippies Are Coming," 21. The planning for the convention, however, had begun much earlier. In January, Superintendent Conlisk created the Convention Planning Committee, which included high-ranking members from patrol, traffic, youth, and community relations, plus the communications

and planning division units. The committee formed working relations with military intelligence, the state's National Guard, the Chicago Convention Committee, and the Democratic National Committee to learn the depth of what was to come by way of protests during the convention. Much of the preparation came in light of the release of the Kerner Report, the result of Johnson's National Advisory Commission on Civil Disorders in March, which suggested that white racists, including some police officers, were in part to blame for some of the rioting in black areas. The report, named after Illinois Governor Otto Kerner, said that the United States was, in fact, becoming two societies, "one black, one white—separate and unequal." It suggested, "white society is deeply implicated in the ghetto. White institutions created it, white institutions maintain it, and white society condones it." See the *Report of the National Advisory Commission on Civil Disorders* (Washington, DC: Government Printing Office, 1968). For the department's planning committee, see the minutes of the Chicago Police Department Convention Planning Committee (CPD-CPC), January and February 1968, NCCPV, A108, Box 5.

46. *Boss,* 175–177.

47. See United States Congress House Committee on Un-American Activities. *Subversive Involvement in Disruption of 1968 Democratic Party National Convention HUAC Hearings of October and December 1968.* Ninetieth Congress, Second Session (Washington, DC: U.S. Government Printing Office, 1968). Subsequent citations are listed as HUAC.

48. See Chapter 3 concerning Daley's reference to shooting and killing arsonists, and his comment during the April peace march that these people had no right to express their views.

49. "Daley City under Siege," *Time,* August 30, 1968, 20.

50. Ibid., and the *Chicago Sun-Times,* August 22, 1968, 3.

51. "Daley City under Siege," 20. See also the *Chicago Sun-Times,* August 12, 1968, 1, 12; August 13, 1968, 19; August 25, 1968, 34; August 27, 1968, 18.

52. *Chicago Sun-Times,* August 22, 1968, 3, 32.

53. Ibid., August 22, 1968, 3, 32, and August 12, 1968, 12.

54. "Daley City under Siege," 21; and *Chicago Sun-Times,* August 26, 1968, 20.

55. *The Sixties,* 323; and Daley City under Siege, 20–21. See also the *Chicago Sun-Times,* August 12; 1968, 1, 12; August 21, 1968, 3, 14; and August 22, 1968, 3, 32.

56. See *Time,* August 30, 20–21.

57. *New York Times,* August 23, 1968, 25.

58. *The Sixties,* 323.

59. *New York Times,* August 18, 1968, 64.

60. "The Yippies Are Coming," 22.

61. *Rights in Conflict,* 27.

62. *New York Times,* August 18, 1968, 64.

63. *The Unraveling of America,* 413.

64. "Who Were the Protestors" *Time,* September 6, 1968, 36.

65. *The Sixties,* 320.

66. *Covering Dissent,* 88–89.

67. *Chicago Sun-Times,* August 21, 1968, 21, and August 23, 1968, 3.

68. Daley is quoted in J. Anthony Lukas, "Dissenters Focusing on Chicago," *New York Times,* August 18, 1968, 64.

69. *The Unraveling of America,* 411.

70. *Chicago Sun-Times,* August 19, 1968, 17.

71. *New York Times,* August 24, 1968, 20.

72. *Fire in the Streets,* 450.

73. *Miami and the Siege of Chicago,* 101.

74. McGovern quoted in the *New York Times,* August 18, 1968, 66.

75. McCarthy's complete plank on Vietnam can be found in the *New York Times,* August 18, 1968, 66.

76. *New York Times,* August, 19, 1968, 32.

77. Ibid., August 18, 1968, 66, 68.

78. Ibid., August 18, 1968, 67.

79. See Charles Lloyd Garrettson, *Hubert H. Humphrey: The Politics of Joy* (New Brunswick, NJ: Transaction Publishers, 1993), 196, 197.

80. *New York Times,* August 23, 1968, 22.

81. Interview with Eddie Kelso, December 11, 1999.

82. *Chicago Sun-Times,* August 21, 1968, 18.

83. *Who Spoke Up?* 184. Interview with Dennis Pierson, January 20, 1999.

84. Interview with Orrest Hupka, September 14, 2002. Both the *Chicago Tribune* and the *Chicago Sun-Times* gave ample coverage to the violence in the Florida city. See the *Sun-Times,* August 9, 2, 22.

85. *Chicago Sun-Times,* August 10, 1968, 3.

86. Interview with Reg Novak, May 27, 1999. See also NCCPV, R502, Box 42.

87. See the *Chicago Sun-Times,* August 9, 1968, 22, and August 10, 1968, 10.

88. *Chicago Sun-Times,* August 23, 1968, 3, 33.

89. *New York Times* August 23, 1968, 22; *Chicago Sun-Times,* August 23, 1968, 24. The *Sun-Times* and David Farber identified the slain youth as "Dean" Johnson.

90. Dellinger was quoted in the *Chicago Sun-Times,* August 23, 1968, 20.

91. Interview with Carl Moore, March 5, 2000.

92. Interview with Tim Markosky, July 8, 2001.

93. Interview with Frank Froese, June 28, 2002.

94. *New York Times,* August 18, 1968, 64; and *Chicago Sun-Times,* August 24, 1968, 14.

95. *Chicago Sun-Times,* August 20, 1968, 14.

96. Jerry Rubin is quoted in *Camelot to Kent State: The Sixties Experience in the Words of Those Who Lived It* (New York: Oxford University Press, 2001), 288. See also the *Chicago Sun-Times,* August 24, 1968, 14; and "The Yippies Are Coming," 21.

97. "The Yippies Are Coming," 22.

98. Reilly is quoted in the *Chicago Tribune,* August 25, 1968, 8.

99. Interview with Jerry Melton, September 20, 2001.

100. *Chicago Sun-Times,* August 24, 1968, 3, 8.

101. *Rights in Conflict,* 84.

102. "The Yippies Are Coming," 22.

103. Interview with Cal Noonan, March 17, 2002. See also NCCPV, R502, Box 42.

104. "The Yippies Are Coming," 22–23.

105. Interview with Ronald Lardo, April 12, 2001.

106. There was no mention of street disturbances or violence in the Sunday edition of the *Sun-Times.* Interview with Milt Brower, January 19, 2001.

107. *New York Times,* August 18, 1968, 64.

108. *The Sixties,* 324.

109. See "The Yippies Are Coming," 21.

110. *Boss,* 178; and Todd Gitlin, *The Whole World is Watching: Mass Media in the Making & Unmaking of The New Left.* (Berkeley: University of California Press, 1980), 169. Gitlin's number of 5,000 seems to be the average; certainly by Wednesday the number could have swelled to 10,000. See "Who Were the Protestors," *Time,* September 6, 1968, 36.

111. *Miami and the Siege of Chicago,* 89–90.

112. See *Rights in Conflict,* 89, 90; *The War Within,* 277; and *New York Times,* August 26, 1968, 25.

113. "The Yippies Are Coming," 23–24; and *New York Times,* August 26, 1968, 25.

114. *Rights in Conflict,* 91, 92; *New York Times,* August 26, 1968, 25; and the *Chicago Sun-Times,* August 26, 1968, 26. See also NCCPV, R502, Box 42; and the Chicago Police Department's Convention Log, A053, Box 5.

115. *New York Times,* August 26, 1968, 25; *Chicago Sun-Times,* August 26, 1968, 5, 26; and *Rights in Conflict,* 92.

116. "The Yippies Are Coming," 24; *Rights in Conflict,* 92–94. See also the *New York Times,* August 26, 1968, 25; and the *Chicago Sun-Times,* August 26, 1968, 5, 26.

117. See the *Chicago Sun-Times,* August 26, 1968, 5, 26; August 27, 1968, 5; "The Yippies Are Coming," 24; the *New York Times,* August 26, 1968, 25; in NCCPV, Richard Schultz, S064, Box 44, and Norman Lapping, R604, Box 43; and *Rights in Conflict,* 96.

118. *Rights in Conflict,* 96; "The Yippies Are Coming," 24; *Chicago Tribune* August 26, 1968, 1, 7; and *New York Times,* August 26, 1968, 25.

119. Interview with Harold Pacnik, June 3, 1999.

120. Interview with Paul Juravinski, January 26, 1999.

121. Jim Miller, *Democracy Is in the Streets: From Port Huron to the Siege of Chicago* (New York: Simon and Schuster, 1987), 299.

122. *New York Times,* August 26, 1968, 25; *Chicago Tribune* August 26, 1968, 1, 7; interview with Darrell Novakovski, October 18, 1999; and *Rights in Conflict,* 97.

123. Interview with Al Ogilvie, September 8, 1999.

124. *New York Times,* August 26, 1968, 25; *Chicago Tribune* August 26, 1968, 1, 7; and *Rights in Conflict,* 97.

125. Interview with Steve Nowakowski, November 1, 1999.

126. See the *New York Times,* August 26, 1968, 25; the *Chicago Tribune* August 26, 1968, 1, 7; and *Rights in Conflict,* 97, 98.

127. *New York Times,* August 26, 1968, 25; *Chicago Tribune* August 26, 1968, 1, 7; and *Rights in Conflict,* 98, 99.

128. For a good description of the events of Saturday and Sunday night, see "The Yippies Are Coming," 22–24. See also *Rights in Conflict,* 99.

129. Interview with Tom Freeborn, May 11, 2001; and NCCPV, R355, Box 41.

130. *New York Times,* August 26, 1968, 25; NCCPV, R284, Box 41, and R621, Box 43; and *Rights in Conflict,* 100.

131. Good general sources for Saturday and especially Sunday prior to convention week can be found in the Walker study team records, including testimony from members of the American Civil Liberties Union (ACLU), the police, and general witnesses. Files consulted included OR143, Box 34, R013, Box 40, S064, Box 44, S066, Box 44, R014, Box 40, S010, Box 44, R284, Box 41, A053, Box 5, R760, Box 43, R656, Box 43, R009, Box 40, R041, Box 40, R773, Box 43, R376, Box 41, and R789, Box 43, and the transcript from *United States* v. *David T. Dellinger* et al., No. 69 CR-180, 1969.

132. *Time,* August 30, 20–21; and The *Sixties,* 318.

133. Interview with Sam Ivanchenko, November 14, 1999, and Randall Bakker, June 30, 2002, and October 11, 2003.

134. Interview with Darrell Novakowski, October 18, 1999, and Brian Ramsey, June 23, 2001.

135. Interview with Murray Sheppard, May 29, 2002, and Jerry Ewaschuck, September 17, 2000; and *Chicago Sun-Times*, August 26, 1968, 5, 26. The police violence, however, was not played up.

136. *United States* v. *David T. Dellinger* et al., No. 69 CR-180, 1969.

137. Interview with Archie Pasis, August 23, 2001, and October 13, 2003. See also David Farber's *Chicago '68*, pages 161–164, for a discussion of the police mood on convention eve.

CHAPTER 5

1. Interview with Darrell Novakovski, October 18, 1999.

2. Mary McCarthy to her father, Senator Eugene McCarthy, as she watched police beat demonstrators from the twenty-third floor of the Conrad Hilton. Quoted in "The Government in Exile," *Time,* September 6, 1968, 37.

3. *Rights in Conflict,* 53.

4. *Chicago Sun-Times,* August 20, 1968, 7, August 27, 1968, 18, and August 17, 1968, 1, 11.

5. Interview with Archie Pasis, August 23, 2001.

6. "The Yippies Are Coming," 24, 25. Article mistakenly refers to Officer Riggio as "Liggio."

7. "The Yippies Are Coming," 25; *New York Times,* August 27, 1968, 29.

8. Interview with Tom O'Malley, July 27, 2000.

9. *Chicago Sun-Times,* August 27, 1968, 6, 21; *Rights in Conflict,* 101; and *New York Times,* August 27, 1968, 29.

10. Hayden's arrest is detailed in *Democracy Is in the Streets,* 300. For comments about plainclothes officers tailing Hayden and Davis, see "The Yippies Are Coming," 24–25. See also the *New York Times,* August 27, 1968, 29. James Ridgeway, writing in the September 7, 1968, edition of *The New Republic,* offers a similar tone but differs in the words attributed to police concerning Hayden as they took him to the station house. Ridgeway quotes police as threatening, "We're going to get rid of you, you son-of-a-bitch." During the Chicago 7 conspiracy trial, officer Frank Riggio denied any such utterances, saying, "No, sir, I never said that."

11. "The Yippies Are Coming," 25; *Who Spoke Up?* 186; and *New York Times,* August 27, 1968, 29.

12. Ibid.

13. Interview with Archie Pasis, August 23, 2001.

14. *Chicago Sun-Times,* August 22, 1968, 32, and August 24, 1968, 14.

15. "The Yippies Are Coming," 25; and *Who Spoke Up?* 186. See also the *New York Times,* August 27, 1968, 29.

16. *New York Times,* August 27, 1968, 29; and *Rights in Conflict,* 103.

17. "The Yippies Are Coming," 25; and *Who Spoke Up?* 186.

18. *Chicago Sun-Times,* August 27, 1968, 6; and *Rights in Conflict,* 105.

19. Interview with Tom Freeborn, March 11, 2001.

20. *Rights in Conflict,* viii.

21. *Chicago Sun-Times,* August 27, 1968, 28.

22. See "Survival in the Stockyards," *Time,* September 6, 1968, 29; *Miami and the Siege of Chicago,* 112–113; the *New York Times,* August 29, 1968, 23; and interview with Carl Moore, March 5, 2000.

23. *Chicago Sun-Times,* August 27, 1968, 6.

24. *New York Times,* August 18, 1964, p. 64.

25. A Harris poll also showed Nixon leading both McCarthy or Humphrey.

26. For a complete discussion of the draft Kennedy campaign, see *The Making of a President, 1968,* 280–285, and the *Chicago Sun-Times,* August 27, 1968, 1, 14, 24.

27. See the *Chicago Sun-Times,* April 2, 1968, 3, and April 3, 22. President Johnson met with Daley on April 2 to discuss the party leadership and the summer convention. The Chicago mayor was seen as a top Democrat to decide on who should run for the party in the fall. In April, Daley appeared to be leaning towards RFK. See also *Sun-Times,* August 14, 1968, 6 and August 16, 1, 14.

28. *Robert Kennedy and His Times,* 903.

29. For a discussion of the Vietnam War plank, see the *Chicago Sun-Times,* August 27, 1968, 3. For convention descriptions, see the *New Republic,* September 7, 1968, 10–11 and "Survival in the Stockyards," *Time,* September 6, 1968, 31.

30. Chicago *Sun-Times,* August 27, 1968, 11, and August 28, 1968, 46.

31. Ibid., August 27, 1968, 3.

32. See "What Happens Now," *New Republic,* September 7, 1968, 7.

33. *Miami and the Siege of Chicago,* 141.

34. *Rights in Conflict,* 106.

35. Interview with Sheldon Bartowski, July 19, 2000.

36. *Chicago Sun-Times,* August 27, 1968, 6; *Rights in Conflict,* 106. See also the *New York Times,* August 27, 1968, 29.

37. *Chicago Sun-Times,* August 27, 1968, 6; and *Rights in Conflict,* 107–108.

38. Interview with Norm Nelson, April 17, 2000.

39. *Chicago Sun-Times,* August 27, 1968, 6; and *Rights in Conflict,* 108.

40. "The Yippies Are Coming," 25; *New York Times,* August 27, 1968, 29; and the *Chicago Sun-Times,* August 27, 1968, 6.

41. *Rights in Conflict,* 108.

42. "The Yippies Are Coming," 25. See also the *New York Times,* August 27, 1968, 29.

43. *New York Times,* August 27, 1968, 29; and *Rights in Conflict,* 108.

44. *Rights in Conflict,* 205.

45. *Chicago Sun-Times,* August 27, 1968, 5; and *Rights in Conflict,* 206. See also *Miami and the Siege of Chicago,* 144–145; and the *New York Times,* August 27, 1968, 29.

46. These incidents are covered in the *New York Times,* August 28, 1968, 36; the *Chicago Sun-Times,* August 27, 1968, 21; *Rights in Conflict,* 206–208; and *Chicago's American,* August 27, 1968, 1, 3.

47. *Rights in Conflict,* 211.

48. Ibid., 209. See also the *New York Times,* August 27, 1968, 29; and *Chicago's American,* August 27, 1968, 1, 3, 24.

49. Interview with Mel Latanzio, August 3, 1999.

50. Interview with Randall Bakker, June 30, 2002.

51. Police interview, October 11, 2003. The former officer, at the author's request, brought out his old service nightstick to look at and feel its heft. During a portion of the

interview, it rested on the table that separated interviewer from interviewee. As the officer finished speaking, as if to add an exclamation point to his comment, he grabbed the baton and swung it down hard onto a phone book resting on the table. It sounded with a terrible crack; the table shook.

52. Interview with Ernie Watson, June 17, 1999.

53. Interview with Sheldon Bartowski, July 19, 2000.

54. *Chicago Daily News,* August 28, 1968, 3.

55. See Les Brownlee in NCCPV, R646, Box 43, 1; *Rights in Conflict,* 117; and *Boss: Richard J. Daley of Chicago,* 183. Twenty reporters needed hospital treatment after Monday night. Larger credentials after Sunday only made them more noticeable to cops, says Royko.

56. Interview with Steven Latz, June 4, 1999.

57. *Rights in Conflict,* 208.

58. Ibid., 210.

59. Ibid., 207.

60. "Dementia in the Second City," *Time,* September 6, 1968, 33.

61. "The Yippies Are Coming," 25–26; and *Miami and the Siege of Chicago,* 143.

62. NCCPV, R402, Box 42, 11, and R401, Box 42, 1, 2, for Commander Robert Lynsky's concerns over the intelligence reports on protestor violence; and *Rights in Conflict,* 109.

63. *Who Spoke Up?* 186.

64. *New York Times,* August 27, 1968, 29; *Rights in Conflict,* 110; and *Chicago Daily News,* August 27, 1968, 1, 3, 4, 8.

65. Interview with Warren MacAulay, January 17, 2000.

66. "Grooving in Chi" Terry Southern, *Esquire,* November 1968; *Chicago Sun-Times,* August 27, 1968, 1; and *Rights in Conflict,* 110–111.

67. Interview with Tom Freeborn, March 11, 2001.

68. Interview with Joe Pecoraro, October 13, 2003.

69. *Rights in Conflict,* 111.

70. "The Yippies Are Coming," 26; and *Chicago Sun-Times,* August 27, 1968, 6.

71. *Chicago Sun-Times,* August 27, 1968, 6; and *Rights in Conflict,* 112.

72. Interview with Dale Jaeschke, November 12, 2001.

73. *Telling It Like It Was,* 38–39.

74. *Chicago Sun-Times,* August 27, 1968, 6; *Who Spoke Up?* 186; and NCCPV, R402, Box 42, 11.

75. *Who Spoke Up?* 187; and *Rights in Conflict,* 112. It's unclear whether authors Nancy Zaroulis and Gerald Sullivan are quoting the Walker report or if they drew from an independent source for the alleged police chant of "Kill, Kill, Kill." David Farber also cites police officer reinforcements yelling the chant as they emerged by bus. Officers questioned on this strongly deny the use of such language. They suggest that people lied to Walker investigators on this issue.

76. *Chicago Daily News,* August 27, 1968, 1, 3, 4, 8; *Chicago Sun-Times,* August 27, 1968, 6; "The Yippies Are Coming," 26; and "Grooving in Chi," Terry Southern, *Esquire,* November 1968.

77. Interview with Ernie Bellows, February 10, 2001.

78. *Rights in Conflict,* 112–113.

79. For a description of these events, see Terry Southern, "Grooving in Chi," *Esquire,* November 1968; and *Rights in Conflict,* 113, and the *Chicago Daily News,* August 27, 1968,

1, 3, 4, 8. A photo of the incident appeared the next day in the *Chicago Daily News* on August 28, 1968, 5. Although most witness reports appear reliable and are easily cross-referenced, at times, some accounts fell victim to a combination of incomplete facts and hyperbole. One example came during the beating of two seminary students near Clark Street. One of the students remained on the ground following the encounter with two officers, prompting a man nearby to yell at police, "You killed a priest, you dirty god-damned mother fuckers killed a priest!" The seminary student ended up in hospital, where he received treatment for numerous lacerations to his head. The attack fractured his skull and damaged the vision in his right eye. Even though the attack was brutal, the perception of what was taking place was not complexly accurate. See *Rights in Conflict,* 113; and the *New York Times,* August 27, 1968, 29. For witness accounts of these incidents of police violence, see NCCPV, R017, Box 40, 3; OR225, Box 35, 1; R215, Box 41, 1; and SOR127, Box 47, 1.

80. Hayden's arrest is detailed in "The Yippies Are Coming," 26; and "The Cops and the Kids," *The New Republic,* September 7, 1968, 12. See also the *New York Times,* August 27, 1968, 29; *Who Spoke Up?* 186; and NCCPV, R008, Box 40, 2–5.

81. *Chicago Tribune,* August 27, 1968, 5; and *Rights in Conflict,* 114.

82. "The Yippies Are Coming," 26; and *New York Times,* August 27, 1968, 29.

83. Interview with, Murray Sheppard, May 29, 2002.

84. A number of sources were used for Monday night's events. They include *Rights in Conflict,* 114, 115, 116; *The Sixties,* 327; *Who Spoke Up?* 187; "The Yippies Are Coming," 26; the *Chicago Tribune,* August 27, 1968, 5; the *Chicago Daily News,* August 27, 1968, 1, 3, 4, 8; *Miami and the Siege of Chicago,* 144; the *New York Times,* August 27, 1968, 29; *Fire in the Streets,* 454–460; and NCCPV, R223, Box 41, 1; R686, Box 43, 1; R603, Box 43, 1; R203, Box 41, 12; SO64, Box 44, 2, 3; OR144, Box, 34, 9–15; SO84, Box 44, 3; R750, Box 43, 1; R502, Box 42, 7–16; OR017, Box 33, 2–4; and R717, Box 43, 3–5.

85. Interview with Fred Jeffery December 8, 2002, and Henry Nostbakken, June 12, 2002.

86. Interview with Kurt O'Grady March 22, 2000.

87. Interview with Sheldon Bartowski, July 19, 2000.

88. *Rights in Conflict,* 116. See also the *New York Times,* August 27, 1968, 29.

89. Interview with Fred Jeffery, December 8, 2002.

90. *Rights in Conflict,* 116; and *Chicago Tribune,* August 27, 1968, 5.

91. Interview with Kurt O'Grady, March 22, 2000.

92. *Rights in Conflict,* 117; and *Chicago Tribune,* August 27, 1968, 5.

93. Interview with Milt Brower, January 19, 2001.

94. Interview with Herbert Bile, May 12, 2002, and Ronald Adler, November 16, 1999.

95. *Chicago Sun-Times,* August 27, 1968, 5, 6.

96. Ibid., August 27, 1968, 33. See also the *Chicago Tribune,* August 27, 1968, 5; and the *Chicago Daily News,* August 27, 1968, 14.

97. *Chicago Sun-Times,* August 28, 1968, 28. See also the *Chicago Tribune,* August 27, 1968, 5; and *Chicago Tribune,* August 28, 1968, 9.

98. *Rights in Conflict,* 211.

99. Ibid., 213.

100. *Chicago Tribune,* August 27, 1968, 5.

101. *Chicago's American,* August 27, 1968, 1, 3.

102. *Chicago Tribune,* August 28, 1968, 11.

103. Interview with Will Gerald, May 6, 2002.

104. Interview with Edward Nochowny, January 11, 2000, and Don Holtz, May 20, 2001.

105. Interview with Reg Novak, May 27, 1999.

106. *Chicago Sun-Times,* August 27, 1968, 21; and *Rights in Conflict,* 117–118.

107. *Chicago Sun-Times,* August 21, 1968, 18; and *Rights in Conflict,* 119.

108. *Chicago Sun-Times,* August 24, 1968, 14.

109. *Rights in Conflict,* 119.

110. *New York Times,* August 28, 1968, 31; *Chicago Sun-Times,* August 28, 1968, 18, 32; and interview with Orrest Hupka, September 14, 2002.

111. "The Cops & the Kids," 13; and "The Yippies Are Coming," 27. See also *Miami and the Siege of Chicago,* 145–146.

112. *Chicago Sun-Times,* August 28, 1968, 18; *The Unraveling of America,* 320; and *Rights in Conflict,* 120.

113. *Rights in Conflict,* 121.

114. Ibid., 126, 127, 129–130.

115. *Who Spoke Up?* 188; the *New York Times,* August 28, 1968, 36; and the *Chicago Sun-Times,* August 28, 1968, 9.

116. Commander Robert Lynsky in NCCPV, R502, Box 42, 16–18; and *Rights in Conflict,* 124.

117. *Chicago Sun-Times,* August 28, 1968, 9; and *Rights in Conflict,* 126.

118. See *Who Spoke Up?* 188; "The Cops & the Kids," 13; *Miami and the Siege of Chicago,* 146–148; *New York Times,* August 28, 1968, 36; and the *Chicago Sun-Times,* August 28, 1968, 9.

119. *New York Times,* August 28, 1968, 36; and *Rights in Conflict,* 126–127.

120. See the *Chicago Sun-Times,* August 28, 1968, 18; *Who Spoke Up?* 188; and "The Cops & the Kids," 13.

121. *Rights in Conflict,* 128; and *New York Times,* August 28, 1968, 36.

122. Silverman's photo appeared in the *New York Times,* on Wednesday August 28, 1968, 36. See also *Rights in Conflict,* 217.

123. *New York Times,* August 28, 1968, 36.

124. *Chicago Tribune,* August 28, 1968, 9.

125. *Chicago's American,* August 28, 1968, 3. For in-depth sources on Tuesday night in Lincoln Park and Old Town, see NCCPV, R502, Box 42, 16–18; A053, Box 5; R760, Box 43, 1–2; R022, Box 40, 12; R028, Box 40, 4–8; and R018, Box 40, 6–7.

126. "The Cops & the Kids," 13.

127. Interview with Ronald Adler, November 16, 1999, Orrest Hupka, September 14, 2000, and Lyall Zedowski, March 16, 2000.

128. See Lance Morrow, "The Whole World Was Watching," *Time,* August 26, 1996.

129. Churchill's account is detailed in the *Chicago Sun-Times,* August 28, 1968, 5.

130. See "The Decline and Fall of the Democratic Party," *Ramparts,* September 28, 1968, 20; *Time,* September 6, 1968, 55; the *Chicago Sun-Times,* August 28, 1968, 23; and *Chicago's American,* August 28, 1968, 5.

131. "The Cops & the Kids," 13.

132. Ibid., 13.

133. *Who Spoke Up?* 188.

134. "The Cops & the Kids," 13.

135. *New York Times,* August 28, 1968, 36; and *Rights in Conflict,* 135.

136. *Rights in Conflict,* 133, 136; and *Chicago Tribune,* August 28, 1968, 1, 9.

137. *Who Spoke Up?* 189. See also *Miami and the Siege of Chicago,* 150. Cop Joe Pecoraro, like several other former officers, held Rochford in high regard. "I think that the best [superintendent] we ever had in my lifetime was James Rochford [who was first deputy superintendent in 1968]. He was right out front; he wouldn't tell his men anything he wouldn't do himself. He was right there. He was a good man—guys would follow him. If you're going to be a leader, be a leader. He was a leader." Interview with Joe Pecoraro, October 13, 2003.

138. *Chicago Tribune,* August 28, 1968, 1, 9; and *Rights in Conflict,* 136.

139. Interview with Ray Mihalicz, July 8, 1999.

140. *Rights in Conflict,* 136; and *Chicago Tribune,* August 28, 1968, 1, 9.

141. *Who Spoke Up?* 189; "The Cops & the Kids," 13; "The Yippies Are Coming," 26; and *Chicago Tribune,* August 28, 1968, 1, 9.

142. *Rights in Conflict,* 138.

143. Interview with Joe Pecoraro, October 13, 2003; and NCCPV, A152, Box 6, 7–8; R703, Box 43, 1–2; R789, Box 43, 9–14; SOR115, Box 47, 1; and SO84, Box 44, 4.

144. *Miami and the Siege of Chicago,* 150–154; *Rights in Conflict,* 137; and *Chicago Tribune,* August 28, 1968, 1, 9.

145. *Miami and the Siege of Chicago,* 150–154. Interview with Carl Moore, March 5, 2000, and Gord Stensill, October 16, 2001; and *Rights in Conflict,* 139.

146. Interview with Randall Bakker, June 30, 2002.

147. Interview with Eddie Kelso, December 11, 1999.

148. *Rights in Conflict,* 141.

149. Interview with Kelly Fredrickson, March 4, 2000.

150. Interview with Dennis Kaminski, June 27, 2001. Walker investigators indicate that there were ten plainclothes police officers in the band shell area. A commander denied that his men "provoked any incident." The department, however, warned those in the uniform division that they would face taunting and baiting and they were to act professionally.

151. *Miami and the Siege of Chicago,* 160–161; and *Rights in Conflict,* 143.

152. Some, including a reporter for the *Chicago Tribune,* suggested that the flag lowering involved undercover cop Robert L. Pierson, who acted as Jerry Rubin's bodyguard. Pierson denied any involvement. See Chapter 6 for a discussion of Pierson's actions that week.

153. *Rights in Conflict,* 145; and *Miami and the Siege of Chicago,* 160–161.

154. Ibid., 145–146; *Miami and the Siege of Chicago,* 160–161. See also, the *Chicago Sun-Times,* August 29, 1968, 30.

155. *Rights in Conflict,* 146. *Miami and the Siege of Chicago,* 161. See also "Who Were the Protestors," *Time,* September 6, 1968, 36; and the *Chicago Sun-Times,* August 29, 1968, 18, 30.

156. See *The Sixties,* 332.

157. *Rights in Conflict,* 146–147; *New York Times,* August 29, 1968, 1, 23.

158. *Miami and the Siege of Chicago,* 160–161; and *Rights in Conflict,* 148.

159. *Rights in Conflict,* 148.

160. *Miami and the Siege of Chicago,* 161.

161. Interview with Dale Jaeschke, November 12, 2001. See also *Rights in Conflict,* 148. A police representative told the Walker Study Team that the flag lowering incident "deeply affected the police." See also *Time,* September 6, 1968, 34.

162. *New York Times,* August 29, 1968, 23; and *Rights in Conflict,* 149.

163. *Rights in Conflict,* 150; and *New York Times,* August 29, 1968, 23. For witness testimony, see NCCPV, SO19, Box 44, 70–73; R229, Box 41, 2; OR146, Box 34, 20–23; SO81, Box 44, 5; and SO84, Box 44, 1.

164. *Miami and the Siege of Chicago*, 161, and *The Sixties*, 332.

165. Dellinger is quoted in *The War Within*, 278.

166. Hayden's words and actions are quoted in *The War Within*, 279; *Miami and the Siege of Chicago*, 161; and *The Sixties*, 332.

167. Interview with Paul Juravinski, January 26, 1999. Indeed Rochford was concerned with intelligence reports that protestors planned to invade the hotels in force. See *United States v. David Dellinger* et al. 8665; and NCCPV, R402, Box 43, 2.

168. *Rights in Conflict*, 153; *New York Times*, August 29, 1968, 23.

169. Interview with Carl Moore, March 5, 2000.

170. Interview with Frank Froese, June 2, 2000.

171. *Chicago Daily News*, August 29, 1968, 1–6; *Rights in Conflict*, 156; and *New York Times*, August 29, 1968, 23.

172. *The Sixties*, 332; and *Chicago Sun-Times*, August 29, 1968, 5, 12.

173. *Rights in Conflict*, 158; and *Chicago Sun-Times*, August 29, 1968, 5, 30.

174. *The Sixties*, 332.

175. Interview with Brian Ramsey, June 23, 2001, and Steve Nowakowski, November 1, 1999. Evidence from the Walker Study Team suggest some confusion among the rank and file police ranks as the crowds pressed against the National Guard lines. See NCCPV, AO53, Box 5.

176. Interview with Walter Jorgenson, May 18, 1999.

177. *Rights in Conflict*, 159.

178. "Who Were the Protestors?" *Time*, September 6, 1968, 36.

179. *New York Times*, August 29, 1968, 1, 23; *Chicago Daily News*, August 29, 1968, 1–6; and *Rights in Conflict*, 162–163.

180. "The Fourth Party Is in the Streets," *Ramparts*, September 28, 1968, 38; *Rights in Conflict*, 163; and *New York Times*, August 29, 1968, 1, 23.

181. *Rights in Conflict*, 167; *The Sixties*, 333.

182. Interview with Harold Pacnik, June 3, 1999, and Steve Nowakowski, November 1, 1999. Much has been made about police officers "losing control" of themselves at this point and refusing to heed the warnings of Rochford and others to hold their positions. But according to several officers, including Joe Pecoraro, Rochford did not want his officers to be hurt in repeated attacks from the crowds and allowed his officers to aggressively defend themselves. The deputy superintendent also did not want the crowd to gain entrance to the Hilton or the Sheraton and understood that force was necessary. As Rochford said later, "I had no intention of allowing a mob to take over the street."

183. *Who Spoke Up?* 191–196; *New York Times*, August 29, 1968, 1, 23; and *Rights in Conflict*, 169.

184. *Rights in Conflict*, 170.

185. Interview with Kurt O'Grady, March 22, 2000, Mel Latanzio, August 9, 1999, and Sam McMaster, September 18, 2000. Indeed, reports in the Walker commission revealed more than one officer reporting being kicked in the groin during confrontations with demonstrators. See *Rights in Conflict*, 173.

186. Interview with Terry Novicki, October 15, 2001, and Sam Ivanchenko, November 14, 1999.

187. *Rights in Conflict*, 170; *Who Spoke Up?* 191–196.

188. Seemingly the only sanity that took place occurred ten minutes before the hour when, following negotiations, David Dellinger, leading Ralph Abernathy's Poor People's Mule Train, was allowed through police lines and up Michigan Avenue.

189. *Miami and the Siege of Chicago*, 164.

190. "Grooving in Chi," Terry Southern, *Esquire*, November 1968.

191. See the *Chicago Tribune*, August 29, 1968, 1, 7; and the *Chicago Sun-Times*, August 29, 1968, 30.

192. For a complete description of the scene at the Hilton, and the events immediately proceeding and following, see "The Fourth Party Is in the Streets," 38; *Rights in Conflict*, 172–173; *The Sixties*, 333; *Miami and the Siege of Chicago*, 162–167; "The Cops & the Kids,"13, 14; *Time*, September 6, 1968, 35; *Who Spoke Up?* 191–196; Terry Southern, "Grooving in Chi," *Esquire*, November 1968; the *Chicago Sun-Times*, August 29, 1968, 1, 5–7; the *Chicago Tribune*, August 29, 1968, 1, 7; the *Chicago Daily News*, August 29, 1968, 1–6; and NCCPV, R402, Box 43, 3–4; R313, Box 41; S100, Box 44, 7; R229, Box 41, 7–18, SO61, Box 45, 1–3; R009, Box 40, 4–6; SO68, Box 44, 5–6; SO71, Box 44, 6–10; R292, Box 41, 2–7; and Boxes 31–47 for general witness statements.

193. *Chicago Sun-Times*, August 29, 1968, 5, 30; and *Chicago Tribune*, August 29, 1968, 1, 7.

194. *Chicago Sun-Times*, August 29, 1968, 5, 10, 18, 30; and *Chicago Tribune*, August 29, 1968, 1, 7.

195. Interview with Ken O'Connor, May 18, 1999.

196. *New York Times*, August 28, 1968, 32.

197. *The Unraveling of America*, 416.

198. *Chicago Sun-Times*, August 29, 1968, 37; *Time*, September 6, 1968, 54; *Miami and the Siege of Chicago*, 172; *New York Times*, August 29, 1968, 23; and *Chicago Tribune*, August 29, 1968, 7.

199. *Time*, September 6, 1968, 6, 54.

200. See *Chicago Tribune*, August 28, 1968, 12; and *Chicago Sun-Times*, August 28, 1968, 5.

201. *Time*, September 6, 1968, 54.

202. Ibid.

203. *Chicago Sun-Times*, August 29, 1968, 17.

204. Ibid., August 29, 1968, 5. McCarthy refers darkly to the battle of 216 B.C.E. where Hannibal crushed the Roman army.

205. *Chicago Sun-Times*, August 29, 1968, 30.

206. Ibid., August 29, 1968, 30; and *Rights in Conflict*, 175–177. See also *Who Spoke Up?* 191–196; "The Cops & the Kids," 13–14; and *Miami and the Siege of Chicago*, 163–168.

207. Lance Morrow, "The Whole World Was Watching" *Time*, August 26, 1996.

208. *Rights in Conflict*, 178–179; *Who Spoke Up?* 191–196; "The Cops & the Kids," 13–14; *Miami and the Siege of Chicago*, 163–168; and *Chicago Sun-Times*, August 29, 1968, 30.

209. *Rights in Conflict*, 180; *Who Spoke Up?* 191–196; "The Cops & the Kids," 13–14; and *Miami and the Siege of Chicago*, 163–168.

210. See *Chicago's American*, August 29, 1968, 1, 3.

211. *Rights in Conflict*, 183; *Who Spoke Up?* 191–196; and *Miami and the Siege of Chicago*, 163–168.

212. *Time*, September 6, 1968, 34, 35.

213. *Telling It Like It Was*, 39.

214. *Rights in Conflict*, 185; *New York Times*, August 29, 1968, 1, 23; and *Chicago Daily News*, August 29, 1968, 1–6.

215. *The Sixties*, 327.

216. *Telling It Like It Was: The Chicago Riots*, 99–100.

217. Ibid., 72.

218. Ibid., 51.

219. Ibid., 54. Particularly helpful for the various accounts of violence are NCCPV witness statements in Boxes 31 to 34 and 40 to 47.

220. Interview with Orrest Hupka, September 14, 2002.

221. Interview with Steve Nowakowski, November 1, 1999.

222. Interview with Joe Pecoraro, October 13, 2003; Ronald Lardo, April 12, 2001; and *New York Times,* August 30, 1968, 15.

223. *Time,* September 6, 1968, 54.

224. *The Sixties,* 327.

225. Ibid., 330.

226. See *Chicago Tribune,* August 28, 1968, 16.

227. Interview with Jim Dziadyk, September 20, 2001; Marlin Rowden, June 21, 2000; and Al Ogilvie, September 21, 1999.

228. *The Sixties,* 328–329.

229. *Time,* September 6, 1968, 34.

230. The officer is quoted in the *New York Times,* August 30, 1968, 15.

231. Interview with George Horsley, July 15, 2001.

232. Interview with Joe Pecoraro, October 13, 2003; and the *New York Times,* August 29, 1968, 1.

233. *Who Spoke Up?* 195; *Miami and the Siege of Chicago,* 174–175; Jonah Raskin, *For the Hell of It: The Life and Times of Abbie Hoffman* (Berkeley: University of California Press, 1996); 166; and the *New York Times,* August 29, 1968, 1. Daley vehemently denied using such a slur during the exchange. See the *Chicago Sun-Times,* September 10, 1968, 7.

234. *Time,* September 6, 1968, 54.

235. "The Fourth Party Is in the Streets," 40.

236. *Rights in Conflict,* 189–190; and *New York Times,* August 29, 1968, 1, 23.

237. The *Chicago Sun-Times,* August 29, 1968, 3.

238. The *Chicago Daily News,* August 29, 1968, 1–3; *New York Times,* August 29, 1968, 1; and *Chicago Sun-Times,* August 29, 1968, 4, 30.

239. *Rights in Conflict,* 188–189.

240. "The Fourth Party Is in the Streets," 40.

241. See *The Making of a President, 1968,* 301–303; the *Chicago Sun-Times,* August 29, 1968, 3.

242. *Chicago Sun-Times,* August 29, 1968, 4.

243. Ibid., August 29, 1968, 30.

244. "What Happens Now," *The New Republic,* September 7, 1968, 7.

245. *Rights in Conflict,* 221–223; and *Who Spoke Up?* 196.

246. Ibid., 218.

247. Ibid., 219.

248. *Chicago Sun-Times,* August 29, 1968, 46.

249. *Chicago Daily News,* August 29, 1968, 14.

250. *Chicago's American,* August 29, 1968, 1, 3, 4.

251. *Chicago Sun-Times,* August 30, 1968, 1, 3; and *Chicago Tribune,* August 29, 1968, 7.

252. *Chicago Sun-Times,* August 30, 1968, 3.

253. *Rights in Conflict,* 224.

254. *New York Times,* August 30, 1968, 12; and *Chicago Sun-Times,* August 30, 1968, 2.

255. *New York Times,* August 30, 1968, 1, 14; and *Rights in Conflict,* 226.

256. *Chicago Sun-Times,* August 30, 1968, 5, 7; *New York Times,* August 30, 1, 14; and *Chicago Daily News,* August 30, 1968, 5–7.

257. *Chicago Sun-Times,* August 30, 1968, 4.

258. Daley appeared on the CBS News, August 29, 1968. *Rights in Conflict,* 219; and *Chicago Sun-Times,* August 31, 1968, 6.

259. For a discussion of these events, see the *Chicago Daily News,* August 30, 1968, 1–5, the *Chicago Sun-Times,* August 31, 1968, 5, 6; "The Fourth Party Is in the Streets," 40–41; *Rights in Conflict,* 230–232; *Who Spoke Up?* 198–199; the *New York Times,* August 31, 1968, 1, 11; *Time,* September 6, 1968, 36; interview with Ernie Bellows, February 10, 2001; and *The Unraveling of America,* 422. Journalists reported seeing people throwing objects at police from the hotel's upper floors. See *Telling It Like It Was: The Chicago Riots,* 111.

260. *Revolution for the Hell of It,* 114, 115; and *Boss,* 189.

261. *New York Times,* August 31, 1968, 1, and September 1, 1968, 1, 37.

262. Interview with Marlin Rowden, June 21, 2000.

263. Interview with Steven Latz, June 4, 1999, and Hank Peterson, February 16, 2001.

264. Interview with Don Holtz, May 20, 2001, and Steve Nowakowski, November 1, 1999.

265. Interview with Ronald Lardo, April 12, 2001, and Tom Freeborn, March 11, 2001.

266. *Chicago Sun-Times,* September 1, 1968, 3; and *Chicago's American,* August 30, 1968, 8.

267. *Chicago Tribune,* September 1, 1968, 2.

268. Interview with Harold Pacnik, June 3, 1999, and October 10, 2003; and *Chicago Sun-Times,* September 2, 1968, 4.

CHAPTER 6

1. Interview with Mel Latanzio, October 12, 2003.

2. City of Chicago Alderman Vito Marzullo quoted in the *Chicago Sun-Times,* December 3, 1968, 5.

3. For Kerr's arrest, see "Dementia in the Second City," *Time,* September 6, 1968; and the *Chicago Daily News,* August 31, 1968, 6.

4. Reston's insightful editorial details the obvious damage to the Democratic Party following the convention. See the *New York Times,* August 29, 1968, 1.

5. See Chapter 7 for a complete look at the opinion polls.

6. See the *New York Times,* September 1, 1968, 1, 36; see also the *Politics of Joy,* 81, 200.

7. *Chicago Sun-Times,* September 1, 1968, 3, and August 31, 1968, 22. See also *A Report of Chicago Crime for 1968,* 5.

8. *Chicago Sun-Times,* September 1, 1968, 3. See also the *Chicago Tribune,* August 30, 1968, 6.

9. The *Making of a President,* 303.

10. *Telling It Like It Was: The Chicago Riots,* 151.

11. The *Chicago Sun-Times,* September 1, 1968, 27.

12. The *Chicago Tribune,* August 30, 1968, 12.

13. The *Chicago Sun-Times,* August 30, 1968, 7.

14. Editorials in the *New York Times,* August 30, 1968, 32, and August 31, 1968, 22, blasted Daley.

15. *Chicago Sun-Times,* August 31, 1968, 8.

16. Ibid., August 30, 1968, 33.

17. *Chicago Daily News,* August 31, 1968, 8.

18. *Chicago Tribune,* August 30, 1968, 1, 9.

19. *Chicago Sun-Times,* September 4, 1968, 4, 6.

20. Ibid., 4, 6.

21. Ibid., September 12, 1968, 16, and interview with Brian Ramsey, June 23, 2001.

22. Official police records indicated that 192 officers received injuries during convention week.

23. *Chicago Sun-Times,* September 10, 1968, 29.

24. "Dementia in the Second City," *Time,* September 6, 1968, 33.

25. *New York Times,* August 30, 1968, 15.

26. *Chicago Sun-Times,* August 30, 1968, 7.

27. *Rights in Conflict,* vii. The witness testimony contained so many expletives that the Government Printing Office refused to print it.

28. "Four-letter Report on Chicago," *New Statesman,* December 6, 1968, 776–777.

29. *Chicago Sun-Times,* December 2, 1968, 3.

30. *Chicago Daily News,* December 3, 1968, 3.

31. *Chicago Tribune,* December 3, 1968, 2.

32. Interview with Ernie Watson, June 17, 1999.

33. *Chicago Tribune,* December 3, 1968, 6, and interview with Joe Pecoraro, October 13, 2003.

34. *Chicago Sun-Times,* December 3, 1968, 5.

35. Ibid., December 3, 1968, 1.

36. Ibid., December 2, 1968, 4.

37. Ibid., December 3, 1968, 8.

38. *Chicago Daily News,* December 4, 1968, 12.

39. *Chicago Tribune,* December 3, 1968, 16.

40. *Chicago Sun-Times,* December 3, 1968, 31. See also the editorial of December 5, where the paper criticizes Daley and Conlisk for their refusal to concede that there were too many instances of police violence to be explained away.

41. *Chicago Sun-Times,* December 4, 1968, 30. A reprint of the *Post* cartoon is found in *Newsweek,* December 16, 1968, 33.

42. *Chicago Sun-Times,* December 6, 1968, 4.

43. Ibid., December 2, 1968, 3.

44. *Newsweek,* December 16, 1968, 33. The grand jury's findings would lead to indictments handed down in March of 1969 against the Chicago 8. See also the *Chicago Daily News,* December 4, 1968, 1, 6.

45. *Chicago Sun-Times,* December 5, 1968, 3.

46. *Newsweek,* December 16, 1968, 33.

47. *Rights in Conflict,* 105.

48. Carl Oglesby, *From Camelot to Kent State: The Sixties Experience in the Words of Those Who Lived It* (Oxford University Press, 2001), 305.

49. *Chicago Sun-Times,* September 1, 1968, 3.

50. Interview with Steve Nowakowski, November 1, 1999, and Herbert Bile, May 12, 2002.

51. Interview with Terry Novicki, October 15, 2001.

52. Interview with Grant Brown, October 17, 2002.

53. Interview with Joe Pecoraro, October 13, 2003.

54. Interview with Jack Ochosky, March 12, 2002.

55. Interview with Sam McMaster, September 18, 2000. McMaster refers to poet Allen Ginsberg.

56. Marlin Rowden, June 21, 2000, and Steve Nowakowski, November 1, 1999.

57. Interview with Harold Pacnik, June 3, 1999.

58. Interview with Norm Nelson, April 17, 2000.

59. Terry H. Anderson, *The Movement and the Sixties* (New York: Oxford University Press, 1995), 222, and interview with Henry Nostbakken, June 12, 2002.

60. Interview with Marlin Rowden, June 21, 2000. Interview with Dennis Pierson, January 20, 1999.

61. "The Government in Exile," *Time,* September 6, 1968, 36–37.

62. See the House Un-American Activities Committee (HUAC) hearings, 2406. Chicago police also had an undercover policewoman gathering information while tagging close to Abbie Hoffman. Officer Mary Ellen Dahl worked the crowds wearing a WWI army helmet. See also John Shultz, *The Chicago Conspiracy Trial* (New York: Da Capo Press, 1993), 128.

63. Interview with Ronald Adler, November 16, 1999, and Mel Latanzio, August 9, 1999.

64. See Terry Southern, "Grooving in Chi," *Esquire* (November 1968).

65. Interview with Sash Sadowski, March 16, 2000; Ray Mihalicz, July 8, 1999; Tom Freeborn, March 11, 2001; and Steve Nowakowski, November 1, 1999.

66. The files of the Chicago Red Squad are archived at the Chicago Historical Society, but they are sealed until 2025.

67. *Rights in Conflict,* viii; and interview with Norm Nelson, April 17, 2000.

68. *Democracy Is in the Streets,* 297. See also Farber's *Chicago '68,* 170.

69. *The Whole World Is Watching,* 189.

70. Interview with Randall Bakker, June 30, 2002; Orrest Hupka, September 14, 2002; and Steve Nowakowski, November 1, 1999.

71. See the *Washington Star,* December 2, 1970, A-8.

72. Quoted in George O'Toole, *The Private Sector: Rent-a-Cops, Private Spies, and the Police-Industrial Complex* (New York: W. W. Norton & Company, 1978), 145.

73. *Chicago Tribune,* April 28, 1968, 8. During the House's Un-American Activities hearings, undercover cop Pierson admitted under oath that he was a former counterintelligence agent with the U.S. army. See HUAC, 2391.

74. See Nelson Black, Cointelpro: *The FBI's Secret War on Political Freedom* (New York: Vintage, 1975), 3–26, 41–45, 119–148; Herbert Mitgang, *Dangerous Dossiers* (New York: D. I. Fine Books, 1988), 268; Ward Churchill and Jim Vander Wall, *The Cointelpro Papers: Documents From the FBI's Secret Wars Against Domestic Dissent* (Boston: South End Press, 1990), 165–230; and Ronald Kessler's *The Bureau: The Secret History of the FBI* (New York: St. Martin's Press, 2002), 148–49, 156.

75. During the HUAC hearings, Chicago Police Department subversive unit officers Joseph J. Healy and Joseph Grubisic detailed their infiltration of the radical groups, in the days and weeks prior to the convention, to collect information and head off any plots to disrupt the convention. Interview with Orrest Hupka, September 14, 2002.

76. *Boss,* 174.

77. Ibid., 174. For a look at the department's Red Squad, see Lois Wille, "The Secret Police in Chicago," *Chicago Journalism Review,* February 1969.

78. Interview with Edward Nochowny, November 28, 1999.

79. *The Whole World Is Watching,* 189.

80. HUAC, 2399–2406.

81. Ibid., 2511–2512.

82. Ibid., 2611–2612.

83. Ibid., 2368.

84. The full color of the proceedings can only be found in reading the complete transcripts. See *United States* v. *David T. Dellinger* et al., No. 69 CR-180, 1969. Also worth reading is John Shultz, *The Chicago Conspiracy Trial* (New York: Da Capo Press, 1993).

85. See *United States* v. *David T. Dellinger* et al.; and the Chicago *Seed,* Vol. 4, No. 8, November 1968, 3, 4, 17; Vol. 4, No. 10, December 1968, 4, 5, 23, 25; Vol. 4, No. 12, February 1969, 2, 3, 29; and Vol. 4, No. 13, February 1969, 6–9. See also Ramsey Clark et al., *Contempt, Transcript of the Contempt Citations, Sentences, and Responses of the Chicago Conspiracy 10* (Chicago: The Swallow Press, 1970).

86. See *Fire in the Streets,* 458, 459.

87. Charles Lloyd Garrettson, *Hubert H. Humphrey: The Politics of Joy* (New Brunswick, NJ: Transaction Publishers, 1993), 200. See also "Hayden Hails Chicago: The Elements of Victory," *The Movement,* October 1968, 4–7.

CHAPTER 7

1. Interview with Steve Nowakowski, October 11, 2003.

2. The use of the term "berserk" to describe police behavior is not uncommon. Its use is also not unique to left-leaning periodicals of the time or to journalists who covered the event who were themselves victims of police actions. Even more conservative scholars in university and high school texts, including Tindall and Shi's otherwise excellent *America: A Narrative History,* ascribe the term to Chicago police. See the Conclusion for discussion of this term's application to police.

3. Interview with Marlin Rowden, June 21, 2000, and October 12, 2003, and Tim Markosky, July 8, 2001. The majority of officers claim that pressure came mostly from some sergeants, commanders, and veteran officers. They believe that Superintendent Rochford was initially hesitant to employ the degree of force that was used, but after he witnessed the brazenness of the first crowds on the streets the Saturday and Sunday before the convention, they suggest he supported officers in their efforts.

4. Interview with Hank Peterson, February 16, 2001.

5. Interview with Edward Nochowny, November 28, 1999.

6. Interview with Al Ogilvie, September 21, 1999, and Daley's promise in the *Chicago Tribune,* October 9, 1967.

7. *Boss,* 164, 165.

8. Interview with Kelly Fredrickson, March 4, 2000.

9. Interview with Tim Markosky, July 8, 2001; and *Time,* September 13, 1968, 56.

10. Interview with Will Gerald, May 6, 2002.

11. Interview with Walter Jorgenson, May 10, 1999.

12. *Chicago Daily News,* December 10, 1968, 10.

13. "Dementia in the Second City," *Time,* September 6, 1968, 33, 34.

14. Interview with Walter Jorgenson, May 10, 1999; Tim Markosky, July 8, 2001; and Walter Jorgenson, May 10, 1999.

15. Interview with Paul Juravinski, January 26, 1999, and Dale Jaeschke, November 12, 2001.

16. Interview with Sam Nuberg, June 15, 1999, and Warren MacAulay, January 17, 2000.

17. Interview with Joe Pecoraro, October 13, 2003.

18. HUAC, 2514.

19. Interview with Gord Stensill, October 16, 2000.

20. Interview with Joe Pecoraro, October 13, 2003.

21. Interview with Tom Freeborn, March 11, 2001.

22. The Chicago Crime Commission report for 1968 indicates that there were only 653 arrests during convention week, whereas the Walker report's tally is slightly higher at 668. See *A Report on Chicago Crime for 1968,* 5, and *Rights in Conflict,* S-5.

23. Interview with Joe Pecoraro, October 13, 2003.

24. Interview with Ray Mihalicz, July 8, 1999.

25. *The Politics of Protest,* 246.

26. *Rights in Conflict,* 191.

27. Ibid., 199.

28. Ibid., 209. See also *Chicago '68,* 185.

29. Interview with Eddie Kelso, December 11, 1999.

30. Interview with Victor Olafson, July 9, 1999.

31. Interview with Paul Juravinski, January 26, 1999. Indeed, as far back as 1965, two-thirds of the department's sergeants believed that the city's newspapers unduly criticized the force. See James Q. Wilson, "Police Morale, Reform and Citizen Respect: The Chicago Case," *The Police* (New York: John Wiley & Sons, 1967), 154.

32. *Telling It Like It Was: The Chicago Riots,* 58; and interview with Greg Parzanski, April 17, 2002.

33. *Telling It Like It Was: The Chicago Riots,* 137.

34. Interview with Norm Nelson, April 17, 2000, and Dennis Kaminski, June 27, 2001.

35. Interview with Will Gerald, May 6, 2002, and Warren MacAulay, January 17, 2000.

36. Interview with Terry Novicki, October 15, 2001.

37. Interview with Carl Moore, March 5, 2000, and Norm Nelson, April 17, 2000.

38. Quoted in *Rights in Conflict,* 220; interview with Eddie Kelso, December 11, 1999.

39. Interview with Joe Pecoraro, October 13, 2003.

40. *Rights in Conflict,* xi; and *Chicago '68,* 185.

41. Interview with Marlin Rowden, June 21, 2000.

42. Quoted in *Time* September 6, 1968, 54.

43. *Chicago Sun-Times,* December 20, 1968, 24.

44. *Rights in Conflict,* xi.

45. Ibid., 201, 202.

46. Interview with Joe Pecoraro, October 13, 2003.

47. Interview with Steve Nowakowski, November 1, 1999, and Ken O'Connor, January 29, 2000.

48. *Chicago Sun-Times,* September 2, 1968, 18.

49. *Chicago Daily News,* September 3, 1968.

50. *Rights in Conflict,* S-6.

51. Interview with Joe Pecoraro, October 13, 2003.

52. See *A Report on Chicago Crime for 1968* (Chicago Crime Commission 1968), 3, 10.

53. Interview with Mel Latanzio, August 9, 1999; George Horsley, July 15, 2001; and Victor Olafson, July 9, 1999.

54. *New York Times,* August 19, 1968, 27.

55. *The Sixties,* 326.

56. Ibid., 233.

57. Interview with Steve Nowakowski, November 1, 1999.

58. Interview with Henry Nostbakken, June 12, 2002, and Lloyd Matthews, January 7, 2001. See also the *New York Times,* August 30, 15.

59. Interview with Brian Ramsey, June 23, 2001; Kelly Fredrickson, March 4, 2000; Sheldon Bartowski, July 19, 2000; and Steve Nowakowski, November 1, 1999.

60. Interview with Hank Pacnik, June 3, 1999.

61. Interview with Eddie Kelso, December 11, 1999; Randall Bakker, June 30, 2002; and Ernie Bellows, February 2001.

62. Interview with Joe Pecoraro, October 13, 2003.

63. Interview with Dennis Pierson, January 20, 1999; George Horsley, July 15, 2001; Grant Brown, October 17, 2002; and the *New York Times,* August 30, 1968, 14.

64. *Telling It Like It Was: The Chicago Riots,* 108.

65. Ibid., 69.

66. Ibid., 37.

67. Dowd is quoted in *The War Within,* 279.

68. See Jean Genet, *Esquire* (November 1968).

69. *New York Times,* August 28, 1968, 31.

70. *Revolution for the Hell of It,* 96. Some police officers, however, were unfazed by demonstrator taunts. "We kind of like the word 'pig,'" cop John Gruber told *Time* magazine. "Some of us answer our officers 'oink, oink, sir,' just to show it doesn't bother us." Gruber was quoted in *Time,* September 6, 1968, 34.

71. *Chicago Tribune,* August 30, 1968, 1.

72. See Lance Morrow, "The Whole World Was Watching: When the Democrats Last Convened in Chicago, the War Broke Out at Home," *Time,* August 26, 1996.

73. See, *Telling It Like It Was: The Chicago Riots,* 50.

74. Columnist Max Lerner writing in the *Chicago Sun-Times,* August 29, 1968, 27.

75. Schlesinger is quoted in *Newsweek,* June 17, 1968, 43.

76. *Revolution for the Hell of It,* 122.

77. *Chicago Sun-Times,* December 4, 1968, 5.

78. *Public Opinion Quarterly,* No. 34, (Spring 1970): 1, 2.

79. Melvin Small, *Covering Dissent: The Media and the Anti-Vietnam War Movement* (New Brunswick, NJ: Rutgers University Press, 1994), 89.

80. *Public Opinion Quarterly,* No. 34, (Spring 1970): 2.

81. Ibid., 3.

82. *For the Hell of It,* 143.

83. *The Sixties,* 335. As Melvin Small has pointed out, "Many television viewers witnessing violence between 'hippies' and police instinctively sided with the police, no matter what they saw on their screens. The country had become polarized and protestors of all stripes were perceived as violent and unpatriotic by the majority of those influenced by media portrayals of dissent." See *Covering Dissent,* 89.

84. *Who Spoke Up?* 199.

85. *Telltale Hearts,* 162. Rubin later said, "The Movement began to turn violent. Every six months there had to be another escalation in tactics, because of boredom. I mean, you're sitting in. 'Well, what else is new since you sat in last week? You're not on page one anymore, you're on page ten.' 'Okay, then we'll block the dean's office.' So you get headlines for blocking the dean's office, but next week you don't get headlines for that, so now you have to blow up the dean's office at 3 A.M. In a sense, we fell into a very American trap: We had to produce more and more." See *From Camelot to Kent State: The Sixties Experience in the Words of Those Who Lived It* (New York: Oxford University Press, 2001), 289.

86. Carpenter is quoted in the *Chicago Tribune,* August 30, 1968, 4.

87. Interview with Terry Noviki, October 15, 2001.

88. *Telling It Like It Was: The Chicago Riots,* 66.

89. Interview with Carl Moore, March 5, 2000, and Tim Markowsky, July 8, 2001.

90. *Time,* September 27, 1968, 31.

91. There are only a couple of vague references in *Rights in Conflict* of police allegedly firing their weapons in the air to disperse crowds. These references are not verified elsewhere. The *Tribune* only cites one account of a shotgun being fired in the air to scatter a crowd. Police officers to a man flatly deny any use of guns at anytime in this manner, maintaining that they never dispersed crowds with guns. Milton Viorst also found no record that firearms were ever used. See *Fire in the Streets,* 461.

92. Interview with Len Colsky, July 12, 2000.

93. Interview with Sheldon Bartowski, July 19, 2000.

94. Quoted in *Chicago's American,* August 29, 1969, 4.

95. Rubin quoted in *From Camelot to Kent State,* 288.

96. Jonah Raskin, *For the Hell of It: The Life and Times of Abbie Hoffman* (Berkeley, CA: University of California Press, 1996), 165.

97. Interview with Joe Pecoraro, October 13, 2003. Jerome H. Skolnick, the director for the Task Force on Violent Aspects of Protest and Confrontation of the National Commission on the Causes and Prevention of Violence, concluded that police officers were in a difficult position. "The predicament of the police in America today can scarcely be overstated, caught as they are between two contradictory developments: their job is rapidly becoming much more difficult (some say impossible), while at the same time their resources—morale, material, and training—are deteriorating. No recent observer doubts that the police are under increasing strain largely because they are increasingly being given tasks well beyond their resources." See *The Politics of Protest* (New York: Simon & Schuster, 1968), 249–250.

98. Interview with Will Gerald, May 6, 2002.

99. Interview with Paul Juravinski, January 26, 1999, and October 10, 2003; Brian Ramsey, June 23, 2001; Joe Pecoraro, October 13, 2003; and Ken O'Connor, October 10, 2003.

CONCLUSION

1. Columnist Max Lerner writing in the *Chicago Sun-Times,* August 29, 1968, 27.

2. *The Final Report of the National Commission on the Causes and Prevention of Violence* (Washington, DC: U.S. Government Printing Office, December 1968), 244. Voter turnout was actually closer to 73 million, as George Wallace, running on the American Independent ticket, captured more than 9 million votes.

3. Interview with Joe Pecoraro, October 13, 2003; and the *Chicago Sun-Times,* August 31, 1968, 20.

4. Interview with Nick Geldon, October 11, 2003; and Carl Oglesby, "Chicago 1968: Street-Fightin' Man" *Against the Vietnam War,* 132. During convention week, 308 U.S. servicemen lost their lives in Vietnam.

Bibliography

U.S. GOVERNMENT DOCUMENTS AND REPORTS

County and City Data Book. Washington, DC: U.S. Government Printing Office, 1952.

Final Report of the National Commission on the Causes and Prevention of Violence. Washington, DC: Government Printing Office, December 10, 1968.

Historical Statistics of the United States, Colonial Times to 1970. Washington, DC: Department of Commerce, 1975. 2 vols.

National Party Conventions 1831–1992. Washington, DC: Congressional Quarterly, 1995.

The Politics of Protest: A Report Submitted by Jerome H. Skolnick, Director Task Force on Violent Aspects of Protest and Confrontation of the National Commission on the Causes and Prevention of Violence, New York: Simon & Schuster, 1968.

Public Papers of the Presidents of the United States, Lyndon B. Johnson: 1963–64.

Records of the Chicago Study Team Investigation, National Commission on the Causes and Prevention of Violence, 1968–1969, Lyndon Baines Johnson Library and Museum.

Report of the National Advisory Commission on Civil Disorders. Washington, DC: Government Printing Office, 1968.

Rights in Conflict: Chicago's 7 Brutal Days: A Report Submitted by Daniel Walker, Director of the Chicago Study Team, to the National Commission on the Causes and Prevention of Violence. New York: Grosset & Dunlap, 1968.

State and Metropolitan Area Data Book. Washington, DC: U.S. Government Printing Office, 1991.

United States Congress House Committee on Un-American Activities. *Subversive Involvement in Disruption of 1968 Democratic Party National Convention HUAC Hearings of October and December 1968.* Ninetieth Congress, Second Session. Washington, DC: U.S. Government Printing Office, 1968.

United States Congress House Committee on Interstate and Foreign Commerce. Special
    Subcommittee on Investigations. *Television Coverage of the Democratic National
    Convention, Chicago, Illinois, 1968: Staff Report.* Washington, U.S. Government
    Printing Office, 1969.
United States v. David T. Dellinger et al., No. 69 CR-180 (a transcript of the proceedings),
    1969.
U.S. Congressional Record. Washington, DC: Government Printing Office, 1965.
U.S. National Guard Bureau, *Annual Report, Fiscal Year 1968.* Washington, DC: 1968.

CHICAGO HISTORICAL DOCUMENTS

Chicago Citizens Commission to Study the Disorders of Convention Week. Records,
    1968–1969.
Chicago Crime Commission 1968. *A Report on Chicago Crime for 1968.*
Chicago Department of Law. *The Strategy of Confrontation: Chicago and the Democratic
    National Convention.* 1968.
Conlisk, James, Jr., "Report of the Superintendent to the Police Board," April, June,
    August 1968, Chicago Police Department.
"Criminal Justice in Extremis: Administration of Justice during the April 1968 Chicago
    Disorders," *University of Chicago Law Review.* Spring 1969.
*Dissent and Disorder: A Report to the Citizens of Chicago on the April 27 Investigating
    Commission. April 27 Peace Parade.* Chicago: American Civil Liberties Union, 1968.

AUTHOR'S INTERVIEWS

All interviews were conducted between March 19, 1999 and October 14, 2003.

MEMOIRS AND OTHER PRIMARY SOURCES

Dellinger, David. *From Yale to Jail.* Marion, SD: Rose Hill Books, 1993.
———. *More Power Than We Know.* Garden City, NY: Doubleday, 1975.
From Camelot to Kent State: The Sixties Experience in the Words of Those Who Lived It.
    New York: Oxford University Press, 2001.
Gettleman, Marvin E., ed. *Vietnam and America: A Documented History.* New York: Grove
    Press, 1985.
Hayden, Tom. *Reunion: A Memoir.* New York: Random House, 1988.
Hoffman, Abbie, *Revolution for the Hell of It.* New York: The Dial Press, 1968.
———. *Soon to Be a Major Motion Picture.* New York: Putnam, 1980.
Horowitz, David, and Peter Collier, eds. *Second Thoughts: Former Radicals Look Back at the
    Sixties.* Lanham, MD: Madison Books, 1989.
Larner, Jeremy. *Nobody Knows: Reflections on the McCarthy Campaign of 1968.* New York:
    Macmillan, 1970.
McCarthy, Eugene J. *The Year of the People.* Garden City, NY: Doubleday, 1969.
Nixon, Richard M., *RN, The Memoirs of Richard Nixon.* New York: Warner Books, 1979.
Rubin, Jerry. *Do It: Scenarios of the Revolution.* New York: Simon & Shuster, 1970.

———. *Growing (Up) at Thirty-Seven.* New York: M. Evans, 1976.
Sayres, Sohnya, ed., et al. *The Sixties, Without Apology.* Minneapolis: University of Minnesota Press, 1984.
Schneir, Walter, ed. *Telling It Like It Was: The Chicago Riots.* New York: Signet, 1969.

FILMS AND TELEVISION

CBS News, Convention Outtakes, August 1968.
———. *"Ten Years After."* August 1978.
Chicago 1968, written and produced by Chana Gazit: A David Grubin Productions, Inc. Film for the American Experience; WGBH Educational Foundation, PBS Video, 1999.
Democratic National Convention 1968 (NBC News Coverage, Parts 1–7), August 1968.
Summer '68, produced by Norman Fruchter and John Douglas, Third World Newsreel, 1969.
"What Trees Do They Plant?" produced by Henry Ushijima, City of Chicago, September 15, 1968.
The Whole World's Watching: 20 Years Later, WBBM-TV (Chicago, IL), 1988.
Yippie, Third World Newsreel, 1968.

NEWSPAPERS, MAGAZINES, AND JOURNALS

Chicago Daily News
Chicago Defender
Chicago Journalism Review
Chicago Seed
Chicago Sun-Times
Chicago Tribune
Chicago's American
Esquire
Harper's Magazine
Liberation
Los Angeles Times
The Movement
Naval War College Review
New Republic
New Statesmen
New York Times
New Yorker
Newsweek
Partisan Review
Public Opinion Quarterly
Ramparts
Realist
Time
University of Chicago Law Review
Washington Star

SECONDARY SOURCES

Algren, Nelson. *Chicago, City on the Make*. Garden City, NY: Doubleday, 1951.

Allswang, John M. *Bosses, Machines, and Urban Voters an American Symbiosis*. Port Washington, NY: Kennikat Press, 1977.

Anderson, Terry H. *The Movement and the Sixties*. New York: Oxford University Press, 1995.

Asinof, Eliot. *Eight Men Out: The Black Sox and the 1919 World Series*. New York: Henry Holt & Company, 2000.

Avrich, Paul. *The Haymarket Tragedy*. Princeton, NJ: Princeton University Press, 1984.

Babson, Steve. *The Unfinished Struggle: Turning Points in American Labor, 1877–Present*. Lanham, MD: Rowman & Littlefield, 1999.

Baumann, Fred E. *Fraternity and Politics: Choosing One's Brothers*. Westport, CT: Praeger, 1998.

Biles, Roger. *Richard J. Daley: Politics, Race, and the Governing of Chicago*. DeKalb: Northern Illinois University Press, 1995.

Black, Nelson. *Cointelpro: The FBI's Secret War on Political Freedom*. New York: Vintage, 1975.

Bodroghkozy, Aniko. *Groove Tube: Sixties Television and the Youth Rebellion*. Durham, NC: Duke University Press, 2001.

Bopp, William J. *O. W. Wilson and the Search for a Police Profession*. Port Washington, NY: Kennikat Press, 1977.

Brick, Howard. *Age of Contradiction: American Thought and Culture in the 1960s*. Ithaca, NY: Cornell University Press, 2000.

Burner, David. *Making Peace with the 60s*. Princeton, NJ: Princeton University Press, 1996.

Capps, Walter. *The Unfinished War: Vietnam and the American Conscience*. Boston: Beacon, 1982.

Carmichael, Stokely, and Charles V. Hamilton. *Black Power: The Politics of Liberation in America*. New York: Vintage, 1967.

Carroll, Wade, Louise. *Chicago's Pride: The Stockyards, Packingtown, and Environs in the Nineteenth Century*. Chicago: University of Illinois, 1987.

Chester, Lewis, et al. *An American Melodrama: The Presidential Campaign of 1968*. New York: The Viking Press, 1969.

Churchill, Ward, and Jim Vander Wall. *The Cointelpro Papers: Documents from the FBI's Secret Wars against Domestic Dissent*. Boston: South End Press, 1990.

Cleaver, Eldridge. *Post-Prison Writings and Speeches*. New York: Vintage Books, 1969.

———. *Soul on Ice*. New York: Dell Publishing, 1968.

Cohen, Adam, and Elizabeth Taylor. *American Pharaoh: Mayor Richard J. Daley: His Battle for Chicago and the Nation*. Boston: Little, Brown, 2000.

Cohen, Lizabeth. *Making a New Deal: Industrial Workers in Chicago, 1919–1939*. Cambridge: Cambridge University Press, 1990.

Coles, Robert. *The Middle Americans*. Boston: Little, Brown & Company, 1971.

Columbia Broadcasting System, CBS News. Special Events Unit. *CBS News, Campaign '68: Democratic National Convention*. New York, 1968.

Cromie, Robert. *The Great Chicago Fire*. New York: McGraw-Hill, 1963.

David, Henry. *The History of the Haymarket Affair: A Study in the American Social-Revolutionary and Labor Movements*. New York: Russell & Russell, 1958.

Dawidowicz, Lucy S., and Leon J. Goldstein. *Politics in a Pluralist Democracy: Studies of Voting in the 1960 Election*. New York: Institute for Human Relations, 1963.

Debenedetti, Charles. *An American Ordeal: The Antiwar Movement of the Victorian Era.* Syracuse, NY: Syracuse University Press, 1990.

Einhorn, Robin L. *Property Rules: Political Economy in Chicago, 1833–1872.* Chicago: University of Chicago Press, 1991.

Emerson, Gloria. *Winners and Losers: Battles, Retreats, Gains, Losses and Runs from the Vietnam War.* New York: Harcourt Brace Jovanovich, 1972.

Farber, David R. *Chicago '68.* Chicago: University of Chicago Press, 1988.

Ferber, Michael, and Staughton Lynd. *The Resistance.* Boston: Beacon Press, 1971.

Flinn, John J., *History of the Chicago Police from the Settlement of the Community to the Present Time.* New York: AMS Press, 1973.

Fogelson, Robert M. *Big City Police.* Cambridge, MA: Harvard University Press, 1977.

Fulbright, William J. *The Crippled Giant: American Foreign Policy and Its Domestic Consequences.* New York: Random House, 1972.

Garfinkle, Adam M. *Telltale Hearts: The Origins and Impact of the Vietnam Antiwar Movement.* New York: St. Martin's Press, 1995.

Garrettson, Charles Lloyd. *Hubert H. Humphrey: The Politics of Joy.* New Brunswick, NJ: Transaction Publishers, 1993.

Gitlin, Todd. *The Sixties: Years of Hope, Days of Rage.* New York: Bantam, 1993.

———. *The Whole World Is Watching: Mass Media in the Making & Unmaking of The New Left.* Berkeley: University of California Press, 1980.

Gleason, Bill. *Daley of Chicago: The Man, The Mayor, and the Limits of Conventional Politics.* New York: Simon & Schuster, 1970.

Goulden, Joseph C. *Truth Is the First Casualty: The Gulf of Tonkin Affair—Illusion and Reality.* Chicago: Rand McNally, 1969.

Green, Paul M., and Melvin G. Holli, eds. *The Mayors: The Chicago Political Tradition.* Carbondale: Southern Illinois University Press, 1987.

Griffith, Winthrop. *Humphrey, a Candid Biography.* New York: Morrow, 1965.

Gronon, William. *Nature's Metropolis: Chicago and the Great West.* New York: W. W. Norton & Company, 1991.

Gropman, Donald. *Say It Ain't So, Joe!: The Story of Shoeless Joe Jackson.* Boston: Little, Brown & Company, 1979.

Guglielmo, Thomas A. *White on Arrival: Italians, Race, Color, and Power in Chicago, 1890–1945.* New York: Oxford Press, 2003.

Guthman, Edwin O. (ed.), et al. *RFK: Collected Speeches.* New York: Viking, 1993.

Halstead, Fred. *Out Now!* New York: Monad Press, 1978.

Harris, David. *Dreams Die Hard.* New York: St. Martin's/Marek, 1982.

Harrison, Carter H. *Stormy Years: The Autobiography of Carter H. Harrison, Five Times Mayor of Chicago.* Indianapolis: Bobbs-Merrill, 1935.

Helmer, William J. *Public Enemies: America's Criminal Past, 1919–1940.* New York: Facts on File, 1998.

Herring, George C. *America's Longest War: The United States in Vietnam, 1950–1975.* New York: Wiley, 1979.

Herzog, Arthur. *McCarthy for President.* New York: Viking Press, 1969.

Hirsch, Arnold R. *Making the Second Ghetto: Race and Housing in Chicago, 1940–1960.* New York: Cambridge University Press, 1983.

Hirsch, Eric L. *Urban Revolt: Ethnic Politics in the Nineteenth-Century Chicago Labor Movement.* Berkeley: University of California Press, 1990.

Hoffman, Dennis E. *Scarface Al and the Crime Crusaders: Chicago's Private War against Capone*. Carbondale: Southern Illinois University Press, 1993.

Hollander, Paul. *Anti-Americanism: Critiques at Home and Abroad, 1965–1990*. New York: Oxford University Press, 1992.

Hormachea, C. R., and Marion Hormachea, eds. *Confrontation; Violence and the Police*. Boston: Holbrook Press, 1971.

Isserman, Maurice, and Michael Kazin. *America Divided: The Civil War of the 1960s*. New York: Oxford University Press, 2000.

Jeffreys-Jones, Rhodri. *Peace Now!: American Society and the Ending of the Vietnam War*. New Haven: Yale University Press, 1999.

Kahn, Melvin A., and Frances J. Majors. *The Winning Ticket: Daley, the Chicago Machine, and Illinois Politics*. New York: Praeger, 1984.

Kaiser, Charles. *1968 in America*. New York: Grove Press, 1988.

Karnow, Stanley. *Vietnam: A History*. New York: The Viking Press, 1983.

Kelman, Steven. *Push Comes to Shove: The Escalation of Student Protest*. Boston: Houghton Mifflin, 1970.

Kessler, Ronald. *The Bureau: The Secret History of the FBI*. New York: St. Martin's Press, 2002.

King, Martin Luther, Jr. *I Have a Dream: Writings & Speeches That Changed the World*. Ed. by James Melvin Washington. San Francisco: Harper, 1992.

Knappman, Edward W., ed. *Presidential Election 1968*. New York: Facts on File, 1970.

Knight, Douglas M. *Street of Dreams: The Nature and Legacy of the 1960s*. Durham: Duke University Press, 1989.

Kurlansky, Mark. *1968: The Year That Rocked the World*. New York: Ballantine, 2004.

Liebovich, Louis W. *The Press and the Modern Presidency: Myths and Mindsets from Kennedy to Election 2000*. Rev. 2d ed. Westport, CT: Praeger, 2001.

Lindberg, Richard, C., *To Serve and Collect: Chicago Politics and Police Corruption from the Lager Beer Riot to the Summerdale Scandal*. Westport, CT., Praeger Publishers, 1991.

Mailer, Norman. *Miami and the Siege of Chicago: An Informal History of the American Political Conventions of 1968*. Harmondsworth: England, Penguin Books, 1969.

Matthews, Christopher J. *Kennedy Nixon: The Rivalry That Shaped Postwar America*. New York: Simon & Schuster, 1996.

Matusow, Allen J. *The Unraveling of America: A History of Liberalism in the 1960s*. New York: Harper & Row, 1984.

Mayer, Harold M., and Richard C. Wade. *Chicago: Growth of a Metropolis*. Chicago: The University of Chicago Press, 1969.

Mehnert, Klaus. *Twilight of the Young: The Radical Movements of the 1960s and Their Legacy*. New York: Holt, Rinehart and Winston, 1976.

Miller, Jim. *Democracy Is in the Streets: From Port Huron to the Siege of Chicago*. New York: Simon & Schuster, 1987.

Miller, Ross. *American Apocalypse: The Great Fire and the Myth of Chicago*. Chicago: University of Chicago Press, 1990.

Mitgang, Herbert. *Dangerous Dossiers*. New York: D. I. Fine Books, 1988.

Murray, Jesse George. *The Legacy of Al Capone: Portraits and Annals of Chicago's Public Enemies*. New York: Putnam, 1975.

Myrus, Donald, ed. *Law & Disorder: The Chicago Convention and Its Aftermath*. Chicago: D. Myrus, 1968.

Nelli, Humbert S. *The Business of Crime: Italians and Syndicate Crime in the United States.* Chicago: University of Chicago Press, 1981.

Oberdorfer, Don. *Tet!: The Turning Point in the Vietnam War.* Baltimore, MD: Johns Hopkins University Press, 2001.

O'Neill, William L. *Coming Apart: An Informal History of America in the 1960s.* Chicago: Quadrangle Books, 1971.

O'Toole, George. *The Private Sector: Rent-a-Cops, Private Spies, and the Police-Industrial Complex.* New York: W. W. Norton & Company, 1978.

Phillips, Michael J. *The Dilemmas of Individualism: Status, Liberty and American Constitutional Law.* Westport, CT: Greenwood Press, 1983.

Pierce, Bessie Louise. *A History of Chicago, Volume I, III.* Chicago: University of Chicago Press, 1937, 1957.

Pinderhughes, Dianne M. *Race and Ethnicity in Chicago Politics: A Reexamination of Pluralist Theory.* Urbana: University of Illinois Press, 1987.

Rakove, Milton L. *Don't Make No Waves—Don't Back No Losers: An Insider's Analysis of the Daley Machine.* Bloomington: Indiana University Press, 1975.

Ralph, James. *Northern Protest: Martin Luther King, Jr., Chicago, and the Civil Rights Movement.* Cambridge, MA: Harvard University Press, 1993.

Raskin, Jonah. *For the Hell of It: The Life and Times of Abbie Hoffman.* Berkeley: University of California Press, 1996.

Regina, Lawrence G. *The Politics of Force: Media and the Construction of Police Brutality.* Berkeley: University of California Press, 2000.

Riess, Steven A. *Touching Base: Professional Baseball and American Culture in the Progressive Era.* Westport, CT: Greenwood Press, 1980.

Rising, George. *Clean for Gene: Eugene McCarthy's 1968 Presidential Campaign.* Westport, CT: Praeger, 1997.

Royko, Mike. *Boss: Richard J. Daley of Chicago.* New York: E. P. Dutton & Co., 1971.

Ryskind, Allan. *Hubert: An Unauthorized Biography of the Vice President.* New Rochelle, NY: Arlington House, 1968.

Sandburg, Carl. *The Chicago Race Riots, July 1919.* New York: Harcourt Brace and Howe, 1919.

Schlesinger, Arthur M., Jr. *Robert Kennedy and His Times.* Boston: Houghton Mifflin, 1978.

Schmidt, John R. *"The Mayor Who Cleaned Up Chicago": A Political Biography of William E. Dever.* Dekalb: Northern Illinois University Press, 1989.

———. *Robert Kennedy in His Own Words: The Unpublished Recollections of the Kennedy Years.* New York: Bantam Press, 1988.

Schultz, John. *No One Was Killed: Documentation and Meditation: Convention Week, Chicago, August 1968.* Chicago: Big Table Pub., 1969.

Sherrill, Robert, and Harry W. Ernst. *The Drugstore Liberal.* New York: Grossman Publishers, 1968.

Shesol, Jeff. *Mutual Contempt: Lyndon Johnson, Robert Kennedy, and the Feud That Defined a Decade.* New York: W. W. Norton, 1997.

Siff, Ezra Y. *Why the Senate Slept.* Westport, CT: Praeger, 1999.

Small, Melvin. *Covering Dissent: The Media and the Anti-Vietnam War Movement.* New Brunswick, NJ: Rutgers University Press, 1994.

———. *Johnson, Nixon, and the Doves.* New Brunswick, NJ: Rutgers University Press, 1988.

Stavis, Ben. *We Were the Campaign: New Hampshire to Chicago for McCarthy*. Boston: Beacon Press, 1969.

Taub, Richard P. *Paths of Neighborhood Change: Race and Crime in Urban America*. Chicago: University of Chicago Press, 1984.

Thomas, Evan. *Robert Kennedy: His Life*. New York: Simon & Schuster, 2000.

Turner, William W. *The Police Establishment*. New York: G. P. Putman's Sons, 1968.

Tuttle, William M., Jr. *Race Riot, Chicago in the Red Summer of 1919*. New York: Anteneum, 1972.

Viorst, Milton. *Fire in the Streets*. New York: Simon & Schuster, 1979.

Wade, Louise Carroll. *Chicago's Pride: The Stockyards, Packingtown, and Environs in the Nineteenth Century*. Chicago: University of Illinois, 1987.

Wainstock, Dennis. *The Turning Point: The 1968 United States Presidential Campaign*. Jefferson, NC: McFarland, 1988.

Wells, Tom. *The War Within: America's Battle over Vietnam*. Berkeley: University of California Press, 1994.

White, Theodore Harold. *The Making of the President, 1960*. New York: Atheneum, 1961.

———. *The Making of the President, 1968*. New York: Atheneum Publishers, 1969.

Wise, David. *The American Police State*. New York: Random House, 1976.

Witcover, Jules. *85 Days: The Last Campaign of Robert Kennedy*. New York: Putnam, 1969.

———. *The Year the Dream Died: Revisiting 1968 in America*. New York: Warner Books, 1997.

Zaroulis, Nancy, and Gerald Sullivan. *Who Spoke Up? American Protest Against the War in Vietnam, 1963–1975*. New York: Holt, Rinehart, & Winston, 1985.

Zinn, Howard. *Disobedience and Democracy*. New York: Random House, 1968.

Index

About the Author

FRANK KUSCH is author of *All American Boys: Draft Dodgers in Canada from the Vietnam War* (Praeger, 2001). He holds degrees in history from Ohio University and the University of Saskatchewan. Historian and editor, he is currently working on a book about Richard Nixon and the antiwar movement.